THE
ALTERNATIVE
MUSIC
ALMANAC

ALAN CROSS

Collector's Guide
Publishing Inc

Toronto • Chicago • London

To my wife, who helped me make beautiful lemonade.

Published by Collector's Guide Publishing Inc., Box 62034, Burlington, Ontario, Canada, L7R 4K2
Editor - Carl Krach

Manufactured in Canada
Alternative Music Almanac / Alan Cross
First Edition
ISBN 1-896522-14-9

ACKNOWLEDGMENTS

This project could not have been completed without the help and support of a ton of people. Here they are in no particular order: My wife (who put up with all the hours I spent on the computer), Mom and Dad (who first exposed me to music by making me take accordion lessons), my grandparents (who, I'm sure, will learn to like KMFDM—one day) along with Allyson, Ivar, all the Club People, Barry the Lawyer, Jay the Accountant, Rob the Sounding Board, Duarte the Computer Guy and Willy (the original Brain Dead Dog and Official Corporate Logo). In addition, I wish to acknowledge a couple of companies in Toronto: Say What! Communications Inc., for their Brain Dead Dog logo design; and Empire Entertainment Ltd. for the Absolute Alternative logo.

I'd also like to thank my friends and co-workers at 102.1 The Edge/Toronto for their support: Hal, Stu, Phil, Rob Johnston, Craig Venn, Jim, Cliff, CVA, Howard, Fred, Maie, Brother Bill, Pete, Martin, Anita, M-K, Chris, Earl, David M., and everyone else at the studios and in the offices. The Edge is my connection to the world of music. Without the people and the resources in that building, this book would have never been possible.

Finally, I'd like to thank the everyone who's ever tuned in to CFNY/The Edge for the music, the other on-air people or *The Ongoing History of New Music* on Sunday nights. You're the reason why we do what we do.

PHOTO CREDITS

David A. Scott 38, 42, 56, 68,
119, 169, 180,
198, 210, 221,
229

Simon White 23, 27, 32, 37,
45, 47, 73, 81,
108, 111, 128,
149

Alan Cross 237, 331, 401

Rykodisc 21, 88, 101

CONTENTS

Acknowledgments | 5
Introduction | 9
So What Is "Alternative Music," anyway? | 11

PART 1 HISTORY | 13
Section 1
The History of Alternative Music | 15
Section 2
This Day In Alternative Music History | 95
Section 3
By Any Other Name: Band Names | 217
Section 4
A Glossary of Musical Terms | 265

PART 2 LISTS & STUFF | 277
10 Classic Alternative Albums · 10 More Essential
Alternative Albums · 20 Mystery Tracks · 3 Examples of
Mystery Audio · Several CDs That Contain More Than Just
Music · 8 Bands Who Recorded Cheap · 11 Cases of
Censorship · 10 Places to Visit on Your Vacation · Crimes
and Misdemeanors · 12 Delightful Oddities · Various
Superlatives · Trivial Trivia · 17 Alternative Artists
Who Appeared in Movies · 4 Things To Do With Movies · 2
Performers Who Tried Big-time Politics · Stories Behind
12 Songs · 7 Heroin Deaths · 11 Loving Music Couples · 16
Ex-Couples · 14 Miscellaneous Relationships · 4 Bad
Career Moves · 11 Cool Indie Labels · Lollapalooza ·
Backstage Passes

PART 3 GETTING MORE INFO | 335
Section 1
Fanclubs | 337
Section 2
Alternative Music and the Internet | 353
Section 3
Record Label Guide | 373
Section 4
Recommended Reading | 383

Alan Cross' ticket from Elvis Costello's
November 15, 1978, concert

INTRODUCTION

I remember the exact moment it happened. It was 8:03 pm November 15, 1978. I was in my seat at the Playhouse Theatre in Winnipeg, Manitoba, wondering why every girl I had asked to the concert had turned me down. I was feeling a little sorry for myself and more than a little pissed that I had wasted seven dollars on a second ticket. Then the lights went down and Elvis Costello walked onstage.

I had never been to a punk show before, but I had this tape called *This Year's Model* that I had bought at K-mart. I'm still not sure what had possessed me to buy it—but I had spent the past summer playing the hell out of it both at home and in the cheap Roadstar cassette player I had installed in my mom's Pinto. When it was announced that Elvis was coming to town, I figured that this would be a good time as any to get exposed to this punk thing firsthand.

When Elvis and the Attractions came on, half the audience immediately ran down to the front of the stage and started pogoing furiously. Yet just as quickly, the security goons (all members of a local biker gang) waded into the crowd and started bashing as many of the kids as they could and heaving them back towards the seats. But Elvis saw what was going on. He stopped singing, stared down at the bikers from behind those geeky glasses and screamed "YOU PIGSHITS LEAVE MY FRIENDS ALONE!"

And then a miracle occurred: The bikers backed off.

I was entranced. I had never seen a singer or band with this kind of relationship with an audience. This wasn't the typical inane banter that I had seen dozens of times at regular rock shows. I couldn't believe that a performer would actually *want* to be this close to the fans. And I had never seen music played with such energy and urgency—with such obvious *zeitgeist*. This was not ordinary rock and roll. This was something *new*. This was something *real*.

At the end of the night, I did something I had never done before. I waited at the stage door until Elvis came out. When the door finally opened and he started for his bus, I muttered something brilliant like "Great show." And then the second miracle of the night occurred. He looked me straight in the eye and said "Thanks, man." Wow.

From that moment on, I became a fan of what was then called "punk" and "new wave." I found other people who felt the same way. When the '70s turned into the '80s, I began to get deeper into what was

9

being called "alternative" music. In fact, I became such a fan that I ended up making the study and promotion of this music my life's work.

This is a book for anyone who has had a similar musical epiphany at some point in their lives. Maybe it happened when you heard "God Save the Queen" by the Sex Pistols for the first time. Or maybe Led Zeppelin seemed old-fashioned the second a friend turned you on to Nirvana. Or maybe you became aware the first time you danced to New Order's "Blue Monday." Whatever the case, I'm willing to bet that you remember the exact moment that you stopped listening to this music and really started *feeling* it.

This book began as a series of radio scripts for a weekly documentary show on 102.1 The Edge in Toronto titled "The Ongoing History of New Music." Those scripts were prepared with countless hours of research using many of the books listed in Part 3, along with hundreds (if not thousands) of magazine articles and the archives of the radio station, which were so graciously made available by management. This is by no means a serious critical and scholarly work—I'll leave that to guys like Greil Marcus, Jon Savage and Simon Frith. Instead, it's a book written by an alternative music fan for other alternative music fans. The idea is to provide fun and factual information that will hopefully allow everyone to get a little more out of their music.

Every effort has been made to ensure that the information in this book is correct, although that occasionally proved to be rather difficult—for example, you wouldn't believe how many different birthdays Brian Eno has. I used as many sources as I could get my hands on, and in cases where there were discrepancies, I made a judgment regarding which source was the most reliable.

If you have any comments or criticisms, or if you spot any mistakes, let me know about it. You can either send a letter to:

The Alternative Music Almanac
c/o C.G. Publishing Inc.
Box 62034
Burlington, Ontario, Canada L7R 4K2

You can also e-mail me anytime. I can be reached at alanc@passport.ca. The more feedback I get, the better version 2.0 of *The Alternative Music Almanac* will be.

Alan Cross
Waterdown, Ontario, Canada
July 1995

SO WHAT *IS* "ALTERNATIVE MUSIC" ANYWAY?

There is a theory of societal evolution that goes like this: Barbarians invent a new culture. A middle class emerges to manage and help perpetuate the culture. An aristocracy eventually develops out of the middle class and devotes their energies to making things comfortable for themselves. Finally, a new set of barbarians smash everything apart and destroy the status quo so that the process must start all over again.

If the culture we're talking about is music, then alternative fans are the barbarians.

A similar sort of evolution goes on within the alternative world itself. A new, unknown band emerges and managed to attract a few die-hard followers. They are the first level of alternative music fans, people who pride themselves on being first to know about a new group or a new type of music. As word of the new group spreads, their popularity reaches a second level of fans. Magazines write stories on the group, college radio plays their indie releases and a major record label or two might show some interest. If the music is good and the market conditions are right, the band is signed, and they may begin to sell records in significant quantities to a third circle of alternative music fans. In very rare cases, the band may go on to become extremely popular and might even invade the mainstream—attracting a fourth level of fans. At that point, they are abandoned by the first level—and they start looking for something new. Then the process starts all over again. This life cycle is crucial to the health of the entire scene because alternative music *depends on constant change* in order to survive.

But that still doesn't answer the our question. What *is* alternative music, anyway?

That's a complicated question worthy of a Ph.D. dissertation. Coming up with an answer that will satisfy everyone is about as difficult as reconciling Einstein's theory of relativity with quantum mechanics (In fact, I'm sure the Heisenberg Uncertainty Principle can be applied here).

For awhile, alternative music was defined by what it was *not*. It was rock music but it wasn't Styx or REO Speedwagon. From there, this idea of "definition by exclusion" expanded to include all the weird stuff that you never saw on MTV or heard on the radio, unless you were listening to some wacko campus station. It was the stuff of cults, indie record labels and dark clubs.

But with the '90s, that all changed. Starting with Nirvana, alternative music slowly took over a good chunk of the mainstream to the point where dozens of formerly culty bands were becoming multi-platinum artists. Even small indie bands were receiving more attention than they ever dreamed as more people were turned on to this new music. The question more and more people began to ask was "an alternative to *what?*"

By 1992, the old definition "alternative music" as being the stuff out on the fringe no longer applied. But at the same time, many people were still uncomfortable with the word "alternative." To them, the word evoked images of weirdos festooned with tattoos and mohawks. Commercial radio stations experimenting with new formats involving this music invented euphemisms like "new rock" or "modern rock" to get around using the word "alternative." In the end, however, there was no fighting it. More and more, bands were classified as "alternative" simply because no one knew what else to call them. The media, the music industry, record stores and just about everyone else has relented and has begun using the "a" word.

But the upshot of all this is that the original spirit of the word "alternative" has been rendered meaningless. It's no longer enough to define something by what it is not. It's no longer necessarily the stuff out on the fringe. And with all the different types of new music out there, it can no longer can be applied to a specific sound or look. What exactly are we talking about?

To me, it all comes down to a common mindset and a common attitude about how music is made. So, for the purposes of this book, this is the definition we'll use. Yeah, it's broad and it's vague, but it's the closest I could come to capturing the spirit and adventure of new music.

Alternative music: *Music made by people who aren't afraid to take chances with musical self-expression.*

Part 1

HISTORY

Section 1

The History of Alternative Music

Everyone pretty well agrees that the alternative music of today grew out of the traditions and aesthetics established by the punk movement of the mid-'70s. But then where did the whole punk thing come from? Good question...

Well, believe it or not, you have to go back a lot further than you may think. This is a quick history of where it all came from and how we got to where we are today.

The Proto-Punk Era
1963-72

One of the essential components of alternative music is *attitude*—the belief that *anyone* can make music. Enthusiasm, energy and attitude are far more important than musical ability. If we're going to use attitude as our yardstick, the roots of punk can be found in the early '60s where, in a garage somewhere in America, a bunch of guys with a half-finished six pack were struggling to learn three chords.

The garage band was the ultimate form of musical democracy. Anyone with access to an instrument and a place to practice could start a band. It didn't matter if you were any good; the idea was to live out a fantasy for a few hours each week. In the early '60s, there were hundreds (if not thousands) of these groups hammering away at whatever songs they could learn or make up. The Ventures, Dick Dale, the Champs and other California "surf music" groups were big inspirations. Many a Saturday afternoon was spent learning the chords to "Walk—Don't Run" and "Tequila." Sure, the results were pretty rough and raw, but so what? It felt *good*.

A few bands became good enough to be able to play somewhere other than in the garage. They'd play parties and school dances—and to their surprise, they found that some people really liked what they were doing. Some even dared to make a record, the greatest of which was the "Louie, Louie" by the Kingsmen. (**See** *The Story of "Louie, Louie"* **sidebar on p. 71.**)

"Louie, Louie" was sloppy, good-time, fratboy rock and the controversy that surrounded the indecipherable lyrics only added to the song's appeal. After the Kingsmen, many people began to look upon the typical garage band as something evil and sinister—and many groups tried to make the most of this. But even as these bands began to hone this new "bad boy" image, something else came along to deflect the public's attention. It was called the British Invasion.

17

The UK had its own version of the garage band in the early '60s. People like Bobby Vinton and the Singing Nun were pushed off the charts by pop groups who flaunted long hair, wild clothes and bad attitudes: the Rolling Stones, the Kinks, the High Numbers (later known as the Who), the King Bees (featuring David Bowie) and even the Beatles (who were known to occasionally appear on stage with toilet seats around their necks). The notorious image of these groups was enhanced by the almost constant brawling between two opposing sets of music fans: the Mods and Rockers.

When this music was exported to North America, many garage bands adopted some of these new British ideas. In Los Angeles, the Music Machine was one band that managed to carve out a new sound— a primordial ooze of garage bands and the British Invasion, along with bits of American folk music and early psychedelia. The Music Machine always dressed in black with one member sporting one black leather glove. They fancied themselves to be "punks" in the '50s tradition of the James Dean leather-clad ne'er-do-well—and "punk" is the term many people used to describe their music. This was the first time anyone had ever used that word in a musical context.

Other groups followed: Count Five, the Seeds, the Shadows of Knight, the Barbarians (who had a drummer with a hook for a left hand), the Leaves, the Standells, and ? and the Mysterions. And although each one of them made it onto the Top 40 charts in the mid-'60s, they were definitely looked upon as something to the left of the musical spectrum.

Meanwhile, something very new was starting to happen in New York. The Velvet Underground had begun to attract the attention of the trendy and cool. When Lou Reed and John Cale formed the group in 1966, they immediately began to write songs about various subculture mysteries: hard drugs, sexual deviancy, social alienation. Their music was propelled by emotional intensity rather than virtuosity. Songs would turn into hypnotic, droning, cacophonous jams that might last for an hour. The Velvets also gave music a strong dose of reality. Sure, other groups were singing about sex and drugs, but the Velvets didn't bother with metaphors and euphemisms. When Lou Reed sang about sticking a spike in his vein in the song "Heroin," you just *knew* that he was speaking from experience. This wasn't pop, folk music, or psychedelic rock—it was uncharted territory.

It didn't take long for the band to become part of the chic New York arts community. They were "discovered" by Andy Warhol, who more-or-less adopted them and used the group in many of his exhibits and projects. Meanwhile, the band continued to make music that was so *out there* for the time that they didn't have a prayer of becoming commercially successful. To the few who understood and/or appreciated the Velvets (and actually bought one of their records), the group was nothing less than a musical revolution. In hindsight, the Velvet Underground was the beginning of a whole different approach to music.

By 1968, several experiments with the garage band/psychedelia mix in the US midwest started to see some results. The MC5 was a loud, obnoxious bunch from Detroit that added some radical politics to the stew. But even more important was the appearance of Iggy Pop and the Stooges in nearby Ann Arbor. They were louder, harder, and weirder than virtually anyone. Songs like "I Wanna Be Your Dog" and "No Fun" preached a type of nihilism that few had heard before. Their musical arrangements were rough and intentionally loose, showing no concern for conventional tastes. Then there was Iggy, who had the goal of becoming the most outrageous rock star in the world. Onstage, he'd cut himself bloody with broken glass, smear himself with peanut butter, bang himself in the head with the microphone (or whatever was handy) and then stagedive into the crowd. But as non-commercial and self-destructive as the Stooges were, some people found this raw, undisciplined, go-for-broke approach to rock fascinating. Soon, there were Stooge imitators popping up all over the place.

By the end of the '60s, there were a number of groups that were obviously not going with the flow of popular music. They weren't satisfied with making "normal" music—they were determined to push the edge of the envelope. Leading the way, besides the Velvet Underground and the Stooges, were the Fugs, the Doors, Alice Cooper and Frank Zappa's Mothers of Invention. The more daring they could be and the more they could blur the lines between sanity and chaos, the better.

Another important figure was Zappa's friend Don Van Vliet, otherwise known as Captain Beefheart. In 1970, he released an album called *Trout Mask Replica*. This was an extremely weird album and most of the planet couldn't stand it. However, it became a very big record for those who were into weird music. These were people who were self-conscious of the fact that they were different from everyone else—something they were quite proud of. They'd go out of their way to be different with their clothes, their hair, their attitudes and of course, their music.

Captain Beefheart became one of their favorites, especially because his stuff really irritated "normal" people. And like the Velvet Underground and Iggy Pop, Captain Beefheart made a big impression on everyone who was bored with mainstream rock and pop.

The early '70s saw the birth of a short-lived British musical fad called "glam" or "glitter" rock. Glam bands specialized in loud pop music with simple melodies enhanced by wild costumes, lots of makeup and elaborate theatrics. Many of these groups also had images that were equal parts androgyny, sexual ambiguity, and science fiction. T. Rex, the Sweet, Slade, Sparks and Gary Glitter were among the first wave of glam bands. They were followed by a more artsy set of groups: Mott the Hoople, BeBop Deluxe and the fashion-conscious Roxy Music.

The most important person to emerge from all the glitter dust was David Bowie. Not only did his albums and singles sell like crazy, but his Ziggy Stardust character was one of the most sophisticated and enduring creations of the glam era. Ziggy had everything: the way-out music, the androgynous appearance, the provocative clothes and costumes, the wild theatrics. And as Ziggy, Bowie did something that no one in rock had ever done before. In a January 1972 edition of *Melody Maker,* Bowie publicly admitted that he was gay. This was a scandalous new twist to the image of the rock star—even for the glam scene—but it was another thing that captured the attention of those were looking for music that was decidedly different and daring.

The Pre-Punk Era
1972-75

By the early '70s, rock had developed to the point where there were dozens of bands who were working on the fringes of mainstream music. Boston had Jonathan Richmond and the Modern Lovers. In Memphis, there was Alex Chilton and Big Star. And in the deep, dark recesses of Manhattan were the New York Dolls.

The Dolls were the first group to successfully incorporate elements of glam, Iggy Pop, the Velvet Underground and Captain Beefheart. They brought so much glamour and camp into rock that they were shocking even in New York. Makeup, high heels, women's clothing, tight Spandex pants, booze, drugs, hints of homosexuality along with their outrageous public statements stirred up more controversy than any other bar band in history. The fact that the Dolls could barely play their instruments only added to the shock value. They were unpre-

20

dictable, threatening and anti-everything—which to many music fans, made them extremely exciting.

A whole new type of music scene developed around the Dolls, and by the end of 1972, the group was getting a tremendous amount of press. The problem was, however, that few record companies were interested. No self-respecting A&R person would dare be seen at a New York Dolls show. The Dolls were just too weird, the places they played were too scary, and their fans were just too hard to understand. This *was* rock music—just not the kind of rock the rest of the world was into. The whole thing just wasn't *normal*.

Eventually, though, the record companies had to look. It was like driving past a bad car accident. Mercury took a chance by signing the band and issuing *The New York Dolls* in April 1973. This was a major milestone for a couple of reasons. First of all, it was the first time in the '70s that a very straight, major record label was willing to take a chance on a band from the weird side of the tracks. Secondly, the signing of the Dolls showed that the press and music fans could convince a label to support a group that didn't fit any conventional commercial stereotypes.

Unfortunately, the world wasn't ready for a group like the New York Dolls. Despite the hype, their two albums were critical and commercial disasters. They were dropped by Mercury in 1974 and all attempts to revive interest in the band failed. However, they did leave a lasting impression on the New York and London underground music scenes—and they certainly had an effect on the man who was their manager at the end: a clothing shop owner from England named Malcolm McLaren. More on him later.

The Dolls had set something in motion, although it didn't become obvious until late 1974. That's when people started flocking to a scuzzy little bar at 315 Bowery in the lower part of Manhattan called CBGBs. "CBGB" stood for "country, blue grass and blues," which described the club's original music policy. No one gave the place much notice. Much of the clientele consisted of residents of the flophouse hotel above the club. The bathrooms behind the tiny stage were a horror and everyone had to watch out for the owner's dog, who could suddenly show up anywhere.

In 1974, a band called Television asked the owner if their group could play on Sunday nights. He agreed and by December, Sunday nights were attracting so many people that CBGBs instituted a "rock

only" policy for the rest of the week. To meet the demand for talent, the club began to book other young groups, many of whom had grown up listening to the Dolls, the Velvet Underground and the garage bands of the '60s. One of the first people to follow Television to CBGBs was Patti Smith, a poet, playwright, and occasional contributor to *Rolling Stone* and *Creem*. At first, her performances consisted of poetry readings backed by someone doodling on a guitar. But when that approach proved to be popular, she began to sing as well as recite. In late 1974, she released an independent 7" ("Hey Joe" b/w "Piss Factory") which many consider to be the first punk single.

Then along came the Ramones. They started their run of gigs at CBGBs on August 16, 1974, in front of a total of six customers—seven, if you count the dog. No one had ever seen anything like these four guys from Queens. The leather jackets and hoodlum image caused some people to describe them as "punks" (they also inspired a fanzine called *Punk* which rekindled the use of that word in regards to music). At a time when fifteen minute guitar solos were the norm, the Ramones were playing fifteen minute *sets*. Their songs were like the simple pop songs of the '60s—short, simple, melodic, but impossibly fast. And most importantly, virtually everyone who saw the band had the same reaction: "I could do *that!*" If the Ramones could be up on stage, then anyone could. One did not have to be a big-time rock star to make

↑ The Ramones

music that people would like. The stuff that was going on with the Ramones was not what was being heard on the radio and stocked in the record stores.

The Ramones and Patti Smith were soon sharing the stage with other groups who were attracted to the New York punk mindset. There was Blondie, Talking Heads, Tuff Darts and the Dictators. Groups like Pere Ubu and the Dead Boys drifted east from Ohio. Dozens of other groups were formed with the sole purpose of impressing their friends by getting on-stage at CBGBs. A lot of these bands were terrible—but the good ones were very good. They were also very, very different.

Once word began to get around, the major record companies were once again forced to overcome their fear of dingy, dark clubs to see what all the fuss was about. Patti Smith was the first CBGBs regular to be signed to a major label, and in late December 1975, she issued *Horses* which featured her famous opening manifesto "Jesus died for somebody's sins, but not mine!" It was a bold and shocking statement that converted kids around the world. Soon, young musicians from Ireland to Athens were hanging on Patti's ever words.

Meanwhile, the Ramones, after being rejected by virtually everyone, obtained a deal with Sire in November and spent the rest of the year getting ready for their first professional recording session. The jury was still out as to whether the Ramones were a revolution in music or just a bad joke—but by early 1976, it was very clear that some of the most exciting new music in the world was coming from the Bowery.

Meanwhile, music had taken a somewhat different direction in the UK. During the whole Beatles era, London clubs were filled with bands who were content to play R&B covers for a few quid a night. In about 1972, a new breed of band began to show up in pubs like Tally Ho and the Hope and Anchor. These groups attracted larger crowds and played more original material, much of it more aggressive than what people were used to hearing. The music press called this "pub rock" and it became quite the rage for a while. Groups like Brinsley Schwartz, Ducks Deluxe and Bees Make Honey didn't sell a lot of records, but they did get people interested in a new type of music that was coming from the street.

The break came in 1975 when a couple of British labels began to take a closer look at the whole pub rock scene. This was a big deal because at the time, British record companies were among the most conservative in the world. As a result, the release of Dr. Feelgood's first album went a long way towards legitimizing this new type of music. This record broke a fair amount of new ground and sold quite well, spreading the word on what was what was going on outside the mainstream music scene. Eddie and the Hot Rods soon followed with a debut album and a younger fan base—specifically music fans who were too young to get into the pubs.

The weak British economy of the mid-'70s also became a factor. For many young people, the choices were simple: get some menial factory job or go on welfare. Seizing the opportunity, some of the new pub rock bands began to act as spokespersons for the young and they were rewarded with the loyalty of an up-and-coming generation of music fans. Other young people were inspired to form their own bands, either to vent their frustration at being blown off by the British social/economic machine or to fight back at those they felt were responsible for their problems.

By late 1975, London was full of young, rag-tag bands who had some interesting musical ideas and a lot of enthusiasm, but who really didn't know where to go or how to get started. One group called London SS (featuring future members of the Clash and Public Image, Ltd.) showed some promise but couldn't seem to get going. However, at a clothing shop at 430 The King's Road in London, someone had started to hatch a plan. Enter Malcolm McLaren.

When Malcolm and the New York Dolls parted ways, he went back to managing his clothing shop. In 1975, it was called "Sex" and it specialized in the sort of torn and abused clothing inspired by the "Teddy Boy" styles of the '50s as well as the wardrobe of Richard Hell from Television. Even though the shop did decent business, McLaren decided that he wanted to take another whack at the music business—only this time, he was determined to be in control from the beginning. The shop would supply the outfits so at the very least, the whole endeavor would be a living, breathing commercial for the store. He recruited four young thugs from the neighborhood and dubbed them the Sex Pistols.

With Malcolm as their acting manager, the Sex Pistols started rehearsing using some stolen equipment. Their first public performance was at St. Martin's Art School on November 6, 1975—and it lasted all of ten minutes. The school's social secretary was so outraged by the Pistols act that the plug was pulled after about three songs. Malcolm, however, viewed this as only a minor setback. He was right because a year later, everyone would be talking about his new band and a new type of music called "punk."

The Year Punk Broke
1976

As the history of music goes, 1976 was one of the biggies. Several major events occurred on both sides of the Atlantic.

By April, the Sex Pistols had begun to attract attention and controversy, due mainly to their surly onstage attitude and the violence that broke out at some of their shows. Despite the bad press, word-of-mouth was good. In fact, the group's popularity was at the point where they were playing bigger clubs like the Nashville Rooms in London. After holding a series of recording sessions, the Pistols began a tour of England in May, which further strengthened the group's cult following and had a huge effect on many people. For example, one of the stops was the Lesser Free Trade Hall in Manchester. Among the 70 people that showed up were Pete Shelley, who was so inspired by what he saw that he decided to form a punk band of his own—the Buzzcocks. Peter Hook and Bernard Albrecht were there and they went on to form the group that would later lead to Joy Division and New Order. Neil Tennant (later of the Pet Shop Boys) was there to cover the event for *Sounds* magazine. And standing at the back of the room was the seventeen-year-old president of the local New York Dolls fan club, Stephen Morrissey, the future lead singer of the Smiths.

Another important series of events surrounded the Ramones. When they released their debut album in the early spring, it caused a sensation. At a time when the English music scene was dominated by art-rock groups like Yes and the macho posings of Led Zeppelin, here were four guys who knew three chords and one tempo. It was stripped down, very basic rock 'n' roll—in fact, it was so basic that it was incredibly different. The simple sound of *The Ramones* was exactly the opposite of what was normal in rock at the time; no songs of epic length, no solos and no pretentious stage patter. This album was nothing short of the beginning of a revolution in guitar-based rock music. That summer, their UK tour helped unite all the unorganized elements that were trying to come together as a new music scene. The Ramones and the Sex Pistols became catalysts in this musical chemistry and literally hundreds of new bands were formed that summer.

At the same time, a new subculture began to appear around bands like Television, the Pistols, the Clash, the Damned, as well as the

Ramones, complete with its attitudes and fashion. There was the underlying sense that after many years, music once again belonged to the fans. The groups making this music weren't pretentious, rich rock stars who had long since lost any connection to the street; the people up onstage were the same as the people in the audience and there was an honesty and sense of reality in the songs that had been missing in regular rock and pop. You didn't even have to be a very good musician; what counted was guts and enthusiasm. Disenfranchised music fans on both sides of the Atlantic had finally found something with which they could identify. And once it became obvious that this new scene was open to everybody, many fans made the leap to performer, introducing new ideas into music that multiplied at a geometric rate.

The punk scene quickly expanded throughout Britain and other parts of the Continent. The European Punk Rock Festival was held in August, followed by the 100 Club Punk Rock Festival in September. Groups like the Stranglers, the Buzzcocks, Subway Sect, the Jam and Siouxsie and the Banshees began to get coverage in the weekly British music press. Record labels started paying attention. On October 22,

27

↑ The Buzzcocks

the Damned became the first British punk act to release a single when Stiff Records issued "New Rose." The Pistols responded with "Anarchy in the UK" on EMI on November 26. But while all this was very exciting to the punk community, the average person knew and cared very little about what was going on. To the outside world, punk was a curiosity, nothing more than a passing fad. But that all changed on December 1.

The Sex Pistols appeared on an early evening chat show called "Today." The interview with host Bill Grundy lasted all of two minutes—but because the group responded to his taunts with all sorts of colorful language, the Pistols created a scandal. The next day, every paper in Britain featured stories on the Sex Pistols, and by that evening, everyone was talking about punk rock. Punk literally went from being a curious youth trend to national scandal overnight.

The Punk Movement Spreads
1977-78

By the beginning of 1977, all sorts of punk bands were releasing records. The Stranglers had a deal with A&M and issued "(Get a) Grip (on Yourself)" while Stiff released "Neat Neat Neat" from the Damned. The Buzzcocks couldn't be bothered with finding a record deal, so they released an EP entitled *Spiral Scratch* on their own New Hormones label. Literally hundreds of other groups were getting ready with their first singles. There seemed to be no end to the constant stream of new groups. However, the focal point and symbol of the entire British punk movement remained the Sex Pistols.

It seemed like the Pistols were always in the news. The Bill Grundy incident had made them synonymous with the word "punk"—but the resulting uproar created all sorts of problems for the band. A week after their *Today* appearance, the chairman of EMI issued an apology for the group's behavior. Many promoters were scared by the publicity and most of the dates on the Pistols' "Anarchy in the UK" tour were canceled. Then, on January 6 (days after a much-publicized vomiting incident at Heathrow airport), EMI dumped the band entirely, buying out the remainder of their contract for £40,000. Another crisis occurred when bassist Glen Matlock was fired over musical differences on February 15.

Malcolm McLaren remained undeterred. He hired the group's number-one fan and the alleged inventor of a dance called the "pogo" as

Matlock's replacement. His name was John Simon Ritchie, otherwise known as Sid Vicious. Malcolm also managed to turn the band's notoriety into another record deal. A month after Sid joined the band, the Pistols signed a new deal with A&M records for £150,000 in an elaborate setting outside Buckingham Palace. However, at the party that followed at corporate head office, the band allegedly got out of hand, spitting on the rug, harassing the secretaries, and dropping things out the window. When word of the Pistols' signing got around to other A&M artists (such as Peter Frampton and Karen Carpenter), they demanded that the label get rid of them. Within a week, the Pistols were again without a record contract—but they were paid £75,000 to get lost.

Once again, Malcolm pressed on and despite all the controversy, Virgin signed the band two months later and on May 27 (just in time for the Queen's Silver Jubilee), the Pistols released their second single, "God Save the Queen." Even though the song was banned by the BBC and most of the big record stores, it sold 150,000 copies in just five days. Two more singles followed: "Pretty Vacant" in July and "Holiday in the Sun" in October. Meantime, controversy continued to follow the band. Singer Johnny Rotten was attacked by a gang with razors on June 18. The next night, drummer Paul Cook was beaten up by five men using knives and an iron bar. Various local authorities became so spooked by the band and their fans that the Pistols had to tour under false names to avoid having their concerts banned. Finally, after two years, three record companies, two bassists, several brutal beatings and more than £120,000 in advances later, the Sex Pistols released their one and only proper album on November 12. *Never Mind the Bollocks— Here's the Sex Pistols* entered the British charts at number one.

While the Pistols were acting as the face of punk, many other groups were putting out great records. The Clash released their first single ("White Riot") in March and their debut album in April. A computer operator named Declan McManus became Elvis Costello and issued *My Aim is True* in August on the new Stiff Records. X-Ray Spex, the Adverts, Generation X and the Vibrators were just a few of the hundreds of British punk bands who managed to release records in 1977.

Some of these bands were signed by large record labels. Others benefited from the rise of the British independent label. These were small companies that sprang up in the back rooms of pubs and record stores in response to the public's demand for punk records. Most of the major labels couldn't be bothered with what most groups were doing, so new labels like Beggar's Banquet, Stiff and Rough Trade took up the slack and eventually became an integral part of the manufacture and distribution of this new music.

The British music press also got involved. The new punk and indie scene was perfect for publications like the *NME, Sounds, Record Mirror* and *Melody Maker*, who needed a constant supply of new bands to fill issues every week. Additional support came in the form of national radio programs on BBC Radio 1, most notably from DJ John Peel.

Things weren't proceeding with quite the same speed in North America for a variety of reasons. Unlike British punk, American punk seemed to lack the characteristics of any cohesive movement, probably because the social, political and economic environments were so much different. North America is also a whole lot bigger than Britain, which means that trends and ideas spread differently. North America also lacks any national weekly music papers, which makes it difficult to get the word out on new bands. The nature of radio is different, too, as there is no national radio voice to champion the cause of this new musical movement.

American record companies reacted differently, too. Instead of embracing the essence of the punk movement and presenting it in its original form, the major labels began to look for ways to water it down, in order to make it more palatable to the general public. The word "punk" was replaced with "new wave" and bands were signed on their salability and image rather than on their punk ideals. For example, the good looks and pop sounds of Debbie Harry and Blondie was looked upon as a better investment than Richard Hell and Voidoids. And unlike Britain, indie labels didn't have the same impact in North America, mainly because it was impossible to get any kind of proper distribution over such a vast geographic area. All this explains why the punk attitude spread much more slowly in North America.

Instead, North American punk grew in localized cells. The biggest one was in New York City. This scene was driven by a somewhat older, more artsy crowd. Groups like Talking Heads and Blondie were attracting most of the attention by the end of 1977, but groups like the Ramones, the Voidoids, the Dictators and Television also getting their share. There was a thriving punk scene in Ohio—although a lot of Ohio groups eventually ended up in New York. Bands like Pere Ubu and the Dead Boys got their start in places like Cleveland where they made music that was similar to what was coming out of Britain. Akron gave the world Chrissie Hynde and Devo. In Toronto, groups like the Diodes opened their own clubs while the Viltetones gained a reputation as the most intense punk group in the country. Los Angeles had developed its own punk community, featuring groups like X, the Germs, the Dils and the Motels. Boston had something going with the Cars and extremely influential Jonathan Richmond and the Modern Lovers. Other cities like Chicago, San Francisco, Vancouver, Philadelphia, Winnipeg and Washington, DC all developed smaller but active punk scenes.

The incredible thing about 1977 was that some form of the punk attitude took hold in all these cities at almost exactly the same time, without much help from the mainstream media. It was a genuine youth culture movement, a true revolt against the status quo. It was also the musical equivalent of the Big Bang.

The year began with one of the worst tours in the history of music. Malcolm McLaren had arranged a record deal with Warner Brothers and he felt it was time that America got a firsthand look at the Sex Pistols. The band was booked on a zig-zag tour of small clubs across the country. The first stop was supposed to have been an appearance on *Saturday Night Live,* but when the group ran into visa problems, Elvis Costello was called in as a replacement. (That's why the Pete Thomas, the drummer in Elvis' band, sported a t-shirt that read "Thanks Malc.")

When things were finally sorted out, the tour started on January 6 in Atlanta where the audience pelted the group with pig snouts. In Dallas, it was beer cans and tomatoes. Violence erupted at shows where the promoter sold too many tickets. The gig in Tulsa was picketed by Baptists from Oral Roberts University. During the flight to Memphis, the band's plane was struck by lightning. Between gigs, Malcolm fought with Johnny Rotten while Steve Jones and Paul Cook formed their own faction.

But the real problem was Sid, who was got weirder and more strung out on junk with each passing day. He'd wander off in search of drugs, miss the bus to the next gig and bring everything to a halt until someone found him. He began to throw strange prima donna fits, refusing to go to sound-check unless he was given a guitar strap with his name on it. During performances, he was all but useless, pounding away on his bass even though he had broken three of the four strings. It became the road crew's job to bathe him whenever he finally passed out.

The final stop on the tour was in San Francisco on January 14 in front of 5,000 people at the Winterland theatre. When the show was over, Johnny and Malcolm had one last blowout over a proposed trip to Brazil. That fight ended with Johnny walking out. The Sex Pistols were finished.

However, the punk movement that the Pistols helped establish lived on. If punk resulted in musical *revolution* between 1974 and 1977, 1978 was the year of musical *evolution*. It was a Darwinian sort of thing. All of punk's best musical ideas survived the confusion and began to mutate, fragment and grow.

For example, the Clash had expanded on both the musical and philosophical tenants of punk. Songs like "Police and Thieves" from their second album, *Give 'Em Enough Rope* incorporated bits of reggae into their sound. And instead of being consumed with the fatalism like the Pistols and so many other early punk bands, the Clash injected a positive energy into their music. They became protesters, the social conscience of this new musical movement.

Elvis Costello emerged as punk's best singer-songwriter. Like the Clash, Elvis didn't go along with the idea that all punk had to be fast and furious. His debut album had featured an American band called Clover (Huey Lewis and Sean Hopper went on to form Huey Lewis and the News; John McFee joined the Doobie Brothers), but by 1978, he and his new band, the Attractions, were working so well together

that Elvis issued two new albums. Each of them displayed new directions for the sound of punk.

More change was happening elsewhere. Although bands like the Stranglers, the Clash, Sham 69 and others carried on with the spirit of 1976 and 1977, it was becoming apparent that the original punk rage was starting to burn out. The anger, the constant turnover of bands, the violence, and the inevitable aging of the audience had begun to take their toll. Plus, it was only natural for some of the raw and rough punks to become better musicians the more they played—and accomplished musicians sound a whole lot different than a bunch of kids learning to play their instruments in public. Punk remained—but it was growing new branches, including something called "new wave."

By 1978, the major American record companies had realized that there really was something to this new music coming from the street. However, they also knew that while punk was the greatest thing ever to a lot of people, there were those who didn't care for it—the music was too heavy, the politics too extreme, the fashion too weird, the violence too scary. What the labels needed was a way of getting around these preconceptions in order to market and exploit this music. Then someone came up with the idea of co-opting the French phrase "nouvelle vague" and using a rough English translation in place of the word "punk." "New wave" was the term used to describe a certain type of new, stripped-down pop music that had the trappings and occasionally the appearance of punk but without the anger. And since this term was an American invention, the first groups to be tagged as New Wave were American: Blondie, Talking Heads, the Cars, Devo.

A form of new wave also began to develop in Britain. Again, these were groups that were inspired by the whole punk thing but whose music had a lot in common with the traditional pop song. In fact, "power pop" was the label applied to groups like XTC, the Tom Robinson Band, Adam and the Ants, the Motors and Squeeze.

Another important development in 1978 was the growing popularity of the keyboard synthesizer. Up until the early '70s, synthesizers were big, ungainly things used mostly by classical composers and experimental groups. The smallest ones were the size of a piano and you had to mess with dozens of patch chords until you got the thing to make the sound you wanted. That all changed in 1970 when Dr. Robert Moog introduced the first truly portable keyboard synthesizer. By 1978, they had become cheap enough for many people to finally try

33

them out.

Some of the first people to take advantage of this new technology were post-punk bands who had grown bored with the traditional guitar/bass/drums set up. These were musicians who not only grew up with the Sex Pistols and the Clash, but also with electronic pioneers such as Brian Eno, Can, Tangerine Dream and especially Kraftwerk, who had set the music world on its ear with their 1974 album *Autobahn* and again in 1978 with *The Man Machine*. Kraftwerk showed that electronic music could also be pop music. And with synthesizers becoming cheaper and easier to use, many young musicians began to understand the potential of this new instrument. Not only could you get original and different sounds from a synthesizer, but this modern technology made it easier to make music. Once you learned a few keyboard and programming basics, you began to sound like a musical genius and writing a song was simple. And what's more, you could make all the music yourself. Who needed a whole band?

Some artists like David Bowie and Ultravox introduced keyboards into their sound slowly, gradually building a bridge between punk, new wave and electronic music. Others dove straight in. Daniel Miller released a totally electronic song called "Warm Leatherette" under the name The Normal. Outside of anything released by Kraftwerk, this was one of the first true post-punk electro-pop singles. Daniel was so entranced by this new instrument that he went on to form Mute Records, a label devoted almost entirely to electro-pop music and the company that eventually discovered Depeche Mode.

By the end of 1978, the musical revolution started by punk was starting to look like the Big Bang theory of creation. A whole new universe of music was expanding outward from a single spark lit by the punk movement—and this universe was about to get a whole lot bigger in a very short period of time.

The Mutations of New Wave
1979-80

By 1979, there was no stopping the spread and exchange of musical ideas. Punk had injected so much life into music that there seemed to no end to the groups who were able to release material with fresh and unexpected twists.

Things were especially interesting in Britain, probably because there were so many young musicians being exposed to so many new ideas in a relatively small area. Not only did a lot of these groups hang out together, but there were other factors, too. The weekly music press needed these new bands to fill each edition (for example, the Cure appeared on the cover of *Sounds* after releasing just one single). BBC Radio 1 (most notably DJ John Peel's national program) was involved in promoting this new music. And while the major labels were interested in some of the major acts, indie labels like Beggar's Banquet, Rough Trade and Stiff released records by hundreds of other new groups whose material was in demand by their fans. More clubs began to book these new acts, and since the UK is a fairly small country, national tours were reasonably easy to arrange. It's no wonder that there was an explosion in post-punk British music and that the resulting fallout spread around the world.

Perhaps the most important release of the 1979-80 era came from the Clash, the most important of all the surviving punk bands. In December, they issued the double-LP set *London Calling*, an album that showed just how far punk had come from the thrash 'n' burn of 1976. It was a huge artistic and commercial success, from the cover shot of Paul Simonon smashing his bass, to "Train in Vain," the mystery track at the end of the side four. The album was so good, so powerful and so influential that *Rolling Stone* would eventually name *London Calling* as the most important album of the '80s.

But things had evolved beyond just punk. New musical mutations appeared almost daily. For example, some of the most exciting developments revolved around synthesizers. Keyboards were attracting more and more converts, mainly because they were so portable (no more big, clunky amplifiers to lug around) and because each new model was more versatile than the one before. Coming up with sounds that no human ear had ever heard before was a breeze—and some of the high-end models could be synched up with a rhythm track on a tape recorder or with this new gadget called a "drum machine." Regular rock bands had been using synthesizers as spice for years, but now more and more artists were basing their entire careers on what they could get these machines to do.

Because this new sound relied so heavily on technology, it eventually became known as "techno-pop" and for a time, "electro-beat." Beggar's Banquet made a huge contribution to this new trend when they had a #1 single with "Are Friends Electric?" from Gary Numan and the Tubeway Army. Orchestral Manoeuvres in the Dark (a four-piece band from Liverpool that included a tape recorder named "Winston" and some homemade electronic noisemakers) released a totally electronic pop song called "Electricity" on Factory Records. Finally, Daniel Miller's Mute Records had expanded beyond The Normal to include new synth bands like Fad Gadget. (See *Techno-Pop Plugs In* sidebar on p. 71.)

And there was more. By the end of the year, it was obvious that post-punk music had begun to separate and cleave into what could best be described as sub-genres. One of the first was ska. It had begun with a small scene in Coventry. Jerry Dammers was a big fan of Jamaican ska and reggae artists like Don Drummond, Desmond Dekker and Prince Buster. He loved the energy and fun of their music. In 1977, he formed a band called the Specials that was devoted to an updated form of ska. Many working-class kids who were tired of the anger of punk immediately latched on to the Specials danceable brand of music and its concept of racial harmony and justice. (See *The Rise and Fall of Ska* sidebar on p. 72.)

In North America, the big thing was new wave. That term was being used more and more, but things were a little confusing. Virtually anyone with a fresh sound was being immediately categorized as being part of the so-called "new wave movement." For example, while the B-52's were called new wave, so was Tom Petty and the Heartbreakers. Groups in suits and skinny ties like the Knack also somehow qualified as new wave. The term was also applied practically every British artist, including the Clash, the Stranglers, Joe Jackson, the Jam, Elvis Costello, XTC, and the Police. As a result, "new wave" evolved into an umbrella term that described an *era* in music rather than a specific *sound*.

But for awhile, any group tagged as "new wave" was almost guaranteed to receive a fair amount of attention. With this variety and constant media hype, it was inevitable that a few of these artists would appeal to mainstream audiences. To North American audiences, new wave was fun, a little quirky and comfortably different from traditional rock and Top 40—and a hell of a lot better than disco. Debbie Harry of Blondie became the most identifiable face of new wave, especially after their crossover disco hit, "Heart of Glass." The Cars did well with their second album, *Candy-O,* plus they got a chance to perform in front of 500,000 people in Central Park. The Talking Heads continued to break new ground with their highly-rhythmic third album *Fear of Music.* Over 5,000 people turned up at the "New Wave Festival" in Min-

nesota to see Devo and 22 other bands, while several other cities held similar events.

As the '80s got underway, it was becoming more and more apparent that the punk scene of the '70s had set off an unstoppable chain reaction. What's more, each of the new sub-genres that kept popping up took on lives of their own.

It was a little difficult to grasp. Here was an obviously new musical culture and mindset coalescing around this huge array of sounds and scenes. There seemed little to link it all together, other than the fact that everything had a common ancestry in punk, a spirit of adventure and a burning desire to do everything differently.

One of the most important new wave debuts came from the Pretenders. Chrissie Hynde was an American who had once worked in Malcolm McLaren's clothing store. The Pretenders had a style that cut across the lines defining punk, new wave, rock and Top 40, making them one of the greatest exporters of post-punk attitudes and influence. By the time they appeared at the Heatwave festival in Toronto that summer, their album had entered the British charts at #1.

Other acts laboring under the new wave label also managed to break new ground. The Talking Heads were making music that was so complex that by the time they appeared at Heatwave, their regular four-piece line up was being augmented by five extra musicians. Funk, jazz and African rhythms were all now part of the Talking Heads' sound and

↑ The Pretenders

their *Remain in Light* album was one of the most influential of the year. Blondie also spread the word on American new wave with their platinum album *Autoamerican* and the single "Call Me" from the movie *American Gigolo*. The B-52's, the GoGos and Devo were some of the other new wave names to receive major attention.

The Clash continued to conquer new frontiers in the name of punk with *London Calling*. By the spring, the album had reached number 27 on the LP charts while the single "Train in Vain" had climbed even higher on the pop charts. The Clash was also accomplishing a rare triple play. Not only were they setting new standards for what a punk band could do, they were also enjoying considerable commercial success while at the same time retaining credibility with their hardcore fans. By the end of the year, the Clash had toured both North America and Europe, completed a movie called *Rude Boy,* released an EP entitled *Black Market Clash* and released the *triple* album *Sandinista!* It's no wonder that people were calling them "the only band that mattered."

Britain continued to be the most fertile place for new ideas. Once punk made it clear that music didn't have any rules, young musicians began to take up this "anything goes, D.I.Y." attitude. Fresh ideas were being introduced almost daily. One of the more dramatic mutations of punk were goth and industrial music. (**See** *The Birth of Goth* **sidebar**

on p. 73 and *The Industrial Revolution* sidebar on p. 74.)

Infiltrating the Mainstream and MTV
1981-82

Although it didn't seem like it at the time, one of the most significant events in the history of music occurred at 12:01 am EDT on August 1, 1981. A new cable TV channel called "MTV" signed on. MTV ("Music Television") was entirely devoted to a new art form called the "music video" which were short, visual interpretations of songs that were used for promotional purposes by some artists. MTV didn't have a lot to work with. When they signed on (with a measly budget of $20 million), all they had were 250 videos and 30 of them were by Rod Stewart. Eventually, they were able to convince record labels that it was in their best interests to invest money into videos because once people realized it was fun to *watch* their favorite songs, they would go out and buy more records. Appropriately enough, the first clip ever shown on MTV was "Video Killed the Radio Star" by Buggles. (See *A Quick History of Music Videos* sidebar on p. 75.)

From the very beginning, MTV had an appetite for stylish and photogenic performers because they looked best on television. Plus, the network had so much time to fill. Where were they going to find enough videos to fill 24 hours a day? The new wave scene. Suddenly, "weirdo" groups like Soft Cell, The Pretenders, the Cars, Duran Duran and Simple Minds had their videos being exposed across North America and around the world, courtesy of MTV. In time, some of these strange, new groups with their weird haircuts, synthesizers and radical musical ideas became superstars, further upsetting the old order of rock and roll. Music would never be the same.

A rich source of material for MTV was an off-shoot of new wave called the new romantic movement. This was a combination of the sound and fashion style created by Roxy Music and David Bowie in the mid-'70s and resurrected in 1980 with the album *Vienna* by Ultravox. *Vienna* was a very lushly textured album, enhanced by an innovative combination of synthesizers and guitars. Groups such as Spandau Ballet, ABC and Visage adopted this style as their own and advanced it further.

Speaking of synthesizers, technology was making it possible for more groups to create all kinds of different sounds. OMD, Human League and Depeche Mode were beginning to ditch recorded backing tracks and reel-to-reel tape machines for computers, sequencers and drum machines. And like their new romantic-pop cousins, techno pop groups were looked upon as some of the most revolutionary and eye-catching performers around.

Adapt and *mutate* continued to be the name of the game everywhere in the world of music. Echo and the Bunnymen's combination of punk and psychedelia was proving to be very popular. They were part of a scene that included the Teardrop Explodes and the Psychedelic Furs. Goth music developed a stronger hold in 1981 thanks to groups like Wedding Present, Bauhaus, and Siouxsie and the Banshees.

The Clash continued to be at the top of the punk heap in Britain, although they had overextended themselves with their *triple* LP *Sandinista!* The Stranglers and the Damned continued to be viable forces, but the most interesting aspect of the punk scene was that a second generation of bands was starting to be heard.

These fell into two categories. The first was made up of members of the punk scene that had moved beyond their original groups. For example, Generation X had broken up, sending Billy Idol off to a solo career. Joy Division regrouped after the death of singer Ian Curtis under the name New Order. Johnny Lydon had firmly established himself with Public Image, Ltd. The second category was made up of the kids who were inspired by the first wave of bands that appeared in the mid-'70s. When they were 14 and 15, they had gone to Clash and Sex Pistols shows. Now they were old enough to have their own groups, like Stiff Little Fingers, Gang of Four and U2. These groups picked up the punk torch and carried it off in many different directions at once. (See *The Death of Ian Curtis* sidebar on p. 79.)

New Pop, College Rock and New Technologies 1982-83

By the summer of 1982, new wave groups had struck deep into the mainstream music scene. British artists (featuring what was dubbed "new pop" or "Euro-pop" sound) were doing particularly well with albums and singles: Human League, Eurythmics, ABC, Thomas Dolby, A Flock of Seagulls. Both radio and MTV ate this stuff up and more and more people were exposed to these new musical ideas.

One obvious by-product of new pop was that making music videos became more important that ever. The general perception was that groups that made videos sold records. Those who didn't soon faded away. Videos had arrived as an essential part of the promotion of every type of popular music. But no one could have predicted the giant boost the entire music industry was about to get from Michael Jackson—and one of the biggest beneficiaries was the alternative scene.

On March 23, 1983, Michael Jackson appeared on the *Motown 25th Anniversary Special* where he performed a song called "Billie Jean" from his new album, *Thriller.* It was an amazing performance, complete with his patented "moonwalk" dance step. Fans raved about the show for months.

The strong public reaction to Michael Jackson resulted in two major events. First, "Billie Jean" became so hot as a single that MTV could no longer ignore it. That song broke the color barrier on the network which brought a whole new audience to MTV. Fans of different genres began to scope each other out, learning the music, the code words and the fashion. Secondly, millions of people were lured into record stores again, looking to buy a copy of *Thriller.* Michael Jackson was responsible for helping to end a big financial slump in the record industry.

The alternative scene felt the effects of this almost immediately. When people tuned in to see "Billie Jean" on MTV, chances were that they also saw a video by a strange new wave act such as the Eurythmics—and liked it. And when people went into the record store to buy the Jackson album, some lingered long enough to check out albums by some of the bands that they caught on MTV by accident. The net result was more exposure for alternative bands.

Two technological events helped get more people involved in music. The first was the introduction of the Sony Walkman. Instead of just having portable radios with earplugs, people now began to use personal stereos with headphones. For the first time, a device was available that allowed the wearer to program *what* music to listen to and *when.* Sales of both pre-recorded and blank cassettes went through the roof. The second milestone happened on February 3, 1983, when Sony and Philips announced that they had jointly developed a new music storage medium called the "compact disc." Both the Walkman and the CD introduced a new level of technology to the general public which made listening to music more flexible and more enjoyable. And when you have more people involved in music and demanding more, there's going to be a greater demand for variety.

Musicians were also taking advantage of new technologies. The members of New Order were big into fiddling with sequencers and

drum machines. They managed to sell 3 million copies of a sequencer-driven 12" dance single entitled "Blue Monday." Yazoo, Blancmange, Art of Noise, Heaven 17 and OMD continued to find new and interesting ways to use keyboards and computers. Helping them was the fact that more and more recording studios were installing special sampling keyboards like Fairlights and Synclaviers. This new equipment allowed musicians to work with new, unimagined sounds that had no equivalent in the real world. Thanks to sequencers and computers, arrangements once considered impossible for a pop group to play could now be performed on-stage. And thanks to the new studio technologies that were coming on-line, the possibilities for creating new sounds for the purposes of making music were endless. (**See** *How New Order Made It Cool to Dance Again* **sidebar on p. 79.**)

(**See** *How New Order Made It Cool to Dance Again* **sidebar on p. 79.**)

This new form of electronic music was an affront to some of punk purists—but there weren't many of them left. The Damned, the Stranglers and the Clash were still around—although things had changed considerably. In 1977, the Clash were so poor that they'd often be forced to eat the flour-and-water paste that they used to stick up the posters advertising their gigs. In 1982, they accepted an invitation to be the opening act on the Who's first farewell tour. And while some fans

42

considered this to be a sellout, the Clash's music continued to be revolutionary. *Combat Rock* was one of the more respected releases of the year and there were those who thought that the album represented a body blow to the mainstream. Punk, they believed, was still in a position to change *all* music for the better.

But just because former hardcore punks like the Clash and Billy Idol were infiltrating the mainstream didn't mean that there was no one out on the fringe. Echo and the Bunnymen, the Psychedelic Furs and the Teardrop Explodes were exploring a new neo-psychedelic sound. The goth scene had really taken off in England and was producing far-out material by groups such as Alien Sex Fiend and Sex Gang Children. And industrial music had begun to evolve from the clank and crash of Throbbing Gristle and Einsturzende Neubauten into the aggressive dance floor melodies of Cabaret Voltaire. And then there was the whole matter of the music being played on college radio.

By the early '80s, there were several commercial radio stations in North America devoted to playing this non-mainstream music, most notably CFNY-FM in Toronto and KROQ in Los Angeles. But the commercial stations were far outnumbered by radio stations that originated from university campuses across the continent. These stations were supported by the schools and not dependent on ratings and advertising revenue. This, in essence, allowed them to play whatever music they wanted, no matter how weird or experimental. For example, the University of Georgia at Athens had a campus station called WUOG and the volunteer DJs would often play stuff that you would never hear on any of the big stations out of Atlanta. If you were within the range of its transmitter in the fall of 1982, you may have heard the station feature material by a new local group called R.E.M. Or you may have heard more from that other local band, the B-52's. Eventually, college radio would organize and become an extremely powerful force in the emerging alternative scene. People soon caught on that if you wanted to hear the newest of the new music out there, the best place to go was your local college radio station.

American "college rock" was different. First of all, it featured a back-to-basics guitar-bass-drums approach that stood out like a sore thumb in what was a very techno-pop world. But at the same time, this wasn't standard rock 'n' roll. There were no guitar solos, drum solos or elaborate stage shows—that and the fact that the people in the band looked, well, like regular people. There were no fancy costumes or wild haircuts. No one had seen this kind of straightforward music since the old punk days.

By the end of 1983, this whole new music scene was spread out over a wide spectrum. The post-punk world scene had cleaved and separated into dozens of different flavors. It was like going to an ice cream stand that offered more selection that you could imagine: punk, college rock, hardcore, goth, industrial, techno-pop, new pop, power pop, new romantics, cold wave, ska—the list seemed endless.

Thanks mainly to Top 40 radio, groups like Human League, Thompson Twins and ABC had managed to establish themselves firmly within the mainstream. But once you began to move to the left, the variety became almost overwhelming. There were "college rock" bands like R.E.M., dreamy poets like Kate Bush, hardcore punks like Black Flag, experimental groups like Psychic TV, serious goths like Alien Sex Fiend and heavy industrial types like Einsturzende Neubauten. The alternative world was getting far more complicated than anyone could have ever imagined.

The Mid-Eighties
1984-86

Amongst the bewildering varieties of styles in the post-punk, post-New Wave world, a star system was beginning to develop. Although they were still firmly outside the mainstream in terms of music and attitude, several groups had achieved enough commercial clout to be set apart from the pack. Depeche Mode, the Cure and New Order were now all major acts in the alternative world and each album and tour was more anticipated than the last.

Two other groups were also promising big things. The Smiths started getting serious attention in November 1983 when they released the single "This Charming Man." That release was followed in February 1984 by *The Smiths*, which was by all accounts an amazing record. This was simple pop, featuring Morrissey's eloquent lyrics and Johnny Marr's tasteful and sparkling guitar. The effect was even more stunning when the Smiths' music was played alongside the techno-pop sounds of the day. This interesting, refreshing and highly emotional change of pace was to change the nature of British music for the rest of the '80s.

The reaction to the Smiths was so strong that there was an immediate demand for more new material. Rough Trade was forced to issue a second album entitled *Hatful of Hollow*, which was really nothing more

that a series of B-sides, radio sessions and studio outtakes. That record further intensified interest in the Smiths, especially after everyone discovered "How Soon is Now?," one of the most enduring and influential singles in the history of alternative music. The Smiths continued to build on their popularity when their much-anticipated third album, *Meat Is Murder*, was released in February 1985. That record had the distinction of blowing Bruce Springsteen's *Born in the USA* out of the #1 position on the British charts. No one had seen *that* coming. And by the time *The Queen Is Dead* was released in 1986, the Smiths (and specifically Morrissey) were being revered as gods in some circles. **(See *The Smiths' Bad Year* sidebar on p. 80.)**

The other group that was living up to its potential was U2. When *Boy* was released in 1980, there were hints that there was something special about them. By 1983's *War*, they had developed into a solid album band who could make a large stadium feel as intimate as a nightclub.

The real breakthrough came in 1984 when the band released *The Unforgettable Fire*. Produced by Brian Eno and newcomer Daniel Lanois, the record was filled with reoccurring themes of freedom and achievement. The album further enhanced U2's position as a rare commodity: a group that managed to sell millions of records and concert tickets while managing to preserve their artistry, integrity and credibil-

45

↑ A very young U2

ity in the eyes of their fans. The "Bono as God" comparison did get a little tiresome, but there was no question that he had developed into a riveting frontman, which transformed U2 into one of the world's most intense live acts. In a world of synthesizers and the posings of traditional rock groups, U2 was very different. (See *Band Aid* sidebar on p. 80.)

British keyboards, however, continued to rule the day. Groups like Simple Minds, Tears for Fears, Thompson Twins, Bronski Beat, OMD and A Flock of Seagulls received the majority of attention from both radio and MTV. The limits of studio technology were being pushed back by artists such as Art of Noise, Howard Jones and Thomas Dolby. Everyone was into using the new keyboards such as the Emulator and the Yamaha DX-7.

But guitars hadn't faded away completely. There were the occasional flashes of neo-psychedelia from Echo and the Bunnymen and the Psychedelic Furs. California hardcore punk was very much alive, thanks to Black Flag, the Minutemen and the Dead Kennedys. Minneapolis had also become a guitar mecca of sorts due primarily to the hardcore work of Hüsker Dü, Soul Asylum and the Replacements. R.E.M. continued to build a following among the "college rock," while at the same time, interest in "roots rock" and the jangly "paisley underground" (Del Fuegos, Guadacanal Diary, Los Lobos, Dream Syndicate, the Bangles) began to take hold. While L.A. had long been a hotbed for punk, things were also starting to get a little funky. The Red Hot Chili Peppers and Fishbone were showing everyone how you could mix punk and funk with bits of ska to create a whole new sound. Funk was also being crossed with metal up in San Francisco by a band named Faith No More.

Goth and pseudo goth music was on the move, too. By this time, it had spread beyond the scene in London—and once that happened, it too began to mutate. The Cult traded their doom and gloom for a dash of psychedelia and released "She Sells Sanctuary," one of the most popular alternative singles of the decade. Love and Rockets attracted a serious following through *The Seventh Dream of Teenage Heaven* (1985) and *Express* (1986). Meanwhile, Peter Murphy (another Bauhaus alumni) was on his way to establishing a solo career with his first album, *Should the World Fail to Fall Apart.* And although Siouxsie Sioux spent much of 1985 battling hepatitis, she and her band continued to add more elements of pop to their sound, which was very apparent of their

46

Cities in Dust EP and on the 1986 album, *Tinderbox.* **(See sidebar *Goth Wars* on p. 82.)**

Gender-bending and expressions of sexuality were back in the news. While the mainstream was contending with Annie Lennox of the Eurythmics, Marilyn, Divine and Boy George, the alternative scene had Liverpool's Frankie Goes to Hollywood. In fact, for awhile, it looked as if Frankie was going to take over the world.

The group was fiercely proud of being gay and let it be known at every given opportunity. Photo shoots often featured leather bondage wear. Interviews talked of decadent weekends in Amsterdam bath houses. Live shows featured half-naked muscle men as stage decorations. Special "Frankie Say" T-shirts were printed up, each sporting a different outrageous saying. Everything Frankie did was orchestrated to create as much controversy as possible. And the BBC was a big part of it.

It all began shortly after Frankie released their first single, "Relax," in November 1983. Although it was an immediate hit, the BBC had problems with the lyrics. Things really hit the fan in January 1984 when (at the urging of BBC Radio 1 DJ Mike Reid) the BBC banned the record. That was exactly what Frankie ordered. The song went to #1 the next week, spreading the Frankie phenomenon throughout Britain and threatening to export it around the world.

Frankie Goes to Hollywood ended up selling millions of 7" singles and several million copies of their debut album, *Welcome to the Pleasuredome.* But their most enduring contribution to the history of alternative music was their use of the 12" remix. The 12" was already a staple in the dance clubs—but few of them were more than extended versions of the single through the use of clever edits or with the addition of extra dance beats. It was like stretching a meal by adding bread crumbs to a pound of hamburger. Frankie changed all that. "Relax" was totally reassembled into at least half a dozen distinct forms. Same thing with the follow-up single, "Two Tribes."

This approach was so successful that it forced everyone to pay much more attention to the concept of the 12" single. As a result of Frankie, producers and engineers were forced to become much more creative and sophisticated when remixing a single. Secondly, record labels were given a real indication of the kind of money you could make with remixes. If you were clever, you could get people to buy multiple copies of the same song. Plus, you could extend the life of the song. Is it any wonder that the number and variety of 12" releases exploded after Frankie? (See *Did Frankie Play on Their Own Record?* sidebar on p. 83.)

Another format was also becoming quite popular. The EP (extended play) was similar to an album except that it contained between three and six songs. Most EPs were built around a single from a current or upcoming album. People were enticed to buy the release because the remaining songs were often unavailable anywhere else. The B-52's, Devo, and the Pretenders were some of the first groups to take advantage of the trend.

The newest trend in studio technology was the use of samples. The Frankie album was full of sample instruments but other artists were incorporating sampled *sounds*. Mick Jones was one of the first. The day after he was kicked out of the Clash in 1983, he began assembling a new band which he called Big Audio Dynamite. By 1985, they were ready with a debut album which featured all sorts of strange snippets of voice and sound effects interspersed within the music. The big single from the album was "$E=MC^2$," featuring dialogue samples from a 1970 movie entitled *Performance* (starring Mick Jagger). "$E=MC^2$" was the first hit rock song anywhere in the world to feature this new concept and it made Mick Jones one of the great musical innovators of the '80s. (See *Live Aid* sidebar on p. 83.)

Another band that continued to show enormous creativity through clever use of technology was New Order. Two years after they came up with the idea of putting a rock bass line to a synthesizer dance beat, their music was changing the very nature of dance music. Their big break in American came when Quincy Jones (Michael Jackson's producer) signed them to his Qwest label. *Power, Corruption and Lies* (1983) was given a proper release in the US, and a new record, *Low-Life* (1986) was issued.

The Late '80s
1987-89

The stock market may have taken a big hit in 1987, but the alternative world was still enjoying a bull market as the music launched another attack on the mainstream. In fact, if you had been able to buy stocks in alternative music in the mid-'80s, you would have seen steady price increases year after year as the alternative scene commanded more attention and more respect.

However, let's get back to the real world. If you wanted to make money by studying musical trends, the place to invest was in technology—and the event that really set things in motion was the release of a record by a studio group called M/A/R/R/S.

M/A/R/R/S came about when Ivo Watts-Russell (the head of 4AD Records) introduced the Colourbox to a group called AR Kane. (The name is made up of the initials of the five principle members: **Martyn, Alex, Rudy**, Ivo Watts-**R**ussell and **S**teven). All five guys were very much into this high-tech musical move called "sampling." They were impressed with what Mick Jones had done with Big Audio Dynamite, but they were ready to take things to the next level.

With the help of a couple of London club DJs, the members of the Colourbox and AR Kane collaborated on a recording using a method that turned the entire music world upside down. They sampled little snatches of songs by Trouble Funk, Eric B. and Rakim, the Last Poets, the Jazzy Five, the Criminal Element Orchestra, Israeli singer Ofra Haza, James Brown and even the Iranian Revolutionary Army Chorus. Then they reassembled these clips into something entirely new: a full song consisting of almost nothing but samples and reconstructions. Vocals, screams, spoken word phrases, basslines, guitar chords, drum sounds—all borrowed from other recordings and used to generate new sounds and new arrangements. Think of it as building a musical version of the Frankenstein monster using hundreds of spare notes and sounds that you were able to isolate and sample.

"Pump Up the Volume" was revolutionary. It showed how a computer could be used as a musical instrument—except that instead of having just notes at your disposal, you had an infinite number of *sounds*. And what's more, there was no limit to the ways you could shape, edit, mold and reassemble those sounds. You didn't even have to be a musician. If you knew how to program a synthesizer and how to run a personal computer, you could make music. This meant that you could become a pop star without a band and without having to tour. In fact, you could quite literally make extraordinarily complex music all by yourself in your bedroom. The result has been that this type of sampling has done more to change the way we make music since the invention of the keyboard synthesizer—and "Pump Up the Volume" was the song that kicked off this revolution.

Meanwhile, several groups had become quite good at using the new keyboards-and-computers technology. The Pet Shop Boys arranged their entire *Actually* album on a Fairlight. Erasure presented an updated techno-pop sound with releases like *The Circus*. Depeche Mode spent a good deal of 1987 creating new sounds at a studio in Spain. Even goth bands were getting more high-tech. The Sisters of Mercy hired Jim Steinman (Meatloaf's songwriting partner!) to produce a heavily-textured album entitled *Floodland*.

There were two remarkable debut records in 1987. Sinead O'Connor was a former shoplifter and Kiss-O-Gram French maid from Dublin who had previously found work as a back-up singer for World Party (she's on the *Private Revolution* album) and with The Edge of U2 (she sings on his *Captive* soundtrack). The first thing people noticed about her was that she was totally bald; the second thing was her incredibly powerful voice. With a little help from her friends in the Irish music industry, Sinead (who was just 20 years old) was allowed to record a debut album. Writing almost all of the material herself and producing the record on her own, Sinead delivered *The Lion and the Cobra*, one of the most astounding debut albums of all time.

The second major debut of 1987 came from the Beastie Boys. Hip-hop, house and rap had once been considered part of the alternative world, but by the mid-'80s, those scenes had grown to the point where they had cleaved away into cultures of their own. However, the Beastie Boys' debut fell right on the fault line. *Licensed to Ill* was full of samples, rapping and rock-style guitars, making it appealing to many alternative fans. However, the rap and hip-hop cultures benefited the most. *Licensed to Ill* assaulted the mainstream and became the first rap album to hit #1 on the *Billboard* charts. From that point on, rap and hip-hop spread like wildfire.

Part of the Beastie Boys success was due to producer Rick Rubin. In the old days, he was known as DJ Double RR, the guy who scratched on the turntables behind the Beasties. By 1987, he had founded Def Jam (now American Recordings), a label that would be responsible for issuing some serious groundbreaking rap records. Rubin also radically changed the sound of the Cult when he was asked to produce the follow-up to the *Love* album. The result was a very chunky, *un*-psychedelic and *un*-gothic record entitled *Electric*. Even though old-time Cult fans were outraged at the results, this album marked a turning point in the Cult's career. It sold millions—and another piece of the alternative world leaked into the mainstream.

The Cure, R.E.M., Depeche Mode and New Order were also getting

51

ALAN CROSS

bigger and stronger. The Cure's double album, *Kiss Me, Kiss Me, Kiss Me*, resulted in their first ever Top 40 single in North America. Many people considered the success of "Just Like Heaven" to be nothing short of a minor miracle—but looking back, it was simply an early indication that there were changes in the air. You could also see it with R.E.M. and "The One I Love," a major single from *Document*, the breakthrough album that they had been working towards since 1983. Depeche Mode set the stage for widespread frenzy with "Strange Love," a single from *Music for the Masses*. And while New Order didn't release much new material in 1987, they consolidated their position as the world's best alterno-dance band with *Substance*, a double collection of their most popular 12" releases.

However, the deepest incursion into the mainstream came from U2. By the middle of the decade, U2's appeal was so universal that they were poised to become the most important band in the world. All they needed was that one album to send them over the top. On March 9, 1987, they delivered *The Joshua Tree*, a brilliant record that straddled a half-dozen genres at once while remaining totally unique.

The effect was immediate. On April 2, U2 started a world tour in Tempe, Arizona—and over the next nine months and 112 shows, only *three* were not sellouts. The first 29 shows were in North America and saw 465,452 tickets sold—a 99.77% sellout rate.

Within weeks, *The Joshua Tree* became the first compact disc to sell a million copies; by the time the tour moved to Europe in May, the album had sold seven million copies and had topped the charts in 22 countries. In Holland, 92,000 tickets sold out in less than an hour. More than 12,000 people lined up to buy tickets in Glasgow. More than 115,000 people attended a single show in Madrid, Spain. When things wrap up in August, the European tour had reached 1,195,000 people who bought 92.7% of all the tickets. In the space of less than a year, U2 had gone from being a band with a large cult-like following to being one of the biggest groups ever.

Meanwhile, two highly influential bands had come to an end. Between 1979 and 1987, Hüsker Dü changed the nature of hardcore punk in America. While Bob Mould was still very much into thrashy loud guitars, he was also fond of strong melodies in his music, an idea which altered the sound and direction of hardcore. Hüsker Dü also became the first hardcore band to sign with a major label, a sign that the music industry was now taking punks seriously. But after years of

← King Ad-Rock aka Adam Horovitz of the Beastie Boys

almost constant touring, Hüsker Dü was tired and beset by internal turmoil. It was time to fold.

Even more significant was the demise of the Smiths. The Morrissey/Marr combination had an incalculable effect on British music—but things had fallen apart. No one in the band was getting along, plus there were ill feelings towards the record company and problems with management. Plus, no one seemed to be talking to each other. The result was a long, ugly protracted break-up that was finally made official on September 12. (See *When Exactly Did the Smiths Break Up?* sidebar on p. 84.)

Guitars made a big comeback in 1988. In California, Jane's Addiction emerged with a heavy post-goth glam-punk sound that first caught on up and down the Sunset Strip. In another part of town, a small label called SST continued its commitment to musical independence by releasing material from bands like the Meat Puppets, Sonic Youth and Black Flag. Meanwhile, Bad Religion's Epitaph label was hard at work preserving California punk.

But there was more to this guitar renaissance than just southern California. Something heavy was happening up in Seattle, featuring bands with names like Soundgarden, Green River and Screaming Trees. Things were also starting to heat up in Boston again, thanks to groups like the Pixies and Dinosaur Jr. Meanwhile, the Sugarcubes came out of Iceland with a sound that incorporated elements of Joy Division, the Cocteau Twins, and Jesus and Mary Chain. And out of England, we started to hear of "grebo" bands like Pop Will Eat Itself, Zodiac Mindwarp and Gaye Bikers on Acid.

There was much growth on the industrial front. New keyboard and computer technology allowed groups to create complex recordings that were more intense than ever before. However, an interesting split was developing. Most industrial music continued to be based in Europe where there was a strong tradition of using aggressive keyboard sounds and noise samples (Front 242, Nitzer Ebb, Einsturzende Neubauten, A Split Second). North American industrial bands were making more use of guitar samples (Ministry, Skinny Puppy, Lard, Big Black). But whatever the flavor, industrial music remained incomprehensible to most people.

That all began to change when a kid from Mercer, Pennsylvania, released an album entitled *Pretty Hate Machine* in 1989. Trent Reznor and Nine Inch Nails were a phenomenon from the start. The industrial crowd loved the record and people who were tired of regular hard rock and metal jumped in because they were looking for something other than another Aerosmith or Van Halen album. It didn't take long for *Pretty Hate Machine* to become the biggest-selling industrial album of all time.

Goth received a dose of Led Zeppelin when John Paul Jones was hired to produced *Children* for the Mission and helped create the band's anthem, "Tower of Strength." There were also releases from Peter Murphy (*Love Hysteria*), a series of singles and EPs from Jesus and Mary Chain, and a very poppy album from Siouxsie and the Banshees entitled *Peep Show*.

More acts that were once totally within the domain of alternative music were now infiltrating the mainstream. After years of being a cult favorite, INXS became a genuine superstar act with the release of *Kick*. Right behind them were two more acts from the southern hemisphere: Midnight Oil and Crowded House.

The five leading groups remained U2, Depeche Mode, the Cure, New Order, and R.E.M. They were all selling huge amounts of records and concert tickets—yet they still managed to retain an image of independence and auras of credibility and integrity. This allowed them to act as ambassadors and recruiters for alternative music. When someone got hooked on, say, Depeche Mode, it was possible for them to discover similar groups like Erasure and OMD. If another person found they really liked New Order, then it wasn't much of a stretch to get into Joy Division. The bigger these groups got, the more people were introduced to alternative music.

And bigger they got. Depeche Mode capped their world tour with a performance at the Rose Bowl in front of 75,000 people—which subsequently resulted in a concert film entitled *101*. The Cure played to big crowds on their 1988 world tour. New Order was summoned to play a club gig for the Duke and Duchess of York. U2 had a theatrical release for their self-produced documentary, *Rattle and Hum*. And R.E.M. continued to gather more fans at an exponential rate. It started with the summer release of a "greatest hits" album, *Eponymous*, followed by the *Green* album and a tour in the fall. *Rolling Stone* put them on the cover with the headline "America's Best Rock 'n' Roll Band" while *NME* listed four R.E.M. records in their "Top 100 Albums of All Time" survey.

Meanwhile, the alternative music lifecycle continued. Some fans had grown bored or were turned off by the commercial success of their

heroes. This meant it was time to look for something new. Some found what they were looking for in Seattle.

Bands in the Pacific Northwest were playing a new type of music that was a mix of heavy mainstream rock and hardcore punk: Soundgarden, Green River, Alice in Chains and Nirvana. The Seattle scene was pretty much a secret at the end of the '80s. Only the locals and those who knew about Sub Pop realized what was going on. But the word was getting out. **(See *The Birth of Grunge* sidebar on p. 85.)**

Almost 5,000 miles from Seattle, another local scene was getting ready to go international. Several local groups had caused a sensation by crossing psychedelic '60s-style pop with the local acid house and rave scene—and the British music press was once again all lathered up.

The whole thing was dubbed the "Manchester Scene." Whether there really was any sort of actual "scene" is up for debate because there were a lot of other groups from this city who weren't into this kind of music. But still, some of these sounds were very exciting.

There were four groups at the center of this storm. Happy Mondays provided an ecstasy-driven form of dance music. Inspiral Carpets were all about updated '60s pop, complete with a cheesy organ sound. Charlatans UK loved their Hammond organ and their baggy pants. But the undisputed champions of Manchester were the Stone Roses.

The Stone Roses were *the* British group of 1989. The first pressing

The Stone Roses ↑

of their brilliant debut album sold out in less than a week. Thousands went to their live shows. Singer Ian Brown and guitarist John Squire were singled out for all sorts of awards. *Melody Maker* called the band "The #1 Brightest Hope." *Sounds* and *NME* named the Roses "The #1 Band of the Year." *NME* went so far as to name the Stone Roses album as the "best indie record of the past ten years." The one thing holding them back was a rather sticky 30-year record contract with Silvertone Records and a running feud with FM Revolver, one of their old labels. These battles would eventually keep the Stone Roses out of sight for almost six years. (See *The Manchester Scene* sidebar on p. 86.)

Let's switch to the mainstream for a moment. Although no one could really see it at the time, a fundamental shift had begun to take hold in the world of rock music during the last eighteen months of the decade. It began with a sharp swing to the right of the musical spectrum.

It was a demographic thing. By the end of the '80s, the Baby Boomer generation had grown up. But due to their economic clout, they were still calling the shots as far as the music industry was concerned. As consumers, most of them weren't interested in anything new—they wanted more of the music they grew up with. That's why the summer of 1989 featured a ponderous array of monster tours from acts like the Rolling Stones, Paul McCartney and Lynyrd Skynyrd. "Classic Rock" and "Lite Rock" radio stations pumped out a continuous supply of familiar, non-threatening music and grabbed huge ratings. And of course, the record companies were only too happy to grab a piece of the action by reissuing old albums on compact disc.

But what if you weren't old enough to be a Baby Boomer? What if you didn't care about Aerosmith and Van Halen? What if you wanted music that meant something to *your* generation?

Things were beginning to move to the left. More and more people were becoming disenchanted with the status quo and there was a growing feeling that things had become stale. The process was inexorably slow, but it was happening.

One of the first indications that something was happening was the rebirth of the B-52's. Although they did quite well in the new wave explosion of the late '70s and early '80s, they had become decidedly uncool by 1985. But in 1989, they issued an album titled *Cosmic Thing* and hit the road for the first time in five years. The record featured "Love Shack," a huge hit single that ended up being named the best of the year by *Rolling Stone*.

This mainstream success was remarkable for the simple fact that (even though they were an old group) their approach to music was campy, fun and comparatively unconventional. If you were watching the situation closely, you got the sense that if the B-52's could sell a million records at a time when classic rock was king, then it was either a big fluke—or something was about to happen. Looking back, it wasn't a fluke at all. It was just the tiniest hint of what was yet to come.

The '90s
1990-95

There's something exciting about the start of a new decade. It's as if you can dump the baggage of the last ten years and start fresh. Eventually—through politics, economics, social trends and other things—the decade takes on a personality of its own.

Naturally, music plays a major part in shaping this personality, and the '90s began with people making predictions about where things were headed over the next few years. Just about everyone who made a prediction got it wrong.

It was apparent that something was going on when Depeche Mode started to sell more records than they had ever sold before. In the fall of 1989, they released "Personal Jesus," which quickly became the top-selling 12" in the history of their American record label. Then on March 20, 1990, a full-scale riot broke out among 25,000 fans who had lined up to see the band during an autograph session at a record store in Los Angeles. The hysteria carried over to the release of their new album, *Violator*, and millions of copies flew out of the stores. In marketing sense, it was a very successful penetration into the mainstream.

These numbers sent ripples through the entire record industry. Executives began asking themselves "Why are *these* guys selling so many records? *And who's buying them?*" Suddenly, major labels began to take more of an interest in the alternative bands on their roster. Their thinking was that if there was such a big market for Depeche Mode, then there had to be a significant number of people who were interested in bands who were making music that fell outside the parameters of the mainstream.

Meanwhile, Depeche Mode was acting as a doorway to thousands of music fans. For them, *Violator* was an introduction to the world for alternative music—and once someone got hooked on Depeche Mode, then the next step was New Order or Erasure or the Smiths. From there, it was easy to branch out even further: goth, grunge, British indie bands, industrial music—it was like discovering a whole new universe that had been right under your nose all along. The result was that the demand for alternative music began to increase dramatically for the first time since the British new wave invasion of the early '80s.

Several fierce indie groups (like the Pixies and Jesus Jones) were snapped up by major labels in quick succession—but before they signed, they made sure that they would retain creative control over their music—a significant victory over the corporate rock establishment. But the biggest shock came when Sonic Youth ended more than a decade of independent recording by signing with DGC (a subsidiary of Geffen which was home to such luminaries as Don Henley, Whitesnake and Cher).

To many hardcore fans, this was the end of the world. "Sonic Youth on a major label? There's no way they're gonna be allowed to make their kind of music. They're gonna be sanitized and sterilized for mass consumption! They've sold out, man! It's over!"

Actually, no. Sonic Youth's *Goo* was as uncompromising as ever, affecting the alternative music in much the same way as *Violator*. It showed the bean counters that there was a market for this kind of material—and if you left creative control in the hands of the groups, you'd get some amazing music. And as a bonus, having these bands on your label gave you a type of new street credibility that had been lacking in rock and roll for many years. In other words, thanks to bands like Sonic Youth and Depeche Mode, alternative music was becoming a priority for the major labels.

Meanwhile, out in the fringe, it was business as usual as groups continued to experiment with the edge of musical envelope. Industrial music was becoming particularly strong, thanks to the work of Nine Inch Nails, KMFDM, Front 242, Ministry, Consolidated and MC 900 Ft Jesus. The "Manchester" scene was going full-tilt, featuring strong contributions from Happy Mondays, Inspiral Carpets and the Charlatans UK. Goth was once again a growing concern due to the work of the Sisters of Mercy, the Mission and Peter Murphy. And people were finally catching on to what the Red Hot Chili Peppers were about, thanks to their punk-funk treatment of Stevie Wonder's "Higher Ground."

There were at least two new music trends to kick off the decade.

One was called "shoegazer," a noisy, deeply introspective type of guitar rock from Britain that was equal parts Jesus and Mary Chain feedback and Cocteau Twins. The leading practitioners were Ride and My Bloody Valentine, an Irish group that almost never made eye contact with the audience (hence the term "shoegazer"). The second was techno, a fast, faceless form of computer-driven dance music that emerged out of the basements of Detroit, the clubs of Chicago and the raves of England. It was an emerging culture where the DJ and the sound systems were the stars and the idea was to get immersed in all the freakiness of the party that surrounded you.

As 1991 began, it was obvious that there was more of an interest in alternative music than ever before. However, the music was still too weird, too "out there" for most and the alternative scene continued to live a relatively isolated existence outside the mainstream. However, two events over the space of four months would alter things forever.

In late 1990, rumors started to spread about a giant caravan tour similar to the kind Dick Clark used to organize in the '50s. The guy who came up with the concept was Perry Farrell, the singer for Jane's Addiction. He wanted to put together a traveling roadshow that would celebrate music, art, free speech, individuality and more. At first, most concert industry people thought that Perry was a little loony. After all, who was going to pay good money to see a bunch of weirdos play music all day? And let's be serious: Why would any of the customers care about art and discussion forums on politics? Still, Perry pressed ahead and on July 18, 1991, the first Lollapalooza began in Phoenix—and by the time it ended late that summer, everyone was raving about the event. The business credibility of alternative music had taken another giant step—not to mention the fact that thousands of people were exposed to this new type of music for the very first time.

The other event occurred on September 24, 1991, when the record stores received their first shipment of an album called *Nevermind*. It was the record that changed things forever.

After it became obvious that Sub Pop was a sinking ship, Nirvana had no choice but to look around for another record company. This wasn't much of a problem because by the summer of 1990, there were a lot of labels expressing interest. The ultimate winner was DGC, that "punk division" of Geffen records. Kurt Cobain figured that if it was cool enough for Sonic Youth, it was cool enough for Nirvana. DGC grabbed Nirvana from Sub Pop for $75,000 in cash and for a share of

61

the profits if the next album sold more than 200,000 units. It would eventually sell more than 10 million.

This is where you can divide the history of alternative music into two eras: "before Nirvana" and "after Nirvana." The effect of *Nevermind* and "Smells Like Teen Spirit" was unexpected and almost unfathomable. Almost twenty years after the Ramones and the Sex Pistols first lit the fuse, music finally exploded with an energy and passion that burned bright all over the world. *Nevermind* was the record that brought alternative music front-and-center for the very first time, creating a situation where this new brand of indie music became the new unifying force in rock. Nirvana was the first rock band in a long time that meant something. It was substance over image—and *Nevermind* became the first album to galvanize the new post-Baby Boomer generation of music fans. To the record companies, it was a sign that this was the music of the future.

It was the beginning of a full-scale assault on mainstream rock. Unlike the new wave explosion of the early '80s (where groups were chosen for assimilation into the mainstream), the Nirvana phenomenon forced the mainstream to deal with alternative music on its own terms, forcing the entire mainstream to move to the left. Fed up with a constant barrage of classic rock, oldies and safe Top 40 music, the music fans of all ages rushed to embrace the new music. And once *Nevermind* opened the door a crack, the rest of the alternative world was there to break it down.

Grunge came first. Since Nirvana was from the Seattle area, it was only a matter of seconds before people began to ask if there was anything else interesting happening in the Pacific Northwest. After years of touring, Soundgarden finally began to get some serious attention. And then there was the matter of Pearl Jam, a group that rose out of the ashes of another Seattle band, Mother Love Bone. They released *Ten* (their debut) at around the same time as *Nevermind* and soon sold even more copies.

Next came R.E.M. They had been flirting with major success for years and finally pulled off The Big One with the release of *Out of Time* in early 1991 which (like *Nevermind* and *Ten*) ended up being a #1 album in North America. U2 shored up their position as one of the most important bands in the world with *Achtung Baby* in the fall. Meanwhile, other bands were nibbling away at the edges. EMF had a huge single with "Unbelievable" while Jesus Jones went with "Right Here,

Right Now" from their *Doubt* album. Morrissey expanded his fanbase with *Kill Uncle* while Big Audio Dynamite did well with a couple of singles from *The Globe*.

By the spring of 1992, most of the media had picked up on the new sounds. Magazines like *Entertainment Weekly* were running cover stories on Lollapalooza. The *New York Times* explored the Nirvana phenomenon in their financial section. Even *Vogue* got into the act, running a pictorial on "grunge fashion" (an oxymoron if there ever was one). New magazines like *Details* and *Raygun* devoted dozens of pages to alternative artists while movie theaters ran *Singles*, a comedy featuring cameos from a bunch of grunge bands from of Seattle. Radio stations and MTV were devoting more of their playlists to this new music. After years of being dismissed as too weird for the general public, alternative music finally had arrived.

Guitars were back in a big way in 1992. Thanks largely to Nirvana, raw, stripped-down bands like the Pixies, Sonic Youth, the Lemonheads, Smashing Pumpkins and Sugar were in big demand. New British indie bands Ned's Atomic Dustbin, Catherine Wheel, Teenage Fanclub, and Manic Street Preachers were finding more fans. Even the old punks were getting their due. The kids who were buying the Nirvana albums were suddenly more receptive to groups like the Sex Pistols and Black Flag and wanted to know more, creating a whole new generation of punks. And Lollapalooza was back, bigger and stronger and more ambitious than the first time around. Looking back, the line-up that year included some truly awesome talent: Soundgarden, Pearl Jam, Red Hot Chili Peppers, and Ministry.

The growth was even more pronounced in 1993. Leading the way was Pearl Jam, who were so hot that they landed on the front cover of *Time* in October. When *Vs.* was released in October, it debuted on the album charts at #1 and sold more than 950,000 copies in the first seven days. No one—not Madonna, not Michael Jackson, not New Kids on the Block—had ever sold records like that before.

Not far behind was Nirvana, who finally managed to released *In Utero*, the follow-up to *Nevermind*. Although it didn't do nearly the volume of the last record, it scored points in another area. Despite enormous pressure to deliver another mega-hit, Kurt Cobain was able to keep the group in touch with its true punk roots, asserting once again that musical integrity was more important than profits. *In Utero* contained no musical compromises. In fact, there were all sorts of rumors about how DGC was horrified at how *un*-commercial the album sounded. It was raw, ragged, and rough, forged in the true traditions of punk—-yet it sold in the millions, spreading the word on alternative music even further.

The third major release of 1993 belonged to Smashing Pumpkins. Ever since the *Gish* album in 1991, Billy Corgan and the Pumpkins had set themselves up to be the Next Big Alternative Thing, the "Next Nirvana"—but it almost never happened. Think about what Corgan was facing: People were expecting him to write an album as good and as successful as *Nevermind*, which was already considered to be one of the most important records of the last twenty years. The excruciating pressure resulted in a long bout of writer's block which spun off into some scary health problems. Fortunately, Billy was able to pull through and by the end of the year, *Siamese Dream* had sold over a million copies and the Pumpkins' reputation in the alternative world was saved.

Speaking of big-selling albums, there certainly was no shortage of those. Depeche Mode sold millions of *Songs of Faith and Devotion;* the Stone Temple Pilots went multi-platinum with *Core;* the Breeders' *Last Splash* become 4AD's biggest-selling record ever; Rage Against the Machine expanded on the punk-funk traditions of the Chili Peppers and Fishbone by adding a little East L.A. Latino attitude and sold a million; and not only did the Lemonheads finally have a commercial breakthrough, but Evan Dando became the year's favorite poster boy. Add to that the successes of albums by the Cure, Midnight Oil, R.E.M. and Kate Bush, and you have the most profitable year yet for alternative music.

The other notable thing about 1993 was how several new British bands finally managed to finally sneak their way into America, albeit in a small way. The last time America had been conquered by the British was in the early '80s when it looked as if bands like Duran Duran were going to take over completely. But in the years since, American tastes had strayed back to guitar bands who were more into a rock 'n' roll attitude. The subtleties of post-Smiths British pop groups were for the most part just not all that important to most American alternative fans. However, in 1993, the situation seemed to be changing. Suede's first American tour was supposed to make them into superstars—-but it was their Irish support act, the Cranberries, that had the breakthrough. They ended up selling more copies of their debut album than any other band in the history of Ireland (including U2!). Then there was Radio-

Adam Yorke of Radiohead ➔

head, the group from Oxford that became an MTV hit thanks to the song "Creep." The results weren't nearly as spectacular as they were in the new wave days, but it was a start. (See *How Alternative Music Took Over* sidebar on p. 87.)

As things moved into 1994, the new alternative world suffered its first great tragedy—it lost the man who was responsible for triggering its growth. Kurt Cobain was found dead of a self-inflicted shotgun blast on April 8. The man who was responsible for much of the explosion of interest in alternative music had apparently found himself unable to cope with fame and health problems. The whole world was stunned by his death and music fans spent much of the year trying to come to terms with the loss. It didn't get any easier when Nirvana's excellent *MTV Unplugged In New York* album came out in the fall, because with each listen, you were reminded how good a band they were and what a talent we had lost. (See *Kurt Cobain's Suicide Note* sidebar on p. 89.)

Many Nirvana fans transferred their attentions to Courtney Love and Hole. Four days after Kurt's body was found, Hole released their second album, the eerily-titled *Live Through This*. For the rest of the year, Courtney was in the news—and not always for her music. She was arrested on drug charges in April, and stalked by a man in June, the same month Hole's bass player, Kristen Pfaff, died of a heroin overdose. Through the summer and fall, there were stories linking Courtney to Evan Dando, Billy Corgan and Trent Reznor. And through much of the year, you could count on catching Courtney venting her spleen on a variety of subjects over the internet.

Meanwhile, other musicians found themselves greatly affected by Kurt's death. Eddie Vedder canceled Pearl Jam's summer tour so that he could spend some time re-evaluating his personal situation. When the band's *Vitalogy* album came out in the fall, it was filled with subtle references to Kurt. Michael Stipe of R.E.M. needed time away from recording the new album just so he could get his head together. (See *The Death of Kurt Cobain* sidebar on p. 90.)

However, the punk attitude was alive and well—and the place to be was California. The West Coast has always been famous for its punk. Back in the '70s, it was the Germs, X and the Dead Kennedys. The '80s saw the rise of such underground bands as Agent Orange, TSOL, Suicidal Tendencies, the Surf Punks and the Amoebas as well as the establishment of "do it yourself" indie labels such as SST (founded by L.A.'s Black Flag), San Francisco's Alternative Tentacles (the DKs label) and

Epitaph (founded in Hollywood by members of Bad Religion). And while very few California punk groups did more than break even, the scene was strong and extremely tightknit—the members of this community are quite possessive when it comes to their music and tend to guard it jealously.

This world was turned upside down in 1994 when two groups from California suddenly found themselves selling more records than they ever thought they would. Always on the hunt for the "Next Nirvana," Warner Music decided to take a chance on a band from Berkeley called Green Day. Green Day was very good at reinventing the '70s sounds of the Buzzcocks and the Diodes, and their two indie albums had sold a grand total of 60,000 copies—a rather respectable number. But by the end of the year, *Dookie* (their major label debut) was pushing 6 *million* copies. The same sort of thing happened with the Offspring. Before *Smash* was issued, an album that sold more than 20,000 copies was considered to be a roaring success. But the Offspring record was so big (also selling in the vicinity of 6 million copies worldwide) that Epitaph was transformed almost overnight into a major player in the music industry. In fact, Epitaph's punk roster and back catalogue became so hot (NOFX, Rancid, Pennywise, Down By Law) that the company entertained buyout offers as high as $50 million.

This created some interesting problems. The first problems were felt by the bands that were selling all the records. Once they made it onto MTV and commercial radio, they were immediately branded as sellouts by the punk community who then sought to have them forever exiled (Green Day especially took a lot of heat). In perhaps an attempt to compensate, some groups requested that once they signed a major deal they be given special concessions. For example, Green Day insisted that the rights to their back catalogue remain with the indie label, Lookout Records. Rancid refused all sorts of mega-dollar offers in order to keep their street credibility. Then there was the case of Beck, who demanded in exchange for signing with DGC that he be allowed to record for indie labels whenever he pleased.

It was very ironic. Twenty years after the Ramones played their first show at CBGBs, punk was back, louder and faster than ever. Things had come full-circle. Maybe it was a backlash against the gloom of grunge. Maybe with Nirvana gone and Pearl Jam staying off the road and away from videos, the music industry needed to feed on something else—the next hip thing. Or maybe it all happened because the music was good

and the time was right.

A group of promoters and corporate sponsors thought that the time was right for another Woodstock. Billed as "Three More Days of Peace, Love and Music," the second Woodstock took place twenty-five years after the original—but not in the same place. Instead, it was held up the road in a field that was a potential dump site in Saugerties, New York, beginning on August 12. Despite criticism that the whole event was nothing more than a cash-grabbing corporate scheme, more than 350,000 people showed up and spent the better part of three days trudging through mud, garbage, and overflowing porta-potties that had collapsed in the torrential rain. Although a number of mainstream acts were booked, the majority of the Woodstock lineup consisted of alternative acts: the Cranberries, Green Day, Porno for Pyros, Live, James, Red Hot Chili Peppers, Primus, Henry Rollins and Nine Inch Nails (the Nails' Saturday night set was especially strong and the moshpit at the front of the stage featured upwards of 30,000 people). The fact that such a massive event could be sold on the strength of these acts was another testament to the growing popularity and power of the entire alternative scene.

Lollapalooza was back for a fourth year. Almost a million people bought tickets to see bands like the Beastie Boys (riding high with *Ill Communication* and the single, "Sabotage"), L7, the Breeders, and headliners Smashing Pumpkins. When it was all over, Lollapalooza was once again among the top ten highest-grossing concert tours of the summer.

Meanwhile, the UK was revisiting the glories of the Manchester scene of the late '80s as the result of three extremely strong releases. The first was *Parklife* from Blur, an album that completed a remarkable comeback for the band after several years of alcoholic and creative despair. The second release was the brash Oasis, who managed to sell a half-million copies of *Definitely Maybe* (their debut release) in less than a week. But most remarkable of all was the fact that after almost six years, the Stone Roses finally released their second album, which came with the cheeky title, *Second Coming*. (See *The Stone Roses: What took you guys so long?* sidebar on p. 92.)

Speaking of second comings, vinyl records were being resurrected with Pearl Jam being the most visible vinyl supporters. The first hint that they were up to something came in the fall when they released "Spin the Black Circle," a song all about playing records. Then, on

← Billie Joe of Green Day

November 22, they released *Vitalogy* as an old-style 12" LP. The cassette and CD versions weren't available until December 6. Other groups soon began to demand that their records also be issued on vinyl.

Pearl Jam was being radical in other respects, too. They had refused to make videos for *Vs.* and weren't going to be pushed into making videos for *Vitalogy*. They also had a big beef with Ticketmaster over concert ticket service charges. That battle made it all the way to the United States Congress. (**See *Pearl Jam vs. Ticketmaster: The Battle So Far* sidebar on p. 93.**)

S I D E B A R S

THE STORY OF "LOUIE, LOUIE"

The Kingsmen were from Portland, Oregon, and in 1963, they released a cover of "Louie, Louie," a standard song in the repertoire of every frat band in the Pacific Northwest. The recording session lasted less than a day and cost about $50. Conditions were primitive, even for 1963. The whole band set up underneath one overhead microphone. This forced singer Lynn Easton to lean his head all the way back and more-or-less shout straight up. It also didn't help that he had these big, clunky braces on his teeth. This combination meant that no one could really make out what he was singing—but since money was tight, the group decided to go with what they had on tape.

Soon after the 45 was issued, rumors started to fly that beneath those garble vocals lay some dirty lyrics. Parents became convinced that "Louie, Louie" featured tales of filth and perversion. The governor of Indiana declared the song pornographic and said his ears "tingled" the first time he heard it. Federal authorities were asked to investigate. The US Congress assigned the FBI's best code-breakers to the case. They spent years trying to figure out the words. The song was played forwards and backwards at different speeds; it was put through various types of audio filters; language experts agonized over it for months. Finally, a 120 page document was presented to the authorities. The conclusion? After an exhaustive study, the lyrics to the Kingsmen's "Louie, Louie" were totally indecipherable and thus *not* pornographic.

Even though the whole controversy was accidental (the Kingsmen repeatedly denied that they had done anything wrong), the effect on other garage bands was tremendous. "Louie, Louie" remains one of the legendary recordings of all-time.✦

TECHNO-POP PLUGS IN

Music through electricity is a concept that goes back further than you might think. It really began in 1928 when Leo Theremin and Maurice Martenot introduced the first electronic musical instrument. This was the start of a revolution in musical instrument design because over the next twenty years, many other inventors followed their lead in constructing devices that could make music using electricity. There was the Electronde, the Obukov and the Dynaphone, to name a few.

This new electronic music caught on the most in West Germany. By 1953, Karlheinz Stockhausen had established his electronic music studio near Cologne and an avant-garde scene began to grow around him and his experimental sounds.

Dr. Robert Moog was responsible

for the next major development. In 1965, he unveiled the Moog synthesizer, an ugly and ungainly thing that was nevertheless far more advanced that previous electronic keyboards. It also had the advantage of being smaller than a railway car. This made it possible for more musicians to experiment.

Once again, Germany was the place to be. In 1967, an all-electronic group called Tangerine Dream was formed. They were followed in 1968 by the avant-garde Stockhausen students in Can. Both groups (as well as others) devoted themselves to exploring the sonic possibilities of oscillators.

The big break came in 1970, thanks again to Dr. Moog. On January 24, he unveiled the mini-moog synthesizer. This one invention made much of today's music possible. The mini-moog could do almost everything that one of the old boxcar-sized machines could do—but because it was about the size of a suitcase, electronic music became truly portable for the first time. And because anyone could now purchase a synthesizer for just a few hundred dollars, the new technology became accessible to thousands of musicians who had grown tired of traditional instruments.

The Germans naturally took the early lead. In 1974, Kraftwerk issued "Autobahn," the first worldwide, all-electronic pop single. By 1977, Kraftwerk's influence had spread everywhere and other groups were trying their hands at an all-synthesizer approach, including early incarnations of OMD and The Normal. And it wasn't long before this pop music-through-technology approach began to take hold in the post-punk world. There were many names for it—but the one that caught on was the most obvious: *techno-pop.*◆

THE RISE AND FALL OF SKA

Within months of their formation, the Specials had a sizable following. They all dressed in suits, porkpie hats, dark glasses and white shirts. Things were going so well that by the spring of 1979, Jerry decided to form his own label. "2 Tone" was totally devoted to ska and acts like the Selecter, the Bodysnatchers, Madness and the (English) Beat as well as the Specials. Within months, the Specials had a large following. It was an incredible mix: white skinheads, black rudeboys, mods, punks, suedeheads. The fans followed the band religiously from gig to gig. The music press fell in love with ska and several 2 Tone artists found themselves with hit singles. Bottom line was that by the beginning of 1980, the ska scene extended all across the UK and was *the* scene of the moment.

Unfortunately, it wasn't meant to last. Because the ska scene had grown so quickly, groups like the Bodysnatchers were thrown into the spotlight long before they were ready. They still couldn't play their instruments properly and became the subject of jokes. The Specials were fighting with the Selecter as well as themselves and everyone was after Jerry

Dammers for the way he was handling the affairs of 2 Tone. And most tragically, the message of racial harmony had broken down. Some of the ska skinheads had gravitated to a form of working class punk music called "oi" where they were exposed to certain fascist and racist ideas. Fights and racial confrontations became more and more common both in the streets at gigs—and it wasn't long before the mainstream media starting making a connection between ska, skinheads and violence. The bands of the ska revival soon found themselves in big trouble. The final straw came when the British music press became enamored with rockabilly (which they assured us would be the "next big thing"), and the heyday of ska was over. ✦

THE BIRTH OF GOTH

A lot of it started with the gloomy, minor key introspection of Joy Division. Then Siouxsie and the Banshees took the next step. When she was part of the Bromley contingent that followed around the Sex Pistols, Siouxsie was into clothes featuring things like see-through blouses and Nazi symbols. But when the Banshees began to get their musical act together, Siouxsie's wardrobe began to change. With her jet-black hair and flowing clothes of velvet, Siouxsie Sioux looked like a cross between something out of *Bride of Frankenstein* and the character from an English gothic novel—and it wasn't long before people began describing the Banshees' music as "English gothic" as well.

Siouxsie's male equivalent was Robert Smith of the Cure. He was also very much into the big, black hair and the black clothes. But then along came the skeleton-thin Peter Murphy and Bauhaus with "Bela Lugosi's Dead," a ten-minute single that talked of the undead and bats in the bell tower. This addition of the occult was crucial. Talk of vampires, corpses,

↑ The Specials

bats, ghouls and zombies allowed the music to grow even more gloomy and foreboding. Goth became and anyone looking for another level beyond plain punk.

Fashion and theatrics took the modern gothic concepts even further. The goth scene encouraged experimentation with make-up, hairstyles and clothes, which made it really appealing to people with intense creative streaks. For example, with their ghostly white makeup and black hair, Nick Fiend of Alien Sex Fiend and Andi Sex Gang of the Sex Gang Children (who actually lived in an apartment complex called "Visigoth Towers") were indistinguishable from real goblins. Fans began to copy this look and called themselves "goths." Black velvet and black leather became the fabrics of choice. Groups like UK Decay, Nick Cave and the Birthday Party, and the Virgin Prunes came along with elaborate stage shows, adding to the art-gloom appeal. By 1982, these groups and many others could be found at a club on Mead Street in Soho in London appropriately called the Batcave. The Batcave was run by a guy named Ollie who also played in a band called Specimen. People went the club to dance to music by Bauhaus, Southern Death Cult, the Cramps—and to check out the newest in goth fashions. ✦

THE INDUSTRIAL REVOLUTION

Like goth, industrial music was once looked upon as punk's twisted, disturbed cousin—the one you locked in the basement whenever you had friends over to supper. Industrial music was perceived as a dark and evil thing that only appealed to people who were into weird extremes.

One of the most proponents of the post-punk industrial revolution was Throbbing Gristle. They were a half punk, half performance art group that originated in 1975 in a place called the Death Factory. The Death Factory was a basement space in a building next to a section of land that used to be a 17th century mass grave for hundreds of bubonic plague victims. With this as a backdrop, it's understandable that the members of Throbbing Gristle became fascinated by death, torture, cults, war, the occult, pornography and societal taboos in general. Their music was harsh, confrontational and occasionally, deliberately unpleasant. Throbbing Gristle displayed aggression in a way no one had every heard before—and in the recession-riddled world of the late '70s and early '80s, many people understood where they were coming from.

Throbbing Gristle was probably the first group to use the term "industrial" to describe their music after they came across the work of San Francisco artist Monte Cazazza. He coined the phrase "industrial music for industrial people"—and it was Throbbing Gristle who took that statement seriously. Their music sounded like it was recorded in a factory. Their record label was called Industrial and their first formal recording had a corporate-industrial sounding title: *Second Annual Report.*

The industrial imagery and attitude was also promoted by groups like SPK, Nurse With Wound, DAF (Deutsche Americakanische Freundschaft, which translates as "German American Friendship"), Controlled Bleeding, and Wire. But the most serious of them all was Einsturzende Neubauten. In the beginning, they didn't even bother with instruments. They didn't care about chord changes or melodies. They had their music with anvils, sledgehammers, breaking glass, lead pipes, sheet metal, power tools and other bits of "found sound." For example, Blixa (the "singer"), once wired his chest with a microphone and had someone give him a bear hug until his ribs cracked. That sound later turned up in a Neubauten composition.

Perhaps the most unheralded founder of the industrial culture was disco-diva Donna Summer. In 1977, she released "I Feel Love," a heavily-sequenced, computerized dance floor hit. While the music didn't appeal to everyone, the nature of the sounds on the record did. More than a few industrial types would copy the techniques first popularized by Donna and her producer, Giorgio Moroder.

Although they would most likely deny it, more than a few industrial-type groups took some cues from Donna and made their aggression danceable (PiL and mid-period Cabaret Voltaire are good examples). Then in 1983, Depeche Mode released *Construction Time Again*, an album full of angry synthesizers and clanking percussion. This record helped fuse some of the elements of techno-pop with the abrasiveness of raw industrial music. It was synthesis of raw sounds of Neubauten and Throbbing Gristle with melodies and structures of conventional pop songs.

Further advancements came every few years in the '80s. The sample-heavy approaches of Canada's Skinny Puppy and the hi-NRG dance beats of England's Nitzer Ebb allowed them to become the first industrial bands to be signed to major record labels. In Europe, Front 242 pushed their keyboard-based "electric body music" while in the US, Ministry's Alain Jourgensen added a touch of heavy metal thrash while performing gigs behind walls of chicken wire. Meanwhile, Chicago's Wax Trax Records established themselves as the pre-eminent industrial label in the world, signing and distributing dozens of groups to a growing audience that was tired of safe '80s pop.✦

A QUICK HISTORY OF MUSIC VIDEOS

Music has always been a visual medium. For centuries, artists have used many different methods of interpreting music through movement—ballet, for instance.

Music and film were first combined in the late 1800s with the invention of the movie camera. Musical scores were composed to complement and enhance the action on the screen. But the real roots of the music video go back to the work of a German composer named Oskar Fischinger.

Beginning in 1921, Oskar began to produce short experimental films that featured abstract images synchronized to jazz and classical music. Many of his films ended up being used as advertisements for products like cigarettes and early models of the television. In essence, they were short, promotional visual music clips. Oskar would later be enlisted to help produce Disney's 1940 landmark animation film *Fantasia* (which, by the way, was one of the first movies to use multi-channel stereophonic sound).

The first attempt to get music videos to a wide audience was in the late 1940s. The Panoram Soundie was a type of video jukebox manufactured by a company headed up by the son of President Franklin Roosevelt. Soundies were coin-operated machines that weighed up to two tons. For the price of a couple of nickels, you could hear a song of the day and watch a short black-and-white that went along with it on a 20" screen. Usually, it was a musical excerpt from a Hollywood movie, but more than 2,000 three-minute films were shot exclusively for the Panoram. Cab Calloway and Louis Armstrong both appeared in Soundie films.

Soundie machines weren't very practical. Each one could only play one "video" which meant that if you were the owner of a cocktail lounge and you wanted to offer your patrons a selection of Soundie films, you had to have a whole wall of these monstrous machines. They were expensive, impractical and difficult to main-

tain. And when television came along in the '50s, the Soundies died a quick death.

In the late '50s and early '60s, a French company put a new spin on the concept with a machine called the Scopitone. The Scopitone was another sort of video jukebox that weighed a little less (1,500 pounds) and could show up to thirty-six different films on its 20" screen. Hundreds of 16mm films were shot (a lot in color) especially for the Scopitone and several dozen artists (including Paul Anka, Nancy Sinatra, Procol Harum and a bunch of European artists) jumped at the chance to experiment with the new medium. But as with the Soundie, the novelty soon wore off with the public and there were headaches for operators. Each new film cost at least $125 and whenever the machines broke down, you had to send all the way to France for replacement parts. By 1967, Scopitone machines had almost totally disappeared.

Meanwhile, television had been delivering music performances to homes around the world since at least 1948. One of the first shows was "Face the Music," a fifteen minute program where a cast of regular singers went through a few of the current hits. The '50s brought shows like "TV Teen Club," "Your Hit Parade" and Dick Clark's "American Bandstand." Live performances by rock 'n' roll acts also became staples of programs hosted by Steve Allen and Ed Sullivan. Meanwhile, the British were forging ahead with regular performance shows like "Top of the Pops." Record labels loved all these TV options and did whatever they could to book their acts on these shows.

A major breakthrough came in the fall of 1966 when "The Monkees" debuted on American TV. The Monkees were put together in late 1965 by executives at Columbia Television as a response to the success to the Beatles' movies. They envisioned four-piece group living together and going on wacky adventures (à la *A Hard Day's Night*). To add some musical legitimacy and as a way of cross-promoting the show using the Top 40 charts, songwriters were hired to write hits for the Monkees. Those singles would be reinforced during each half-hour episode with at least one "music video" segment—some sort of offbeat sequence set to music. It was all a roaring success.

At about the same time, British acts like the Kinks and the Who were experimenting with conceptual promotional films like the famous and very surreal "Strawberry Fields" clip. British TV shows were only too glad to run them again and again. Unfortunately, most American programs that tried to incorporate these music films had dismally low ratings, and in the late '60s, the whole concept of using moving visual images to promote music died out.

However, some record labels weren't about to give up. Warner Brothers recognized the potential of visual music and formed an office dedicated to the idea. One of the very first "videos" designed to promote the retail sale of an album was con-

structed for Captain Beefheart's *Lick My Decals Off, Baby*. Promotional films were also commissioned by record labels in order to familiarize other branches of the company with the product. It became standard practice at some labels to hire a director to shoot films for up to sixty artists for a ninety minute promotional film that would be screened at sales conferences around the world. Some of these reels cost up to half a million dollars each. When it wasn't possible to shoot the act itself, the directors would go with a conceptual visual idea and set the band's music to that. This is where a lot of the ideas for the modern music video began to be formed.

There was another major event in 1975. Bruce Gowers spent $7,000 and two days on a short clip for the song "Bohemian Rhapsody." The song was considered so different at the time that the band figured they needed some sort of hook that would get the song played in record stores and the odd clubs. But when the song finally appeared, it caused a tremendous sensation and "Bohemian Rhapsody" became one of the most unlikely hit singles of the '70s—and a lot of the credit was given to the video.

Nothing breeds imitation like commercial success. Suddenly, everyone wanted to shoot videos. Most were quickie productions, rarely costing more than $10,000 and were usually put together in just a few days. But there still wasn't a place where the public could see these videos. Several companies started up in the late '70s to distribute videos to a network of bars and clubs that were equipped with TVs—but this still wasn't enough.

Once again, the answer was television. A few network shows popped up—but the real savior was cable. Cable channels could afford to dabble in specialized programs and video shows debuted in places like New York and San Francisco and were hosted by people like comedian Howie Mandel and ex-Monkee Mike Nesmith, two of the first "VJs."

In 1980, Warner Communications merged with American Express and created a company called Warner Amex Satellite Entertainment Corp. The head of the company was John Lack and he had this vision of a 24-hour music video channel that would focus mainly on the music that was being ignored by rock radio at the time. It took a lot of convincing and arm-twisting, but John got his way. MTV made its debut at 12:01 am EDT, August 1, 1981.

The effect was incredible. Once Buggles' "Video Killed the Radio Star" started being shown, sales all over the country went up dramatically. It didn't take long for record labels start budgeting for more and more video shoots for their favorite artists. MTV and music videos became integrated elements in the marketing and promotion of music—and it didn't take long for the concepts (and the budgets) to get bigger and bigger. British new wave acts benefited the most for two reasons. First, there was a long tradition of music performance on TV, thanks to shows like "Top of the Pops." Secondly, with their make-up, costumes and theatrical approach to music, they looked great on TV. This got them on MTV, which gave them more exposure, which lead to higher record sales. The British New Wave Invasion was on.

The most perfect video band of the early '80s was Duran Duran. In 1981, their label, EMI, raised the stakes and the standards of video production by spending $200,000 to send the band to Sri Lanka to shoot three clips, including the early MTV favorite, "Hungry Like the Wolf."

One more bit of history. Michael Jackson has to receive a lot of credit for advancing the video medium. His "Beat It" video set ultra-high standards, thanks to its budget of $150,000. The clip was also one of the first to feature added sound effects like the flick of a switchblade and opening of a garage door. The approach was a huge success. Before the clip appeared on MTV and other video programs, the *Thriller* album had sold three million copies. After it started airing, sales went up to 200,000 *a week*. Finally, Jackson has to be credited as breaking the color barrier on MTV. Up until he came along, the channel was all about white rock 'n' roll. Jackson's success changed all that, opening up opportunities to artists of color everywhere.

These days, MTV is right up there with CNN as far as impact and influence go. The network has the potential to reach more than a billion people in more than sixty countries.✦

THE DEATH OF IAN CURTIS

Ian Curtis of Joy Division was never a happy guy, but in 1980, his battles with depression, epilepsy and relationships took their toll. As the *Unknown Pleasures* album was about to be released, the other members of the band (Peter Hook, Bernard Sumner and Stephen Morris) became very concerned with Ian's manic personality. It was around this time that the group decided that they would change their name should anything happen to one of the members.

On April 7, Ian attempted suicide by overdosing on his epilepsy medication, a drug called Phenobarbitone. He was rushed to the hospital where he had his stomach pumped and his mental condition assessed by a psychiatrist. However, the doctor concluded that Ian was not suicidal.

On the evening of May 16, Ian played pool with Peter Hook at a Manchester pub and everything seemed fine. The next night, he canceled a scheduled meeting with guitarist Bernard Sumner. Returning to his house at 77 Barton Street in Macclesfield, he watched a Werner Herzog film called *Stroszek*, a movie about a German musician who travels to America and ends up killing himself after he's unable to choose between two women (It should be noted that although Ian had a wife, Deborah, he was also having an affair with a Belgian women named Annik Honore, and was having trouble juggling the two relationships. The parallels are even more eerie when you consider that Joy Division was just hours away from leaving on a major North American tour).

After the movie, Ian drank a couple cups of very strong coffee and a little bit of whiskey. Then he went over to the stereo where he put on *The Idiot*, his favorite Iggy Pop album. Sometime after 1 am, he wrote a long letter in big capital letters to his wife. Then, before the sun came up, he hung himself in the kitchen using rope taken from a clothesline. His wife found him at about noon on Sunday, May 18th.

Ian was buried a few days later. His headstone reads "Ian Curtis 18-5-80. Love will tear us apart."✦

HOW NEW ORDER MADE IT COOL TO DANCE AGAIN

The members of New Order were never really much into playing live. What they were most concerned about was the party after the gig. Encores just delayed the fun.

One day in 1983, they came up with the idea of turning on Stephen Morris' drum machine and letting it go while everyone walked offstage. To add a little spice (and to keep the audience slightly interested), they programmed a sequencer to run a line from Gillian Gilbert's keyboards. That seemed to work well, so they had another sequencer add a Peter Hook bass-line—and before they knew it, they had the foundations for a new song.

Legend has it that New Order got loaded up on LSD and took these programs into the studio. They managed to get all the tracks down but were told by the engineers to go sleep it off while the song was pieced together. When it was finished, they had a very danceable eight-minute song that was pressed as a 12" single entitled "Blue Monday"

The record was distributed to dance clubs around England. At the time, the big dance tracks were "Physical" by Olivia Newton-John and "I Love Rock and Roll" by Joan Jett. No one had ever heard anything quite like this New Order track. It caught on very quickly, selling more than 3 million copies around the world. In the process, the song forged all sorts of links between alternative music, new wave, rock and regular dance music. Dozens of musicians were moved to expand on these concepts, adding a new dimension to music in the post-punk world. In short, "Blue Monday" made it cool for many people to dance again.

And it all started because one band hated doing encores.✦

THE SMITHS' BAD YEAR

While the Smiths were selling albums and singles by the millions, things were not going well. The band continued to fight with their label, Rough Trade, over contracts and money. (Listen to "Frankly, Mr. Shankly" from *The Queen is Dead* and substitute the name Geoff Travis for Mr. Shankly and you'll get a good idea of the Smiths' position). Andy Rourke's drug problems were creating havoc to the point where he was actually kicked out of the band for a

week. Craig Gannon was brought in to pick up some of the slack—but then Morrissey sacked him, creating more legal problems. And then Morrissey's 23-year-old cat died.

But the scariest event happened on November 11 when Johnny Marr crashed his new BMW after an evening of tequila and wine. The wreck was so bad that Marr was lucky to have escaped with his legs. The official story was that Marr's wife had been driving when the car hit the brick wall. This was false. Angie Marr had been miles away from the crash but this was the story to cover up the fact that Johnny had been driving without a license.

BAND AID

By the end of 1984, the situation in Ethiopia had grown beyond desperate. The drought, civil war and famine was affecting so many people that relief workers could only help a few hundred out of every ten thousand people they encountered. Yet few people in the West knew what was going on.

That all began to change in November 1984. Bob Geldof of the Boomtown Rats had just finished supper when he turned on the TV to find a BBC documentary on Ethiopia. He was so appalled by what he saw that he became determined to make some kind of a difference.

The concept was simple: a charity single release where no one would make a profit. Where possible, time and material would be donated with the goal being to raise as much money

Sir Bob Geldof ➔

as possible for African relief efforts. Within a couple of days, Bob had written a song entitled "It's My World." He called up Midge Ure of Ultravox and asked him to write a tune around it. The result was an arrangement called "Do They Know It's Christmas/Feed the World."

Once the song was finished, Bob got to work mobilizing the recording industry. Trevor Horn's SARM West Studio was booked. Calls went out to manufacturers and retailers. And calls were made to all the big names in British music.

On November 25, 1984, 36 stars gathered to record the song. Bono and Adam Clayton flew back from an American tour to take part. Spandau Ballet cut short a Japanese tour to be there. Sting and Paul Weller showed up along with members of the Boomtown Rats, Heaven 17, Duran Duran and others. The session took twelve hours from start to finish.

The single was released on December 7, 1984. The retail price of the 7" was £1.35. Out of that, only 17.46p would go to manufacturing and distribution. The remainder would go to Africa.* One million copies were sold during the first week, making it the fastest-selling record of all time. A 12" mix was also issued, featuring David Bowie, Holly Johnson and other performers who couldn't make it to the original session. More than 8 million copies were sold all over the world and the project inspired additional fundraising through the "USA for Africa" effort in America and the "Northern Lights" single in Canada.

By March 1985, the first supplies paid for by Band-Aid reached Ethiopia.✦

The Thatcher government wouldn't budge on the 18p VAT. However, Ireland dropped the tax.

GOTH WARS

In 1984, the Sisters of Mercy split down the middle. Singer Andrew Eldritch and Docktor Avalanche (his drum machine) went one way and Wayne Hussey and Craig Adams going the other.

For awhile, it wasn't very clear to anyone on the outside if the group was finished or if the name "Sisters of Mercy" had been retired. However, Eldritch knew exactly what he wanted. He wanted to retain the name just in case; meanwhile his next band was to be called the Sisterhood.

That caused some problems. Wayne Hussey and Craig Adams were also in the process of forming another band called the Sisterhood. As a result, it became a race to see who's lawyers could nail down the name. Eldritch won, mainly because he rush-released an EP called *Gift* in 1986.

Eventually, though, it was decided that no one could use the name and that Eldritch had title to the name Sisters of Mercy. Eldritch and Doctor Avalanche moved to Germany to start a new version of the Sisters while Hussey and Adams changed the name of their project to the Mission.✦

DID FRANKIE PLAY ON THEIR OWN RECORD?

Almost immediately after Frankie Goes to Hollywood starting releasing records, people became suspicious as to whether the band actually participated in the recording. There was no doubt that it was Holly Johnson singing—but what about the rest of the group?

The Lads (as the musicians in Frankie were known) started recording "Relax" with producer Trevor Horn at SARM Studios in July 1983. He was very concerned by what he heard. Mark, Nasher and Ped were between 16 and 18 years old and really didn't have a clue what they were doing. That's when Horn and his assistant (J.J. Jeckzalic, co-founder of the Art of Noise) started constructing a rhythm track using a Fairlight. Ian Dury's Blockheads were brought in for musical support, but things didn't work out and the sessions were scrapped. Finally, members of Art of Noise were hired to create the backing tracks. Holly was then called in to sing. Meanwhile, an engineer was busy out by the pool recording the sounds Mark, Nasher and Ped made when they dove into the water. Those sounds were the only contributions they made to the record.

When it was time to record *Welcome to the Pleasuredome*, the Lads were once again left out. Most of the guitar parts were played by Steve Lipson, another Horn assistant. The rest of the parts were assembled using sequencers, samplers, synthesizers and drum machines. It's no wonder that the Lads spent most of their time feeling very insecure.◆

LIVE AID

Soon after Band-Aid began shipping famine relief materials to Ethiopia, rumors started to circulate that Bob Geldof was trying to organize a special charity concert to raise even more money for the cause. The £8 million raised by "Do They Know It's Christmas" was starting to run out and the situation in Africa was still very desperate. By the end of June 1985, everyone was talking about what could be done. That's when Geldof made the announcement—but no one could quite believe the scope of what he had planned.

The event was to be a one-day affair involving Wembley Stadium in London and JFK Stadium in Philadelphia involving dozens of the biggest names in music with the rest of the world joining in via satellite. The BBC, NBC, MTV, RTE and other broadcasters were persuaded to give up television and radio airtime while the national networks of other countries were given the satellite feeds for free. Promoters, stage crews, catering companies, staging companies, ticket agencies, trucking firms and limo companies were convinced to get involved free of charge. Money would be raised through ticket sales, merchandise sales and donations in the form of pledges from the viewing audience. At first, no one thought it could be pulled off.

But they did it. At 12:15 on Saturday, July 13, 1985, Geldof walked out on stage in front of 72,000 people at Wembley Stadium and Live Aid was on. By the time things ended in Philadelphia 18 hours later, almost 2 billion people had seen part of the show. Almost $100 million was raised.✦

WHEN EXACTLY DID THE SMITHS BREAK UP?

Smiths fans spent most of 1987 wondering what was happening to their heroes. New rumors about a breakup circulated daily and the confusion became so great that no one—not even the Smiths themselves—was really sure what was going on.

January: Band finally hires a new manager. Johnny Marr really likes Ken Friedman. Morrissey is not so sure. Craig Gannon is officially turfed.

March: While recording the new album, there is friction between Morrissey and Friedman. Marr is upset by this. Gannon sues for songwriting royalties he says are owed to him.

April: Rumors of animosity between Morrissey and Marr surface in the British music press.

May: Morrissey and Marr continue to fight over the Smiths' future musical direction. Marr meets Mike Joyce and Andy Rourke for dinner and tells them that he intends to leave the group. The members spend a couple of weeks apart to cool off. On May 19, the Smiths finish recording "I Keep Mine Hidden," the last song

they will ever do together. Marr heads to L.A. to rethink his future, but everyone expects him to come back to the band.

June-July: Deafening silence from the Smiths camp. Meanwhile, Marr tells a friend that he's definitely out. Morrissey denies there are problems.

August 1: *NME* reports "Smiths to Split." Both the band and Rough Trade deny that there's any truth to the rumors.

August 2: Thinking that Morrissey is behind the *NME* story, Marr breaks his silence and confirms that the Smiths have dissolved. Morrissey denies he had anything to do with the breakup story.

August 8: Marr reconfirms that he has quit the group. There are whispers that the Smiths will continue with another guitar player.

August 18: Producer Stephen Street receives a letter from Morrissey stating that the Smiths are finished. Street keeps the information to himself.

August 29: *NME* speculates about possible replacements for Marr. One name that keeps coming up is Mike Murray of Easterhouse.

September 5: Sick of the rumors, Mike Joyce leaves the Smiths.

September 12: The contents of the letter to Stephen Street are made public. It becomes official: The Smiths are finished.✦

THE BIRTH OF GRUNGE

Once California labels like SST and Alternative Tentacles were up and running, it wasn't long before this music started getting around. Records and tapes featuring Hüsker Dü, Sonic Youth, Black Flag, Dinosaur Jr. and the Dead Kennedys made the rounds between friends and acquaintances. This music became very popular among bored suburban kids and people who were tired of all the posings of rocks stars. And more than a few of these tapes made it up to Seattle.

In the mid-'80s, Seattle was best known as the place where they built Boeing 747s. It was also where a nerdy looking guy named Bill Gates was working on a little computer company called Microsoft. Beyond that, it was fishing, the seaports and the forestry industry.

Amidst all this heavy industry, high-tech and blue collar jobs was the world headquarters of Muzak. You know them—the people that supply that wonderfully inoffensive music for elevators and shopping malls. However, the offices of Muzak were the setting for one of the most delicious ironies in the history of alternative music. For deep in the warehouse where they stored all those sickly sweet orchestral versions of songs by Whitney Houston and REO Speedwagon, a rough beast was born: Sub Pop.

In the late '70s and early '80s, most of the city was into traditional hard rock: Led Zeppelin, Black Sabbath, Judas Priest, Neil Young. But very slowly, punk started to creep in, thanks in large part to Black Flag, who regularly went up the coast to play gigs in Washington state. The result was that Seattle rock began to mutate into a hybrid of American hardcore and mainstream metal. It was as aggressive as California punk, except a little slower. Plus, it was as melodic as mainstream rock but without all the stereotypical rock star posing.

Enter Sub Pop. Bruce Pavitt was an employee of the Muzak Corporation who worked in the warehouse as the "tape returns coordinator." He loved the kind of music that was being made in the area, especially the kind you heard on one of the local campus stations and on small labels like K. It got to the point where his sole ambition was to form a label based on the SST model that would be devoted to releasing indie music.

In 1986, often during his shifts at Muzak, Pavitt began working on gathering local material that could be released on compilations issued by his own label. One of them featured a song by his buddy and co-worker, Mark Arm, who had this group called Green River and they became the first band to release an album on Sub Pop. In fact, it was Mark that would come up with a name for this heavy, loud, sludgy guitar music: grunge.

In 1988, Pavitt went into a partnership with Jonathan Poneman, a concert promoter and sometime radio DJ. They scraped up $20,000 and officially formed Sub Pop on April 1. They continued to issue 7" singles from local bands like Mudhoney, Soundgarden, Tad and Screaming Trees along with the odd out-of-town group—like that trio from Aberdeen called Nirvana.

The company operated on a shoestring budget for years, often teetering on the edge of bankruptcy. There were many times when there was no money at all in the company account—but that all ended in 1991 with the release of Nirvana's *Nevermind*. (In 1995, Pavitt and Poneman sold a 49% share in Sub Pop to Warner Music for $20 million.)

One thing about the history of grunge is that it's characterized by a series of pivotal breakups. The breakup of Green River in 1987 was crucial. Mark Arm and two other guys went on to form Mudhoney while the other half ended up in a group called Mother Love Bone. When Mother Love Bone was forced to break up when singer Andrew Wood died, his bandmates and friends recorded a tribute album under the name Temple of the Dog. It was during those sessions that the several of the guys decided to stick together in a new group that they would call Pearl Jam.◆

THE MANCHESTER SCENE

A travel writer once picked Manchester as one of the twelve worst cities in the world to visit. He was obviously not a music fan.

Beneath the smokestacks and factories lies one of the most vibrant local music scenes anywhere in the alternative world. But when someone mentions "Manchester" music, most people from outside the city thinks about the loopy, trippy, neo-psychedelic stuff of the late '80s: the so-called "Manchester" scene with all the baggy pants and ecstasy. Truth is that there is much more to the city than that "sound" of the late '80s and early '90s.

The first great Manchester band was the Buzzcocks, a punky, Sex Pistols-inspired outfit that became one of the first alternative groups to issue material on their own record label. Then there was Joy Division, the group that managed to capture the economic and social mood of the late '70s. Their music became the soundtrack for a brutal recession that kept many young people from getting any kind of work. (To make matters worse, the city's 19th century sewer system was crumbling which resulted in an awful smell during hot summer days. That probably didn't make the unemployed feel any better about their situation). The early '80s saw the rise of New Order, the Smiths and the Fall. Factory Records was born and began issuing material. Clubs opened, bands got gigs and everyone danced—just like in every large city.

But then it happened. Several local groups all began releasing records at almost the same time. About the only thing these bands had in common was that their music was a cross between pop and the local rave/acid house scene. It was fresh, exciting, faintly psychedelic-sounding and very danceable. Suddenly, the British music press was swarming all over Manchester, hyping everything out of proportion.

At the center of the storm were a total of four quality groups: the Stone Roses, Happy Mondays, Inspiral Carpets and Charlatans UK. But once the media decided to make Manchester the center of the universe, a number of other bands were uncovered in rapid succession: the Mock Turtles, the High, Northside, 808 State. Once the idea of a "Manchester Sound" became familiar, groups from other cities were classified as "Manchester." The list included the Farm (who were from Liverpool), Ride (Oxford) and the Soup Dragons (Glasgow).

The "Manchester" craze continued for almost three solid years, and most of the time, it was hard to dispute what was going on because group after group kept releasing one great song after another. TV documentaries were made, gigs sold out and it seemed that everyone expected the party to last forever.

But as with any kind of media frenzy, there was bound to be a backlash. By the end of 1991, no one wanted to hear about the "Manchester scene" anymore. It was just as well, too. The Stone Roses were in court and out of commission; Happy Mondays were all drugged out; and Charlatans UK were in trouble because their keyboard player was convicted of armed robbery. Without its superstars, the concept of "Manchester" sputtered and died.◆

HOW ALTERNATIVE MUSIC TOOK OVER

Here's an analogy: if the alternative music scene were a stock market and you purchased a few shares in January 1991, you'd have been a millionaire many times over by Christmas 1994. If you find that hard to believe, consider that K-mart was selling pre-distressed grunge wear in time for back-to-school and that the 1993 Lollapalooza was the seventh-highest grossing tour of the year, raking in over $17 million in revenues.

When everything was totaled up at the end of the year, Pearl Jam, Nirvana, R.E.M., the Stone Temple Pilots and Depeche Mode accounted for almost 10 million albums. This doesn't sound like a very "alternative" number. What was going on? How did alternative music end up taking over mainstream rock?

There are several reasons:

(1) The Death of the Spandex-and-Hair Bands:

The '80s were a great time for bands like Warrant, Trixter, Ratt, White Lion, Poison, Cinderella and hundreds of other groups that played riff-heavy melodic metal—but then they all became the victims of their own success, especially after they all discovered the economic benefits of the "power ballad." By the end of the decade, these hair metal bands were everywhere: on every type of radio station, on MTV a dozen times a day, on movie soundtracks. It was a simple case of overexposure. People got sick of them.

Record companies tend to be much more fashion-conscious than the average music consumer. Realizing that the melodic metal thing had been almost tapped out, A&R reps started looking for The Next Big

Thing. They found it in Seattle.

(2) The Nirvana Factor:

The grunge scene of the Pacific Northwest was the answer to the major labels' dreams. Here were all these groups that played a melodic form of rock but with a completely different twist. They did it without spandex, poodle haircuts and the tedious rock star posing. All that was needed to break things wide open was a group good enough and exciting enough to capture the public's attention. That group was Nirvana.

Make no mistake; Nirvana was expertly marketed to the masses using all the vast publicity resources of the recording industry. Yet at the same time, this music was *different*. Unlike the fluffy metal of the '80s, this music really seemed to mean something—and the public responded by stampeding to the record stores. The huge success of Nirvana was a watershed event for all music. *Nevermind* showed the world (including the major record labels, commercial radio stations and MTV) that alternative music could have broad appeal; it wasn't just necessarily for weird people out on the fringes of pop and rock.

Once Nirvana broke big, capitalist interests started mining the alternative scene, hoping to find another group or artist that would do the same. Suddenly, there was a flurry of interest in other Seattle groups like Pearl Jam, Soundgarden and Alice in Chains. Once the Pacific Northwest had been thoroughly scoured, the major labels started signing virtually any group that sounded even vaguely grunge. Say hello to Stone Temple Pilots, Sugar, Smashing Pumpkins and dozens of others.

(3) The Classic Rock Factor:

In the '80s and early '90s, mainstream rock radio relied heavily on classic rock artists such as Led Zeppelin, Aerosmith, Van Halen and the Eagles. Stations all over North American spent the better part of a decade rehashing the same songs from the same old bands. For awhile, this strategy worked and many stations with a classic rock format enjoyed high ratings and fat revenues. Record companies did well too, making millions by reissuing old inventory again and again.

But this maneuver turned out to be very shortsighted. Since so much time was spent on old rock music, very little emphasis was placed on developing new rock talent. Any bands that did break through were of the lightweight variety: Poison, Warrant, Ratt—groups that didn't have any real longevity and who were suffering from severe overexposure. In other words, old resources were being used up and new ones weren't becoming available. You can only survive on the past for so long before you stagnate and burn out.

Realizing that they were in trouble and that they had to find some new groups in a hurry (and intrigued by the success of Nirvana), mainstream rock stations started looking to the music scene where things new talent was still a cherished thing—alternative music. What they found was a gold mine. The alternative scene provided them with dozens of well-developed, highly talented guitar-based groups that didn't sound too out of place alongside mainstream groups. This is how Nirvana, Pearl Jam, Stone Temple Pilots, Soundgar-

den, Green Day and the Offspring found themselves being played alongside Eric Clapton and Metallica. The result was more public exposure and thus greater penetration into the mainstream.

(4) The Demographic Factor:

With the dawn of the '90s came a whole new generation of music fans—kids that might not have even been born when the original punk movement hit in the '70s. These kids do not want to listen to their parents' music. They have wants, needs and concerns of their own—and they want their own music. The situation was very similar to what faced the punks of the mid-'70s. Unable to identify with Mick Jagger or David Lee Roth, the new generation latched on to artists with which they felt something in common: Kurt Cobain, Eddie Vedder, Tori Amos.

(5) The Good Music Factor:

The music created by the alternative mindset is just too good and too exciting to be kept a secret forever. Maybe it was just a matter of time before the rest of the world caught on.✦

KURT COBAIN'S SUICIDE NOTE

"This note should be pretty easy to understand. All the warnings from the Punk 101 courses over the years, since by first introduction to, shall we say, ethics involved with independence and embracement of your community, have proven to be very true.

"I haven't felt the excitement of listening to as well as creating music, along with really writing something, for too many years now.

"I feel guilty beyond words about these things—for example, when we're backstage and the lights go out and the roar of the crowd begins, it doesn't affect me the way in which it did for Freddy Mercury, who seemed to love and relish the love and adoration of the crowd. Which is something I totally admire and envy. The fact that I can't fool you, any one of you, it simply isn't fair to you or to me. The worst crime I could think of would be to pull people off by faking it, pretending as if I'm having 100% fun.

"Sometimes I feel as I should have a punch-in time clock before I walk out on stage. I've tried everything within my power to appreciate it, and I do, God believe me I do, but it's not enough. I appreciate the fact that I and we have affected and entertained a lot of people. I must be one of those narcissists who only appreciate things when they're alone. I need to be slightly numb in order to regain a much better appreciation of all the people I know personally, and as fans of our music, but I still can't get out the frustration to gather the empathy I have for everybody. There's good in all of us and I simply love people too much. So much that it makes me feel just too fucking sad. Sad little sensitive unappreciative Pisces."

[The next few lines contain a personal message to Courtney Love and Frances Bean.]

"I had a good marriage, and for that I'm grateful. But since the age of seven, I've become hateful toward all humans in general only because it seems so easy for people to get along that have empathy. Only because I love and feel for people too much, I guess. Thank you all from the pit of my burning, nauseous stomach for your letters and concern during the last years. I'm pretty much of an erratic, moody person and I don't have the passion anymore."✦

Peace, Love, Empathy,
Kurt Cobain

THE DEATH OF KURT COBAIN

January 1992: As *Nevermind* sits at the top of virtually every album chart in the world, stories start to circulate about Kurt's heroin habit.

February 24, 1992: Kurt marries Courtney Love in a private ceremony in Hawaii.

August 18, 1992: Frances Bean Cobain is born. In the delivery room, Kurt collapses to the floor with withdrawal symptoms.

September 21, 1994: Kurt comes clean about his drug abuse in an interview in the *Los Angeles Times*.

Early 1993: Kurt says that his drug problems are behind him. He credits the birth of his daughter with turning things around. However, the chronic stomach pains he's suffered since childhood continue. He consults nine different specialists, one of whom suggests the problem could be a pinched nerve in the spine. That could explain why only certain painkillers like Percodan, morphine and heroin worked. Kurt is given a prescription for physical therapy and a drug called Bruprenex.

July 1993: Police are called to investigate a domestic dispute at the Cobain residence in Seattle. A large quantity of guns and ammunition is seized.

Early 1994: Disturbing stories about Nirvana begin to circulate. Some rumors say the band members aren't getting along and a break-up is imminent. Others tell of a very depressed Kurt Cobain who may be back to using heroin again.

March 2, 1994: Using the pseudonym Kurt Poupon, Kurt, Courtney and Frances Bean check into room 541 of the Excelsior Hotel in Rome.

March 4, 1994:
12:00 am: Kurt has one of the hotel staff run out for a prescription drug called Roypnol (a tranquilizer/-sleeping aid). A suicide note is found nearby.

6:15 am: Courtney finds Kurt unconscious on the floor. He apparently had taken a large quantity of Roypnol and washed them down with champagne.

6:30 am: After being taken by ambulance to Umberto I Hospital, Kurt has his stomach pumped. The next five hours are spent administering emergency treatment for the overdose.

12:00 pm: Kurt is transferred to American Hospital, a private luxury clinic. Meanwhile, CNN reports that he has died.

3:45 pm: Kurt wakes up on his own and appears to be out of danger.

6:00 pm: Nirvana's record company issues a statement saying that Kurt has been admitted to hospital suffering from "exhaustion and the flu."

March 9, 1994: Kurt and the family return to the house at 171 Lake Washington Boulevard in Seattle. All European dates on the tour are postponed indefinitely.

March 18, 1994: During a fight with Courtney, Kurt locks himself in a room with his gun collection and threatens to kill himself. The police are called and the situation is diffused.

March 20, 1994: Courtney arranges a "tough love" intervention session in hopes of getting Kurt to straighten out. He agrees to seek professional help.

March 28, 1994: Kurt enters a twelve step program at the Exodus Recovery Center at the Daniel Freeman Hospital in Marina Del Ray, California.

March 30, 1994: Kurt walks away from the treatment center and heads back to Seattle. Once he gets there, he convinces his friend Dylan Carlson to buy him a 20-gauge shotgun.

April 1, 1994: While in Los Angeles promoting the release of the new Hole album, Courtney receives a call from Kurt at her hotel. It's the last time they speak.

April 2, 1994: Worried about Kurt's state of mind, Courtney hires a private detective and orders him to find Kurt.

April 4, 1994: Kurt's mother reports him missing to the police. Meanwhile, Kurt apparently phones a friend to ask about the best way to shoot one-self in the head.

April 5, 1994: Kurt returns to the house at 171 Lake Washington Boulevard in Seattle. Despite the fact that the place is supposed to be staked out by friends, family and the police, he slips in unnoticed. Sometime that evening (or perhaps in the early morning hours of April 6), he moves to the room above the garage out back where he writes a long letter and takes a mixture of heroin and Valium. He then shoots himself by placing the shotgun in his mouth and pulling the trigger with his thumb.

April 7, 1994: The phone at the house rings constantly. No one answers.

April 8, 1994: An electrician finds the body at 8:40 am PDT. By noon, the whole world knows.✦

THE STONE ROSES: WHAT TOOK YOU GUYS SO LONG?

There aren't many bands who can disappear for six years and still find someone waiting for them when they finally showed up again. But then the Stone Roses aren't exactly your average band.

When they released their debut album in May 1989, they were the most interesting thing to hit the British indie scene and years and for the next eighteen months, they were at the very front of the so-called "Manchester scene." But at the height of their popularity, things began to go terribly wrong. Here is a chronology of what happened:

Late 1989: FM Revolver reissues "Sally Cinnamon" complete with a tacky video without the band's permission.

January 1990: The Stone Roses visit the offices of FM Revolver and stage a vandalism attack on president Paul Birch in retaliation. By the time they're finished, Birch's offices were redecorated to the tune of $50,000 in damage. Charges are laid and each member of the band is eventually fined £3000.

September 1990: The beginning of The Wait. Legal action against Silvertone Records begins. The band wants out of the contract which binds them to the label for thirty years. Meanwhile, a bidding war over the Roses erupts between several major labels.

January 1991: The Roses reluctantly announced that recording sessions for their new album have been delay indefinitely due to their legal problems with Silvertone.

March 1991: Court case begins in London. Meanwhile, Geffen offers the band a deal worth $4 million.

April 1991: Gareth Evans (the band's manager) announces that the Stone Roses will play two giant comeback shows in America. It never happens.

May 1991: The court decides that the

Silvertone contract is one-sided and unfair and releases the band from the agreement. Silvertone is also ordered to pay all costs. Geffen wins the bidding war, offering the group a contract worth an estimated £23 million.

February 1992: The band loses their manager (who eventually files a lawsuit against the group for £10 million).

March 1992: The band goes into the studio for a while—but nothing much happens so they decide to take some time off.

March 1993: They record about a dozens songs with producer John Leckie, but things still weren't going right, so they decide to take more time off. Geffen announces that the release of the band's second album has been delayed until August.

July 1993: Leckie gets tired of waiting and quits. Geffen announces that the album will not be out in August as scheduled but that October looks likely. The Roses attempt some sessions with producer Paul Schroeder.

October 1993: Geffen lets it slip that the Stone Roses album won't be out anytime soon. Meanwhile, the group continues to cash the checks that Geffen keeps sending over.

February 1994: Paul Schroeder quits and his assistant, Simon Dawson, takes over as producer. The promised single for February 14 doesn't materialize.

May 1994: Geffen finally sends a representative over to England to see how their money is being spent. He returns relieved.

October 1994: Final mixes of the new album are finished and the artwork for the album is completed. Geffen announces the album will be out soon. No one believes them.

November 21, 1994: A copy of the first single, "Love Spreads" is delivered under armed guard to the BBC who are allowed to play it once. The single is then removed from the building.

December 5, 1994: Sixty-six months after the first album, Second Coming is released. More than 3,470 hours of studio time were used to complete 75 minutes of music.✦

PEARL JAM VS. TICKETMASTER

April 17, 1994: At the Palladium in New York, Pearl Jam plays their last performance before announcing that they were canceling their summer tour. The tour is on hold until they can make an arrangement to sell tickets without using Ticketmaster. The band accuses the agency of charging too much in service charges and fees. Pearl Jam wants services charges to be no higher than 10% of the face value of the ticket.

May 1994: Pearl Jam files a complaint with the US Justice Department that accuses Ticketmaster of threatening to sue promoters who work with Pearl Jam on setting up an alternative tour featuring lower ticket prices and lower service charges.

June 8, 1994: The *Los Angeles Times*

93

reports that the Justice Department has subpoenaed the records of Ticketmaster.

Late June 1994: California Congressman Gary Condit calls Pearl Jam to testify before a House of Representatives subcommittee investigating anti-trust charges against Ticketmaster. In his testimony, guitarist Stone Gossard alleges that it is almost impossible for a band to launch a large-scale tour of America without using Ticketmaster. He cites exclusive contracts between Ticketmaster and "significant" concert promoters.

July 30, 1994: Pearl Jam files a complaint with the Justice Department, saying that Ticketmaster had made potentially misleading statements in its testimony.

November 22, 1994: Pearl Jam releases *Vitalogy*. The Justice Department doesn't appear in a hurry to make a decision on the Ticketmaster matter. Meanwhile, R.E.M. announces that they support Pearl Jam's stance. However, R.E.M.'s 1995 tour uses Ticketmaster to distribute tickets.

January 12, 1995: Pearl Jam jams with Neil Young at a Rock 'n' Roll Hall of Fame ceremony. Eddie Vedder later jokes about how the band was seated next to the Ticketmaster table.

Spring 1995: After much fanfare, Pearl Jam announces that they will tour America in the summer using a new computerized ticket distribution company called ETM.

June 14, 1995: In a statement to the press, band manager Kelly Curtis drops hints that Pearl Jam may abandon its attempts to fight Ticketmaster.

June 16, 1995: Pearl Jam's summer tour starts in Caster, Wyoming. Eddie tells the crowd that they are not giving up the battle. Meanwhile, no other bands have joined Pearl Jam's boycott.

June 20, 1995: Pearl Jam plays Red Rocks outside of Denver. Fans give the show mixed reviews.

June 24, 1995: At show in San Francisco's Polo Grounds, Eddie leaves the stage after seven songs, complaining that he was ill with the flu (He was treated at an emergency ward the night before). Neil Young takes over for the rest of the show. Complaints are heard about the ETM ticket arrangement.

June 25, 1995: Pearl Jam announces that they are canceling the remaining dates on a planned fifteen date, twelve city tour. They cite "continued controversies associated with attempting to schedule and perform at alternate venues." The battle for Ticketmaster is turning out to be more trouble than it's worth.

June 27: 1995: Pearl Jam announces that they will play shows in Milwaukee and Chicago. Ironically, tickets for the Milwaukee show are handled by Ticketmaster.

July 5, 1995: The Justice Department drops its investigation of Ticketmaster.◆

94

Section 2

This Day In Alternative Music History

January

January 1st

1979: The Invaders play their last gig in London, before renaming the band Madness.

1977: The Clash headlines on opening night at the Roxy Club in London.

1964: "Top of the Pops" debuts on the BBC.

January 2nd

1979: Sid Vicious goes on trial in New York for the murder of his girlfriend, Nancy Spungen. The trial is never completed because Sid dies of a heroin overdose on February 2.

Birthdays: Keith Gregory (Wedding Present), 1963.

January 3rd

1992: A Red Hot Chili Peppers/Pearl Jam concert in Seattle is canceled, when Anthony Kiedis comes down with the flu.

1984: Stiff merges with Island.

1981: David Bowie plays his final night in *The Elephant Man* on Broadway.

Birthdays: Raymond McGinley (Teenage Fanclub), 1964.

January 4th

1994: Green Day's management announces plans to set up their own label. It will be called 510 Records, after the band's Berkeley area code.

1991: Nirvana announces they've signed a two album deal with Geffen records.

1965: Fender Guitar, which made Stratocasters and Telecasters, is bought by CBS for $13 million.

Birthdays: Martin McAloon (Prefab Sprout), 1962. Ian Masters (Pale Saints), 1964. Michael Stipe (R.E.M.), 1960. Bernard Sumner (Electronic/New Order), 1956.

January 5th

1978: The Sex Pistols kick off their first (and only) US tour in Atlanta. Nine days later the band announces they are splitting up.

1940: The first FM radio broadcast takes place in the US.

Birthdays: Grant Young (Soul Asylum), 1964. Chris Stein (Blondie), 1950.

January 6th

1983: The Smiths headline their first show at Manhattan Sound in Manchester. It features a gay go-go dancer complete with stilettos and maracas.

1982: Lynval Golding of the Specials is attacked and stabbed by skinheads in Coventry, England. They miss his jugular by less than an inch. He needs 20 stitches to close the wounds.

1977: Following the "Today" incident with Bill Grundy the previous December 1, EMI drops the Sex Pistols.

Birthdays: Mark O'Toole (Frankie Goes To Hollywood), 1964.

January 7th

1982: The Stranglers' Hugh Cornwell is convicted of drug possession and sentenced to eight weeks in jail and fined £300. He starts serving his sentence in March after losing his appeal. While in jail, he keeps a diary which he later turns into the book *Inside Information.*

1958: Gibson patents its "Flying V" guitar design. Bob Mould would later use a Flying V on dozens of Hüsker Dü tours between 1981 and 1987.

January 8th

1991: Sixteen year-old Jeremy Wade Delle puts the barrel of a .347 magnum in his mouth in front of his English class in Richardson, Texas, and pulls the trigger. He was distraught over being chewed out for skipping school. The incident is the inspiration for Pearl Jam's "Jeremy."

Birthdays: Andrew Wood (Mother Love Bone), 1966. Matt Johnson (The The), 1961. David Robert Jones aka David Bowie, 1947. Peter Gill (Frankie Goes to Hollywood), 1964.

January 9th

1991: Mr. Blackwell, calling her the "bald-headed banshee of MTV," puts Sinead O'Connor on his worst dressed list.

1981: Jerry Dammers and Terry Hall of the Specials are fined £400 on charges that they incited violence at a Cambridge concert in 1980.

Birthdays: David Johansen (New York Dolls), 1950.

January 10th

1984: Soft Cell plays their final concert in London.

1979: The Ramones release "I Wanna Be Sedated" b/w "She's The One."

1978: The Sex Pistols play The Longhorn Ballroom in Dallas, a country and western bar. Trouble between punk fans and cowboys never materializes but Sid Vicious is offered oral sex by a groupie who makes it on stage.

January 11th

1992: *Nevermind* by Nirvana knocks Michael Jackson's *Dangerous* out of the number one spot on the Billboard album chart.

1984: A BBC DJ announces he won't play "Relax" by Frankie Goes To Hollywood any more because of its sexual lyrics. The BBC eventually bans the song entirely.

1980: The Pretenders release their self-titled debut LP.

January 12th

1981: The Recording Industry Association of America donates 800 LPs to the White House. Among the records President Ronald Reagan and visiting British Prime Minister Margaret Thatcher can dance to are *Never Mind The Bollocks–Here's The Sex Pistols.*

1970: A Pan-Am 747 touches down at Heathrow Airport, completing the first transatlantic 747 flight.

January 13th

1995: R.E.M. play their first full electric concert in more than five years in Perth, Australia.

1986: Former members of the Sex Pistols sue former manager Malcolm McLaren for £1 million in unpaid royalties. The suit is eventually settled out of court.

1984: BBC Radio 1 bans "Relax" by Frankie Goes to Hollywood because of the song's perceived "homosexual undertones."

Birthdays: Suggs McPherson aka Graham McPherson (Madness), 1961.

January 14th

1995: Pearl Jam, Neil Young and L7 play charity shows for Voters For Choice in Washington, DC, and Jack Irons, formerly of the Red Hot Chili Peppers debuts as Pearl Jam's new drummer.

1978: The Sex Pistols play their last live show at the Winterland in San Francisco. Following the gig, Johnny Rotten has a huge fight with Malcolm McLaren and quits, breaking up the band.

1966: David Jones became David Bowie to avoid being mistaken for Davy Jones of the Monkees.

Birthdays: David Grohl (Nirvana/Foo Fighters), 1969. Patricia Morrison (Sisters of Mercy), 1962. Chas Smash aka Cathal

David Bowie ➜

Smythe (Madness), 1959.

January 15th

1977: David Bowie releases *Low*, the very electronic and dispassionate Brian Eno-produced album that ends having an impact on everything from techno-pop to industrial music.

Birthdays: Martha Davis (Motels), 1951. Captain Beefheart aka Don Van Vliet, 1941.

January 16th

1978: Sid Vicious ODs and is sent to the hospital. Meanwhile, Virgin Records declares there will be no more Sex Pistols releases.

Birthdays: Brendan O'Hare (Teenage Fanclub), 1970.

January 17th

1984: The US Supreme Court rules on "The Betamax Case," and decides home videotaping for private, non-commercial use does not constitute copyright infringement.

1975: The Talking Heads start their first rehearsals in New York.

January 18th

1981: Police in Milwaukee arrest Wendy O. Williams during a Plasmatics concert for simulating masturbation with a sledgehammer. During the bust, Wendy is pinned to the floor and needs twelve stitches to repair cuts to her head and face.

1971: New rules regarding Canadian content in radio music programming go into effect. Between 6 am and midnight, 30 percent of the music broadcast has to be by Canadians.

Birthdays: Tom Bailey (Thompson Twins), 1957.

January 19th

1994: Bob Marley is posthumously inducted into the Rock and Roll

Hall of Fame.

1988: A Chicago music critic sues the Beastie Boys for a half-million dollars, accusing them of breaking into his Hollywood hotel room while he slept, pouring water on him, and filming the prank for a video.

1988: The Sugarcubes re-edit their "Cold Sweat" video after the producer of a British television show complained about the part showing Elinar having his throat cut. The band substitutes shots of monkeys playing.

1978: Johnny Rotten is fired from the Sex Pistols for "not being weird enough anymore."

Birthdays: Mickey Virtue (UB40), 1957.

January 20th

1991: Cait O'Riordan aka Mrs. Elvis Costello sues her former bandmates in the Pogues for £6,000 in unpaid royalties.

1990: Sinead O'Connor's *Nothing Compares 2 U* is released.

1987: The Cure ask radio stations not to play "Killing an Arab." They plan to attach stickers to their album explaining the song was really anti-violence.

1984: Ministry's Al Jourgensen marries Patty Marsh in Chicago.

January 21st

1995: Courtney Love is arrested, strip-searched and subjected to a police interrogation upon arriving at the Melbourne Airport from Brisbane. She pleads guilty to abusing a Qantas attendant, pays a £245 fine and is put on a one month, good behavior bond.

1988: U2 is named the most profitable live act in the US, grossing $35 million on their American tour.

1967: The Velvet Underground kick off a week long gig at Expo '67 in Montreal.

Birthdays: Wendy James (Transvision Vamp), 1966.

January 22nd

1983: Three months after they announced they would split up, the Jam makes recording industry history by having nine re-issued singles hit the UK charts at the same time. Doesn't matter. The band still wants to call it quits.

1972: During an interview with *Melody Maker*, David Bowie professes to be gay.

Birthdays: Michael Hutchence (INXS), 1962. Malcolm McLaren, 1946.

January 23rd

1990: David Bowie tells the press he's launching his final, global concert tour, *The Sound and Vision* tour. Fans are able to request their favorite hits via local radio stations

1977: During a show in Tampa, Florida, Patti Smith falls off the stage and breaks a vertebrae in her neck.

1976: The Easy Cure have their first proper rehearsal in a church hall in Crawley, England.

1974: John Cummings and Douglas Colvin get drunk after work and decide to buy a couple of guitars. They go to Manny's Guitar Center on 48th Street in New York where John picks up a blue Mosrite and Douglas buys a DanElectro bass. The following Sunday, they start a band which will end up being known as the Ramones.

Birthdays: Earl Falconer (UB40), 1957. Kevin Staples (Rough Trade), 1950.

January 24th

1980: Malcolm McLaren gets his way and Adam Ant leaves Adam and the Ants. Malcolm then pairs the Ants with Annabella Lwin to form Bow Wow Wow.

← Courtney Love of Hole

1979: The Clash release their first American single, a cover of the Bobby Fuller Four's "I Fought the Law."

1970: Dr. Robert Moog unveils the "mini-moog," the first truly portable keyboard synthesizer. Professional musicians express concern, saying that the machine could soon put them all out of work.

Birthdays: Julian "Jools" Holland (Squeeze), 1958.

January 25th

1980: The Specials play their first American gig at a club called Hurrah in New York City.

1973: Because of his fear of flying, David Bowie begins his world tour by crossing the Atlantic on the QE2.

Birthdays: Gary Brian Tibbs (Adam and the Ants/Roxy Music), 1958. Andy Cox (English Beat/Fine Young Cannibals), 1956.

January 26th

1993: David Rockola, the manufacturer of the jukebox, dies in Illinois at the age of 96. Rock-Ola and Wurlitzer were the top two jukebox makers until 1974 when Wurlitzer stopped making them.

1978: Workers at EMI's record-pressing plant refuse to manufacture copies of the Buzzcocks single "What Do I Get" because the B-side is entitled "Oh, Shit."

Birthdays: Norman Hassan (UB40), 1958.

January 27th

1994: Oasis make their London debut at the Water Rats in Kings Cross. More than 200 people are turned away because the club is so full.

1990: Billy Idol wins a libel suit against a British tabloid.

1981: David Bowie signs a five-year, ten-million dollar contract with EMI.

1974: The Ramones hold their first rehearsal.

Birthdays: Gillian Gilbert (New Order), 1961. Wolfgang Amadeus
  Mozart, 1756.

January 28th

1984: The Smiths dominate the UK indie charts with singles in the
  top three slots.

1988: *Never Mind the Bollocks–Here's The Sex Pistols* finally goes gold
  in the US.

1984: "Relax" by Frankie Goes To Hollywood hits number one on the
  charts.

1983: WDHA in New Jersey becomes the first radio station in the US
  to air a compact disc.

Birthdays: David Sharp (Alarm), 1959.

January 29th

1979: Brenda Spencer brings a gun to her school in San Diego and
  murders two people. When asked why she did it, Brenda replies,
  "Because I don't like Mondays." The incident inspires Bob
  Geldof to write "I Don't Like Mondays" for the Boomtown
  Rats.

1977: The Stranglers release their first single, "(Get a) Grip (on Yourself)."

Birthdays: Roddy Frame (Aztec Camera), 1964. Tommy Ramone aka
  Thomas Erdelyi (Ramones), 1949.

January 30th

1986: Spandau Ballet splits with Chrysalis Records over musical direction and image marketing.

1972: More than a dozen Roman Catholic civil rights marchers are
  shot by British soldiers in Londonderry, Northern Ireland. The
  event became known as "Bloody Sunday" and is the inspiration

for U2's "Sunday Bloody Sunday."

January 31st

1988: The Beastie Boys deny reports of a split.

1976: David Bowie releases *Station To Station.*

Birthdays: Al Jaworski (Jesus Jones), 1966. Lloyd Cole (And The Commotions), 1961. Phil Manzanera (Roxy Music), 1951. Johnny Rotten aka John Lydon (Sex Pistols/PiL), 1956.

February

February 1st

1995: Richey Edwards of Manic Street Preachers disappears. His car is found abandoned two weeks later, on a bridge that spans the Bristol Channel.

1983: Tears For Fears release "Change."

1949: RCA Victor introduces the 45 rpm single to rival Columbia's 33 1/3 LP, which has been on sale for about a year. Both took on

Johnny Lydon aka Johnny Rotten ↑

the old 78s, and because the change in formats confused people at first, record sales actually drop for awhile. Eventually, the LP is adopted for classical music and the 45 becomes the preferred speed for popular music. By the way, the first single ever pressed was "Gaite Parisienne" by the Boston Pops Orchestra. The first pop 7" was "The Waltz You Saved For Me" by Wayne King and His Orchestra. It was pressed in April.

February 2nd

1992: Pearl Jam kick off their first tour of the UK and have their first run-in with British music critics.

1981: Duran Duran release their first single, "Planet Earth."

1980: More than 1,000 punks march to Hyde Park in London in honor of the first anniversary of Sid Vicious' death. Sid's mom was supposed to join the march but she overdosed the night before and is in hospital.

1979: Sid Vicious dies of a heroin overdose at a friend's New York City apartment. He apparently took too much of a stash that his mother had bought for him. Sid was awaiting trial in connection with the death of his girlfriend, Nancy Spungen. To this day, no one really knows if Sid did it.

February 3rd

1983: The Smiths play the Hacienda in Manchester which is decked out in flowers, which Morrissey says "offered hope."

1983: Sony of Japan and Philips of The Netherlands announce that they had developed a new music storage device called the "compact disc."

1877: The piano composition entitled "Chopsticks" is registered at the British Museum by Euphemia Alten, a sixteen-year-old girl. She uses the alias Arthur de Lull.

Birthdays: Laurence "Lol" Tolhurst (Cure), 1959. Tony Butler (Big Country), 1957.

February 4th

1994: Blur finishes recording *Parklife*.

1993: While Europe sleeps, Russian scientists deploy a giant mirror in orbit which momentarily flashes sunlight across the continent.

1983: Karen Carpenter dies of a heart attack brought on by her long struggle with anorexia. She was only 32.

February 5th

1993: Hackers on Prodigy offer a sneak peak of Depeche Mode's *Songs Of Faith And Devotion*, including reviews gleaned from bootleg copies. Sire/Reprise Records tracks down some of the leaks and blames alternative radio stations.

1977: Iggy Pop signs a solo record deal with RCA.

Birthdays: Nick Laird-Clowes (Dream Academy), 1957.

February 6th

1995: Martin Kemp of Spandau Ballet recovers from emergency brain surgery after having a tumor removed in London.

1990: Billy Idol breaks his arm and leg in a motorcycle accident in Los Angeles after recording the final tracks for *Charmed Life*. Police reports indicate he wasn't wearing a helmet when he ran a stop sign.

1945: The accepted birthdate of Bob Marley. The problem is that birth records in his hometown of St. Ann's, Jamaica are rather sketchy. His passport lists his birthday as April 6.

Birthdays: Melissa Brooke Belland (Voice Of The Beehive), 1966.

February 7th

1995: Pop Will Eat Itself cancels some American dates on the NIN tour after singer Graham Crabb collapses with nervous exhaustion. Nine Inch Nails is blamed for adding new dates all the time.

Iggy Pop ➔

1987: The Smiths play their final performance at the San Remo festival in Italy, sharing the bill with the Pet Shop Boys, Style Council and Spandau Ballet.

1982: Kraftwerk becomes the first German act to top the UK singles chart with "Computer Love/The Model."

Birthdays: Brian Travers (UB40), 1959.

February 8th

1980: David and Angela Bowie get divorced. He gets custody of son Zowie, now called Joe.

1964: The publisher of "Louie, Louie" offers $1,000 to anyone who can prove that the song features pornographic or suggestive lyrics.

February 9th

1995: L7 cancels the rest of their European tour following the death of guitar roadie Umbar, who died of a heart attack after a London show.

1995: Simple Minds launch their world tour in Seattle, their first tour of the US in more than three years.

1987: The Housemartins win the Best British Newcomer title at the BRITS, though the tabloids claim the group isn't from Hull in Yorkshire, but rather from Horsham in the south of England.

1981: New Order's first London date is supposed to be secret, but the one thousand tickets available for the Heaven club sell out in minutes.

Birthdays: Graeme Naysmith (Pale Saints), 1967. Holly Johnson aka William Johnson (Frankie Goes to Hollywood), 1964.

February 10th

1988: The British High Court rules the contract between Holly Johnson of Frankie Goes To Hollywood and ZTT records, was "nonsensical" and an "unreasonable restraint on the singer." The judge orders ZTT to pay Johnson's half-million dollar legal bill. Johnson can now sign with MCA as a solo artist.

1942: The first-ever gold record is awarded to the Glen Miller Orchestra for "Chattanooga Choo-Choo."

February 11th

1994: The Ramones play their 2,000th show in Tokyo.

1988: London fans of the Butthole Surfers go on a rampage when a gig at the Mean Fiddler sells out.

1979: Stiff Little Fingers release their debut album, *Inflammable Material.*

1972: David Bowie introduces his new alter-ego at a concert in Tolworth, England. He calls the character "Ziggy Stardust." It didn't take long for fans to start showing up to his shows wearing the Ziggy make-up.

1847: The inventor of the phonograph, Thomas Alva Edison, is born in Milan, Ohio.

February 12th

1995: Soul Asylum fire drummer Grant Young in a fight over style.

1990: Sexual assault charges against David Bowie are dismissed by a Texas judge.

1981: Deborah Harry leaves Blondie.

Birthdays: Gary "Gaz" Whelan (Happy Mondays), 1966. Neil Conti (Prefab Sprout), 1959. Fruitbat aka Leslie Carter (Carter The Unstoppable Sex Machine), 1958.

February 13th

1994: Lol Tolhurst testifies at his bitter divorce suit against the Cure. The former keyboardist is demanding a bigger slice of the royalties even though he was bounced for his drinking problem.

1982: The Jam's "A Town Called Malice" hits #1 in the UK.

1981: Island Records ticks off the British music industry by introducing their One Plus One series of half pre-recorded/half blank tapes, which appears to promote home taping.

1980: London police raid Johnny Lydon's house but leave when the only illegal substance they can come up with is a canister of tear gas, which Johnny says he needs to keep out intruders.

Birthdays: Henry Rollins, 1961. Les Warner (The Cult), 1961. Peter Hook (Joy Division/New Order), 1956. Peter Gabriel, 1950.

February 14th

1985: The Smiths release *Meat Is Murder.*

1981: Generation X breaks up and Billy Idol goes solo.

1977: The B-52's play their first gig on Valentine's Day, in a greenhouse on the grounds of the University of Georgia in Athens.

1958: CBS News reports that the government of Iran has banned rock music on the grounds that it is against the concepts of Islam. It's also officially declared a health hazard.

February 15th

1993: The video for "I Feel You" debuts on MTV. It's the first from Depeche Mode's new *Songs of Faith And Devotion* LP.

1977: Sid Vicious replaces Glen Matlock as the bassist in the Sex Pistols. Matlock was officially fired for "liking the Beatles." A few days later, Sid Vicious is hired as his replacement, despite the fact that he can't play a note.

1972: The Anti-Bootlegging Bill goes into effect in America. It gives copyright protection for sound recordings and forbids unauthorized reproduction.

Birthdays: Ali Campbell aka Alastair Campbell (UB40), 1959.

February 16th

1991: Sinead O'Connor announces she won't accept a Grammy award, even though she's nominated four times.

1979: Elvis Costello plays an announced show at the Palamino, a country music club in Hollywood. The performance includes many of Elvis' country favorites, including a bunch by George Jones.

Birthdays: Tony Kylie (Blow Monkeys), 1962. Andy Taylor, (Duran Duran), 1961.

February 17th

1995: R.E.M.'s Michael Stipe goes Hollywood with a film production company called Single Cell Pictures (or, as he calls it, Pond Scum). Stipe insists he won't learn how to "talk the talk," and hopes to remain somewhat naive about how the business works.

1988: Jim Reid of the Jesus and Mary Chain is given an absolute discharge after pleading guilty to bashing two fans with a microphone stand during a show in Toronto. They had been yelling "boring" all through the Chain's set. Jim later apologizes to the fans and donates $1,000 in their names to the Salvation Army.

1979: The Clash kick off their first US tour, dubbed "Pearl Harbor '79." The first show was at the Palladium in New York; the first song was "I'm So Bored With the USA."

1978: Kate Bush's debut album *The Kick Inside* is released in the UK.

1962: The chair of the Radio Trade Practices Committee proposes that all pop lyrics be screened by the National Association of Broadcasters Code Committee because of "the proliferation of songs dealing with raw sex and violence."

February 18th

1995: Bob Stinson, the ex-Replacements guitarist, is found dead in his Minneapolis apartment. He had been diagnosed as suffering from manic depression. A syringe was found nearby.

1978: *Sniffin' Glue,* the original punk fanzine, folds.

1971: Captain Beefheart and The Magic Band make their New York debut at Unganos.

Birthdays: Brian James (Damned/Lords Of The New Church), 1961.

February 19th

1991: INXS has about $2,000 stolen from their hotel room in Mexico. That's not the band's only brush with crime during this tour. The roadie for Garry Beers is detained by two Mexican cops who demand $120 before they will set him free.

1983: Paul Weller announces the formation of the Style Council.

Birthdays: Falco (1957). Dave Wakeling (English Beat/General Public), 1956.

February 20th

1995: For the first time in the history of the British Music Awards, a band wins four times. Among the honors, Blur is named Best British Band. During the dinner, Blur tosses bread rolls at Prince.

Birthdays: Kurt Cobain (Nirvana), 1967. Ian Brown aka Ian George Brown (Stone Roses), 1963.

February 21st

1992: While playing in Manchester, Pearl Jam's tour bus is robbed by a gang of toughs who hold their manager at knifepoint as they make off with whatever they can carry.

1990: Sinead O'Connor debuts as an actress, playing a schoolgirl in a British made-for-television movie which premieres at the Dublin Film Festival.

Birthdays: James Dean Bradfield (Manic Street Preachers), 1969. Ranking Roger aka Roger Charlery (English Beat/General Public), 1961. Jean Jacques Burnel (Stranglers), 1952. Jerry Harrison (Talking Heads/Casual Gods), 1949.

February 22nd

1987: Andy Warhol died in New York. He was 58.

1987: Gary Numan shuts down his Numa Records label.

1978: The Police dye their hair blond to star in a television commercial for Wrigley's gum. This was before the band had released any records.

Birthdays: Graham Lewis (Wire), 1953.

February 23rd

1985: The Smiths' *Meat Is Murder* knocks Bruce Springsteen's *Born In The USA* out of top spot on the UK album chart.

1983: The Hammersmith Odeon cancels the second night of the Stranglers show in London after a riot on opening night, during which fans tear up several rows of seats.

Birthdays: David Sylvian aka David Batt (Japan/Raintree Crow), 1958. Howard Jones aka John Howard Jones, 1955

February 24th

1992: Kurt Cobain and Courtney Love marry in Waikiki.

1979: The soundtrack to the Sex Pistols' movie *The Great Rock 'n' Roll Swindle* is released.

1979: "Roxanne" by the Police is released as a single in the US.

1956: Cleveland police drag out a 1931 law that bars people under the age of eighteen from dancing in public unless accompanied by an adult.

1897: Emile Berliner takes out a Canadian patent on his gramophone talking machine. He built the first version at his Washington home a decade before and had already licensed his invention in the US. Berliner's invention used lateral-cut discs, versus the vertical-cut cylinders Thomas Edison used for his gramophone. Eventually, Berliner's format will make Edison's efforts obsolete.

February 25th

1995: Elastica is ordered to give up nearly half the publishing rights from "Waking Up" to the Stranglers because it sounds suspiciously like "No More Heroes." They also reach an agreement with Wire over their appropriation of the intro to "Three Girl Rhumba" for the song "Connection."

1994: Suede announces they will be known as London Suede in the US, after being sued by a singer from Washington, DC, who has been using the name Suede professionally for years.

1991: The Farm releases *Spartacus*.

1977: The Jam sign with Polydor for £6,000. They renegotiate the four year deal after 90 days.

Birthdays: Mike Peters (Alarm), 1959.

February 26th

1994: Kevin Key of Skinny Puppy breaks his kneecap and left arm and will need cosmetic surgery to his face because of an accident filming a fight scene for *Doom Generation*.

1982: Killing Joke splits in two when Jaz and Geordie move to Iceland to escape the impending apocalypse. When the world fails to end, they return to Britain.

1955: The 7" single outsells the 78 rpm record for the first time.

Birthdays: Timothy Brown (The Boo Radleys), 1969.

February 27th

1992: The Recording Industry Association of America announces as of 1993, CDs won't be sold in longboxes but in jewel boxes. Environmental concerns outweigh retailers' worries about shoplifting.

Birthdays: Paul Humphreys (OMD), 1960.

February 28th

1989: G.G. Allin, lead singer of the Toilet Rockers, defecates on stage during a show in Milwaukee and then tosses his leavings into the audience. He's convicted of provoking a disturbance and slams the jury as "a bunch of narrow-minded, robotic puppets of society that look like my dead grandmother."

1983: U2 releases *War.*

1981: The Tourists split up and two members, Annie Lennox and Dave Stewart, go on to become the Eurythmics.

1979: During a Cure concert in Bournemouth, a girl pulls off her boyfriend's ear.

1966: CBS Labs report that they've developed a metal disc capable of storing video images for playback through a TV set.

Birthdays: Philip Gould (Level 42), 1957. Ian Stanley (Tears For Fears), 1957. Cindy Wilson (B-52's), 1957.

February 29th

1992: U2 opens their Zoo TV tour in Lakeland, Florida—the band's first US concert date in five years.

1960: Hugh Hefner opens his first Playboy Club in Chicago.

March

March 1st

1995: Drummer Bill Berry has to leave the stage ninety minutes into an R.E.M. concert in Lausane, Switzerland complaining of a migraine. It turns out to be two aneurysms and emergency surgery is ordered.

1989: R.E.M. begin their first arena trek, "Green World Tour," in Kentucky.

1980: Patti Smith and Fred "Sonic" Smith of MC5 get married in Detroit. Some joke Patti chose her groom because marrying

Fred meant she wouldn't have to change her name.

March 2nd

1993: Nirvana's Krist Novoselic gives a spoken-word performance in London as part of a show to raise money for children injured in the war in the former Yugoslavia.

1988: U2 wins two Grammys for *The Joshua Tree*, including Album of the Year.

1983: Sony, Phillips and Polygram introduce us to the compact disc.

1974: Television play their first gig at the Townhouse Theatre in New York.

Birthdays: Lou Reed (Velvet Underground), 1944.

March 3rd

1995: Bill Berry of R.E.M. undergoes emergency surgery to remove two brain aneurysms. The band postpones the rest of their European tour.

1991: A London paper reports Sinead O'Connor will play Cathy in a Paramount remake of Emily Bronte's *Wuthering Heights*.

1980: Sotheby's in London hold their first pop memorabilia auction.

Birthdays: Simon Scott (Slowdive), 1971. Paul Jamrozy (Test Department), 1959. Chris Hughes (Adam and the Ants), 1954. Robyn Hitchcock, 1952.

March 4th

1994: At 6:15 am in Room 541 of the Excelsior Hotel in Rome, Courtney Love finds Kurt Cobain on the floor in a coma. He has taken at least 50 Roypnol pills. Kurt is taken by ambulance to Umberto I hospital where he has his stomach pumped. From there, he is transferred to American Hospital, a private luxury clinic. All concerned insist this was an accidental overdose. While all this is going on, CNN reports that he has died.

1994: CNN announce they are changing their name to XC-NN to avoid being sued by Ted Turner, owner of the news network.

1984: Chris Stein of Blondie checks into a New York City hospital and spends the next two months being treated for a mysterious metabolic blood deficiency. He is diagnosed as suffering from a genetic disease known as pemphigus.

1980: Morrissey and a friend claim to see a fleet of flying saucers and he comes away convinced aliens have landed.

Birthdays: Patrick Hannan (Sundays), 1966.

March 5th

1994: Kurt Cobain regains consciousness at American Hospital in Rome following his drug overdose.

1965: The Mannish Boys release their debut single "I Pity The Fool." David Bowie sings in this band.

Birthdays: Damon Albarn (Blur), 1968. Mark E. Smith (Fall), 1957.

March 6th

1970: Charles Manson releases an album called *Lie*. Proceeds from its sales will help pay some of his legal bills.

March 7th

1995: Dave Jordan, the producer of Bob Marley, the Specials and the Pogues LPs, dies in France of an apparent heart attack. He was 43.

1987: *Licensed to Ill* by the Beastie Boys becomes the first rap album to top the charts in the US.

1975: David Bowie releases *Young Americans*.

Birthdays: Paul Davis (Happy Mondays), 1966.

March 8th

1994: Morrissey releases *Vauxhall And I*.

1990: *Rolling Stone* readers vote U2's Bono "Sexiest Male Rock Artist."

1965: David Bowie's television debut with the Mannish Boys on "Gadzooks! It's All Happening" is almost canceled because producers say his hair is too long.

Birthdays: Peter Gill (Frankie Goes To Hollywood), 1964. Gary Numan aka Gary Anthony James Webb, 1958

March 9th

1992: *The Manson Family,* the first opera album to carry a parental warning label, is released. It features Iggy Pop among others.

1987: U2's *The Joshua Tree* is released and becomes the first album to sell more than a million copies on CD.

Birthdays: Martin Frye (ABC), 1958.

March 10th

1979: Roxy Music begin a North American tour in support of *Manifesto,* their first album in three years.

1977: The Sex Pistols sign with A&M Records in a cheeky ceremony outside the gates of Buckingham Palace. The label drops them ten days later—but not before paying them £75,000 to get lost.

Birthdays: Jeff Ament (Pearl Jam), 1963.

March 11th

1977: The Slits make their live debut supporting the Clash. They are considered to be the first all-female punk band.

Birthdays: Bruce Watson (Big Country), 1966. Nina Hagen, 1955.

March 12th

1912: Juliette Gordon Lowe founds the Girl Guides in the US.

Birthdays: Graham Coxon (Blur), 1969. Jack Kerouac, 1922.

March 13th

1995: After an appearance on MuchMusic (the Canadian music video channel), Annie Lennox and her band head to a party arranged by her record label, BMG. But on her way to the top of the Toronto high-rise, the elevator gets stuck and the fire department had to be called to set them all free. It took an hour. Ironically, Lennox new album *Medusa* contained a cover of Bob Marley's "Waiting In Vain."

1987: Bryan Adams "Heat of the Night" becomes the first commercially released cassette single in the US.

Birthdays: Adam Clayton (U2), 1960.

March 14th

1990: The last of the big independent labels, Geffen Records, is sold to MCA.

1981: Roxy Music's cover of John Lennon's "Jealous Guy" is released as a tribute to the murdered ex-Beatle.

Birthdays: Boon Gould (Level 42), 1955.

March 15th

1995: Board Aid '95, is held in California. The event features airboarding and a mosh pit. Porno for Pyros and Ned's Atomic Dustbin perform to raise money for safe sex education.

1987: Frankie Goes to Hollywood announce that they're breaking up.

1980: *Rude Boy*, the Clash's movie, premieres in London.

1979: Elvis Costello makes some stupid remarks about Ray Charles and James Brown to Stephen Stills in the lounge of a Holiday Inn in Columbus, Ohio and a fight breaks out. The media picks up on the story and Elvis is later forced to apologize for the what he said at a press conference in New York.

1968: The Diocese of Rome okays the use of rock music during Roman Catholic masses.

Birthdays: Brian Eno, 1948.

March 16th

1990: Andrew Wood of Mother Love Bone OD's on heroin after spending 116 days clean and sober.

1981: Only a dozen people show up for a U2 concert in Los Angeles because nobody realizes the band was playing a second show in the area.

March 17th

1978: *This Year's Model* by Elvis Costello is released in the UK.

Birthdays: Billy Corgan (Smashing Pumpkins), 1957. Mike Lindup (Level 42), 1959.

March 18th

1995: Seventeen-year-old Ryan O'Donnell of Orlando files a misdemeanor battery complaint against Courtney Love, saying she slugged him in the chest after stage diving into the crowd during a Hole concert four days earlier.

1994: Kurt Cobain locks himself in a room with his gun collection at his house in Seattle and threatens to kill himself. The police are called and the situation is defused.

1977: The Clash release their first single, "White Riot."

1944: WQXR of New York bans singing commercials.

Birthdays: Jamie West-Oram (The Fixx), 1953.

March 19th

1995: Pearl Jam's tour wraps up in Melbourne. 13,000 tickets were sold, but 35,000 fans show up and there's trouble. Dozens are taken to hospital with minor injuries

1990: After three days on life support, Andrew Wood, lead singer of Mother Love Bone, dies of a drug overdose in Seattle. His parents had given doctors the okay to pull the plug and Andrew dies as Queen's *A Night At The Opera* plays in his hospital room.

1988: Les Warner decides to drop out as the Cult's drummer, when the band announces they are moving to Los Angeles.

Birthdays: Terry Hall (The Specials), 1959. Ricky Wilson (B-52's), 1953.

March 20th

1995: INXS' Michael Hutchence loses it when the press intrudes on his rendezvous with Paula Yates, the estranged wife of Bob Geldof.

1994: Concerned about his escalating heroin use, a five hour "tough love" intervention is held by Kurt Cobain's friends at his house in Seattle. During the meeting, his management threatens to drop Nirvana if he doesn't shape up. Kurt doesn't take things well and says he's quitting the band.

1990: There is a big crush and mini-riot at a Depeche Mode autograph session in Los Angeles. Seven fans are injured and the promoters have to pay the $25,000 bill for fire and police services.

1970: David Bowie marries Angie Barnett in Bromley, England.

1954: *Billboard* magazine reports that a number of record labels are introducing "high fidelity" recordings.

March 21st

1995: Bill Berry is released from a Swiss hospital after undergoing surgery on a pair of brain aneurysms.

1991: Leo Fender dies in California at the age of 88. He perfected the electric guitar and in the late 1940s the first mass produced solid-body electric guitar rolled off his assembly line. His company's Telecaster and Stratocasters are still favored by musicians.

1988: The Pixies release *Surfer Rosa*.

1976: David Bowie and Iggy Pop are arrested for drug possession in New York City. The case is adjourned and charges will later be dropped.

March 22nd

1995: Andy Creggan of the Barenaked Ladies quits, leaving the band without a keyboard player.

1994: The Charlatans UK release *Up To Our Hips*.

1978: The Police sign a deal with A&M in the UK, who thought the trio could be sold as a more palatable strain of punk than the Sex Pistols, which the label dropped the previous year.

March 23rd

1995: Bob Marley's former manager writes a bio about the singer called "Too Much Things To Say" in which he credits Marley with guiding the spirit of his dead son back in the form of another son, born exactly nine months later.

1993: Butthole Surfers release *Independent Worm Saloon*.

1993: Depeche Mode officially release *Songs Of Faith And Devotion*.

1985: Wembley Stadium takes flack for refusing to offer the venue free of charge for the upcoming Live Aid concert. They later change their minds.

1975: Following a gig at CBGBs, Richard Hell announces that he is quitting Television.

Birthdays: Julian Swales (Kitchens Of Distinction), 1964. Ric Ocasek (The Cars), 1949

March 24th

1995: Courtney Love throws a post-Oscar bash in Los Angeles and is cheesed she doesn't get to meet Keanu Reeves, who was staying at the same Chateau Marmont. Apparently someone was calling hotel rooms at random looking for the latest Hamlet.

1990: Ziggy Marley headlines a concert to celebrate Namibian inde-

pendence from South Africa. Ten years earlier, his dad Bob played a concert in honor of Zimbabwe independence.

1973: While onstage during a show in Buffalo, New York, an over-enthusiastic fan bites Lou Reed on the bum as he performs "Waiting for the Man."

1966: The New York State Assembly is the first legislative body in the world to ban bootleg recordings.

Birthdays: Lene Lovich, 1949.

March 25th

1995: Eddie Vedder has a close call in New Zealand. While swimming with Tim Finn, ex of Crowded House, he is carried away from shore by a riptide and has to be rescued by a life guard.

1980: The Police become the first Western band to play in Bombay in more than a decade.

Birthdays: Steve "Spiny" Norman (Spandau Ballet), 1960. Nick Lowe, 1949.

March 26th

1995: The Tragically Hip win two Junos (Canadian music awards) including Group of the Year, and Entertainer of the Year.

1993: Jack Sherman sues his former bandmates in the Red Hot Chili Peppers. He was fired in 1985. The suit says not only was he never given a reason but that Anthony Kiedis and Flea "giggled" while they let him go.

1983: Duran Duran is mobbed by five thousand fans outside a New York video store.

1977: Stiff Records releases "Less Than Zero," the first single from Elvis Costello.

Birthdays: Susanne Sulley (Human League), 1963. Martin Price (808 State), 1955.

← The Police

March 27th

1990: The King County Medical Examiner concludes Andrew Wood of Mother Love Bone died of an accidental heroin overdose.

1992: During a Detroit concert, Bono is switching channels after "Even Better Than The Real Thing." When a pizza ad comes up on one of the large onstage video screens, he decides to order 10 thousand pies for the crowd. Speedy's manages to deliver about 100 pepperoni pizzas. The incident leads to the hot T-shirt of the Zoo-TV tour, which reads "I'd like to order 10,000 pizzas."

1987: U2 stops traffic in L.A. when they shoot a performance video for "Where the Streets Have No Name" on the roof of an office building.

Birthdays: Andrew Farriss (INXS), 1959. Billy MacKenzie (Associates), 1957.

March 28th

1994: Kurt Cobain enters the 12-step program at the Exodus Recovery Center at the Daniel Freeman Hospital in Marina Del Rey, California.

1994: Miami riot police move in when 2,000 people without tickets push through fences to get into a Pearl Jam concert, tossing rocks and bottles as they go. Five people are hurt, four arrested.

1993: Sinead O'Connor is one of 15,000 protesters in Dublin, rallying against an IRA bombing that killed two children in England.

1964: Radio Caroline, Britain's first pirate radio station, takes to the air.

Birthdays: Rupert Greenall (The Fixx), 1951.

March 29th

1995: Seven New York State legislators table a bill which would cap the service charges ticket handling agencies can slap on concert-goers.

← Gord Downey of the Tragically Hip

1989: Crowded House play a neat gig in Calgary—performing for 80 people in the basement of Grant Harvey's house. He won the concert when his homemade video was judged the best entered in a MuchMusic contest. The four minute long, $87 video answered the question "What would your house look like if Crowded House came over?"

1985: Tom Bailey of Thompson Twins is found on the floor of his hotel room suffering from exhaustion. His doctor orders him to take a total break from work.

1984: The Federal Communications Commissions in the US approves stereo television broadcasts.

Birthdays: Perry Farrell (Psi Com/Jane's Addiction/Porno For Pyros), 1969.

March 30th

1995: U2 accuses a pirate condom company of exploiting their image by selling three packs of rubbers in pub vending machines throughout Britain. Even though they are bootlegs and don't come with the legally required expiration date and safety standard mark, they are collectors items.

1995: Rage Against The Machine admit work on their next album is stalled, after they come to blows in the studio. The working title is *Did You Spill My Pint, Motherfucker?*

1994: Kurt Cobain walks away from the rehab center in Marina Del Rey and returns to Seattle. Once he gets home, he convinces his friend Dylan Carlson to buy him a 20-gauge shotgun from Stan's Gun Shop on Lake City Way, saying that he needs it "for protection." Dylan agrees and purchases a Remington Model 11 for $300. After he hands the gun over to Kurt, he never sees him alive again.

1981: U2 demands cash for a concert in Lubbock, Texas at which point the club owner pulls out a gun and tells them they will take a check like everybody else.

1978: While still in school, U2 wins £500 and a CBS audition in a Guinness talent contest in Limerick, Ireland.

1976: The Sex Pistols play the 100 Club in London for the first time. Only fifty people show up.

1974: The Ramones play their first gig. About thirty people show up to see them at the Performance Studio on East 23rd Street in New York.

Birthdays: Tracy Chapman, 1964.

March 31st

1994: Morrissey's upcoming show in Los Angeles sells out in a record two minutes and thirty-one seconds.

1973: Lou Reed has a hot single in Britain with "Walk On The Wild Side."

April

April 1st

1994: Kurt Cobain phones Courtney Love, who is in Los Angeles to promote the new Hole album. He tells her "No matter what happens, I love you." It's the last time she and Kurt speak.

1988: With a $20,000 loan, Bruce Pavitt and Jonathan Poneman start Sub Pop records in Seattle. In 1995, they sell 49% of the company to Warner Music Group for $20 million.

1966: David Bowie releases his first solo single on Pye Records. It's called "Do Anything You Say."

Birthdays: Billy Currie (Ultravox), 1952.

April 2nd

1994: Worried about her husband, Courtney Love hires a detective to find him. They stake out the house at 171 Lake Washington in Seattle but Kurt is nowhere to be seen.

1992: Soundgarden's concert in Bristol is marked by a protest against the artwork for "Jesus Christ Pose" by a local religious group.

1971: David Bowie's *The Man Who Sold The World* is released.

Birthdays: David Robinson (The Cars), 1953.

April 3rd

1979: Kate Bush plays her first live show at the Liverpool Empire.

1882: Jesse James is shot in the back by a member of his own gang in St. Joseph, MO.

April 4th

1995: Duran Duran release *Thank You*, an album of covers.

1994: Kurt Cobain's mother reports to the police that her son is missing and claims that he's suicidal. They check the house on Lake Washington a number of times but find no one. Meanwhile, Kurt allegedly phones a friend to ask about the best way to shoot oneself in the head.

1987: Kate Bush is one of the artists to record a cover of The Beatles "Let It Be" for FerryAid, to raise money for the victims of a car ferry disaster in the North Sea. One hundred and eighty-seven people drowned when the boat capsized.

1987: RCA is taken over by the Betelsmann Music Group, or BMG, but gets to keep Nipper as its corporate logo.

1960: RCA announces that from now on, all albums on the label will be released in both mono and stereo.

Birthdays: David Gavurin (Sundays), 1963.

April 5th

1994: Kurt Cobain returns to his house at 171 Lake Washington Boulevard in Seattle. Sometime during the evening, he moves to the apartment about the garage. After writing a long letter, he takes a mixture of heroin and valium. He then puts the 20 gauge Remington shotgun in his mouth and pulls the trigger with his thumb.

1980: R.E.M. play their first gig at an old church in Athens, Georgia. The event was a birthday party for a friend.

Birthdays: Michael McCready (Pearl Jam), 1964. Stan Ridgeway (Wall Of Voodoo), 1955. Everett Morton (English Beat), 1951.

April 6th

1994: A Los Angeles court tosses out a lawsuit filed against the Red Hot Chili Peppers by ex-guitarist Jack Sherman. The court said he waited too long to legally complain about being fired in 1988 and didn't buy Sherman's explanation that childhood abuse made him passive.

1993: David Bowie releases *Black Tie White Noise*, his first solo effort in almost six years.

1988: The Mission entertain fellow stranded ferry passengers by busking on Folkestone dock.

Birthdays: Andy McClure (Sleeper), 1970. Stan Cullimore (Housemartins), 1962. Bob Marley (according to his passport), 1945.

April 7th

1994: Nirvana's management company announces that the band will not perform on the 1994 Lollapalooza tour. Meanwhile, the phone rings and rings at the house on Lake Washington. No one answers.

1994: Courtney Love is arrested at a Beverly Hills hotel and charged with drug possession. The charges are dropped within a month, when they find out the substance tested was not a narcotic.

1980: Ian Curtis of Joy Division attempts suicide by overdosing on Phenobarbitone, an epilepsy drug. He's rushed to hospital where he has his stomach pumped. A psychiatrist concludes that he is not suicidal.

1927: A New York audience takes in television for the first time, an appearance by then Commerce Secretary Herbert Hoover.

Birthdays: Patrick Fitzgerald (Kitchens Of Distinction), 1964.

April 8th

1994: At 8:40 am PDT, electrician Gary Smith finds the body of Kurt Cobain in a room above the garage of his Seattle home. Smith calls his boss, who calls a Seattle radio station with the news and by mid-afternoon every copy of every Nirvana album had been sold out in Seattle. In Los Angeles, Courtney Love learns of the situation on MTV. At 11:45 am PDT, police confirm that they have found a body. By 7:05 pm PDT, a positive ID is made.

1993: Hole issues the single "Beautiful Son." The cover shows a young Kurt Cobain.

1988: R.E.M. leaves IRS records for Warner Brothers. Their advance is so big that even their boss at IRS, Miles Copeland, tells them to accept the offer.

1977: The Clash release their self-titled debut album.

April 9th

1994: A crowd of between 5,000 and 7,000 people attend a candlelight vigil for Kurt Cobain. Courtney Love's pre-recorded message is played for the hometown fans, including quotes from Kurt's suicide note.

1988: Pet Shop Boys have their fourth #1 single in two-and-a-half years with "Heart."

1977: The Damned become the first British punk band to play American when they perform at CBGBs.

1969: David Bowie meets Angela Barnett for the first time at a King Crimson concert.

April 10th

1995: During a record store autograph session in Beverly Hills, Simon Le Bon kisses, nibbles and fondles the breast of an obliging Duran Duran fan.

← Brett Anderson of Suede

1993: Suede's self-titled album goes straight to #1 in the UK.

1991: Martin Hannett, the producer of Joy Division and the Buzzcocks, dies of a heart attack at the age of 42.

1982: Andy Partridge of XTC collapses with an ulcer and his health problems force the cancellation of the band's planned tour.

1980: The Cure kick off their first US tour in Cherry Hill, New Jersey.

Birthdays: Kenadid Osman (Sleeper), 1968. Reni aka Alan John Reni (Stone Roses), 1964. Bunny Wiler aka Neville O'Reilly Livingston (The Wailers), 1947.

April 11th

1994: Daniel Kaspar, a 28 year-old in Seattle, becomes the first documented case of copycat suicide following the death of Kurt Cobain.

1988: David Byrne and two collaborators (Cong Su and Ryuichi Sakamoto) win an Academy Award for the musical score of the Bernardo Bertolucci film *The Last Emperor.*

1981: The Cure releases *Faith.*

Birthdays: Stuart Adamson (Big Country), 1958. Neville Staples (The Specials), 1956. Chris Difford (Squeeze), 1954.

April 12th

1994: Hole releases their second album, *Live Through This.*

1994: The Rollins Band releases *Weight.* The LP was recorded in a log cabin in California.

1993: Lisa Bonet files for divorce from husband Lenny Kravitz.

1982: Thompson Twins play their last show as a 7 piece band. The group doesn't miss Chris Bell, Pete Dodd, John Roog and Matt Seligman. Tom Bailey, Alanah Currie and Joe Leeway do much better as a trio.

Birthdays: Will Sergent (Echo And The Bunnymen), 1958. Tony

James (Generation X), 1958. David Letterman, 1948.

April 13th

1995: *Dookie* by Green Day goes sextuple platinum. (Six million copies sold.)

1995: Juliana Hatfield collapses from nervous exhaustion after a concert in New York.

1986: The Alarm visits Disneyland and Snow White and Pluto ask to pose for pictures with singer Mike Peters.

1978: The Easy Cure shortens its name to The Cure.

Birthdays: James Destri (Blondie), 1954. Ron Loney (Flaming Groovies), 1946.

April 14th

1994: Kurt Cobain is cremated. Courtney Love sprinkles his ashes at the foot of a willow tree in the backyard. More ashes are placed under a Buddha in her bedroom as well as under an altar in the living room. A portion is also shipped off to India to be incorporated into a shrine that is blessed by the Dalai Lama. His death certificate lists his occupation as "poet/musician." More than a year later, she enters some of his remains in the Seattle Calvary Graveyard under a headstone inscribed with the lyrics from the Nirvana song "Dumb."

1983: Pete Farndon, fired from the Pretenders the previous year, dies of a drug overdose. He was 30.

1980: Warner Home Video releases the first commercial rock video. It's a concert by Gary Numan called *The Touring Principle*.

1967: Deram Records release "The Laughing Gnome" by David Bowie. No one seems to care. However, the song does much better on the UK charts when it is re-released in 1973.

Birthdays: Carl Hunter (The Farm), 1965.

April 15th

1995: Sarah McLachlan's *The Freedom Sessions* is the first CD-ROM to hit *Billboard's* charts, debuting at #78.

1988: The Pogues accuse the British television show *Friday Night Live* of censoring their song "Birmingham Six."

1986: Jello Biafra (leader of the Dead Kennedys) has his home raided by members of the San Francisco and LAPD. They're looking for "harmful material" related to the DK's 1985 album *Frankenchrist*. They seize several copies of the album along with posters by H.R. Giger which were included with the record.

1986: Simple Minds does a benefit concert in Los Angeles, and raises $50,000 for Amnesty International.

April 16th

Birthdays: Dave Pirner (Soul Asylum), 1964.

April 17th

1995: Courtney Love becomes the first America Online subscriber to have the plug pulled on her e-mail account. The company took the action because of "a high number of violations in terms of service, including a death threat."

1980: Bob Marley is the guest of honor at Zimbabwe's Independence Day celebrations.

Birthdays: Pete Shelley aka Peter McNeish (The Buzzcocks), 1955.

April 18th

1988: The Pet Shop Boys hightail it out of their Florida hotel, claiming they saw a ghost.

1982: The Cure kicks off their Fourteen Explicit Moments Tour in Plymouth to promote *Pornography*.

Birthdays: Les Patterson (Echo And The Bunnymen), 1958.

April 19th

1995: The Cult announce that they are breaking up.

1995: David Bowie, "the artist," unveils his paintings at a South London Gallery to mixed reviews.

1978: Patti Smith releases "Because The Night," a song co-written by Bruce Springsteen.

1978: Dead Boys drummer Johnny Blitz is stabbed after leaving a gig at CBGBs in New York.

April 20th

1995: Perry Farrell announces Lollapalooza fans that can't make the concert can keep up thanks to a souvenir CD-ROM called *Teeth*.

1995: Matthew Sweet kicks off a tour in Hollywood for *100% Fun*.

1980: The Cure's *17 Seconds* debuts and is panned by the British music press as "cold."

1979: 2 Tone Records is formed in Coventry by Jerry Dammers of the Specials.

April 21st

1995: MTV Asia launches a Mandarin service.

1982: Joe Strummer of the Clash disappears, forcing the band to cancel their tour. He turns up three weeks later living in less-than-luxurious conditions in Paris.

Birthdays: Michael Timmins (Cowboy Junkies), 1959. Mike Barson (Madness), 1958. Robert Smith (The Cure), 1957. Iggy Pop aka James Jewel Osterberg, 1947.

April 22nd

1994: Andrew Fletcher announces he won't be playing all the dates on Depeche Mode's impending tour so he can look after business matters and await the birth of his second child.

1990: Three-quarters of a million people celebrate Earth Day in New York's Central Park with a concert featuring the B-52's.

1977: The Jam release their first single "In The City"; the best it can do is #40 in the UK.

Birthdays: Carol Van Dijk (Bettie Serveert), 1962.

April 23rd

1994: Courtney Love gives the gun Kurt Cobain used to commit suicide to the Mothers Against Violence In American and sets up a College Scholarship in his name at Aberdeen High, where Cobain and Krist Novoselic both went to school. As well, ex-Hüsker Dü drummer Grant Hart announces a Kurt Cobain Memorial Fund to educate people about heroin.

1994: Autopsy results for Kurt Cobain are made public and they show the level of heroin in the singer's blood stream was 1.52 milligrams per litre. Half that amount could prove fatal. There were also traces of the tranquillizers valium and diazepan. Pathologists say this makes it uncertain whether Cobain meant to overdose or whether he was aware of what he was doing when he shot himself.

1991: Johnny Thunders of the Heartbreakers was found dead under mysterious circumstances.

1987: A 90-minute film called *The Cure In Orange* debuts at a French film festival.

1978: Sid Vicious films his version of Paul Anka's "My Way" in Paris. The sequence eventually turns up in the film *The Great Rock 'n' Roll Swindle*.

Birthdays: Gen aka Simon Matthews (Jesus Jones), 1964. David Gedge (Wedding Present),1960. Captain Sensible aka Ray Burns (Damned), 1955.

April 24th

1995: Courtney Love gets into a brawl with fans at an Amsterdam club after somebody douses her with a cup of a liquid during a

Hole show.

1992: David Bowie marries supermodel Iman in a private Swiss town hall ceremony.

1984: *Stop Making Sense*, the Talking Heads' feature film directed by Jonathan Demme (*The Silence of the Lambs*), debuts in San Francisco.

1974: David Bowie releases *Diamond Dogs,* and there is trouble over the art on the album's cover: a photo of Dave as a dog complete with canine privates runs into censorship problems.

Birthdays: Paul Ryder (Happy Mondays), 1964. Robert Gould (Faith No More), 1963. Boris Williams (The Cure), 1958.

April 25th

1995: The sister of a Kurt Cobain copycat suicide victim starts a petition demanding a better parental warning sticker on albums whose lyrics may promote suicide. Besides Nirvana, the B.C. woman says Nine Inch Nails is another group that isn't appropriate for troubled teens.

1989: The Depeche Mode concert film *101* premieres in North America.

1979: *Rock 'n' Roll High School* (featuring the Ramones) premieres in Los Angeles.

1978: Alternative TV headlines on the last night of punk bands at the 100 Club in London.

1968: The Confederation of British Industry complains that listening to BBC Radio 1 makes workers less productive.

Birthdays: Andy Bell (Erasure), 1964.

April 26th

1980: The English Beat release "Mirror in the Bathroom." It's the first digitally-recorded single in Britain.

Birthdays: Roger Taylor (Duran Duran), 1960.

April 27th

1990: David Bowie kicks off the US leg of his Sound and Vision tour, the last time he will sing the old hits like "Fame" for the fans.

1976: Russian border guards give David Bowie a hard time after finding Nazi material in his luggage. He said he was researching a movie on Goebbels.

Birthdays: Marco Pirroni (Adam Ant), 1959. Kate Pierson (B-52's), 1948.

April 28th

1995: The Beastie Boys launch their first North American tour in three years in California. Besides music, they are offering interactive computer stations in something called the Carpet Compound.

1994: The Sleestacks, a California band, releases "Cobain's Dead," done to the tune of "Girlfriend In A Coma" by the Smiths.

1986: Arista Records announces Joe Leeway is leaving the Thompson Twins, leaving Alannah Currie and Tom Bailey to carry on.

1981: Gary Numan makes his "last public appearance" at Wembley Stadium in London.

Birthdays: Roland Gift (Fine Young Cannibals), 1961. Saddam Hussein, 1937.

April 29th

1994: Peter Gabriel is backing a neighborhood campaign to protect Solsbury Hill from being destroyed by a new road. The ancient fort site in Bath inspired his debut hit single.

1993: The Cure finally has a number one album in the UK with *Wish*.

1991: Warner Brothers will no longer accept unsold LPs from retailers.

Birthdays: Simon Edwards (Fairground Attraction), 1958. Bill Drummond aka William Butterworth (Big In

Japan/JAMMs/Time Lords/KLF), 1953.

April 30th

1994: Drummer Brendan O'Hare leaves Teenage Fanclub.

1994: The Cranberries cancel a series of UK dates because of singer Dolores O'Riordon's knee injury. She hurt herself two weeks earlier in a skiing accident.

May

May 1st

1995: New Order's Bernard Sumner announces the first record attributable to Prozac. He took the drug to overcome writer's block. The record is from Electronic. His use of the antidepressants has been documented in a British TV special called *Prozac Diaries*.

1977: The Clash begin their debut tour, named "White Riot" after their first single, with a date at the Roxy in London. The Jam, the Slits and the Buzzcocks are also on the bill.

1923: The first dance marathon in the US ends with Alma Cummings still dead on her feet in New York City after hoofing away for 27 hours.

Birthdays: D'Arcy Wreztky (Smashing Pumpkins), 1968. Phil Smith (Haircut 100), 1959. Nick Feldman (Wang Chung), 1955.

May 2nd

1995: After being turned down by Oasis, British women's magazine *For Women* releases its wish list for musical male centerfolds. They would pay $48,000 for INXS Michael Hutchence to pose nude, but only $500 for ex-Pogue Shane MacGowan.

1993: Kurt Cobain suffers a heroin overdose at a party.

Birthdays: Dr. Robert aka Bruce Robert Howard (Blow Monkeys),

1961. Joe Callis (Human League), 1951.

May 3rd

1995: Courtney Love turns down a $1 million offer from Playboy to pose nude, saying she doesn't need the money or the publicity.

Birthdays: Simon Smith (Wedding Present), 1965. David Ball (Soft Cell), 1959. Steve Jones (The Sex Pistols), 1955.

May 4th

1995: U2 announce plans to launch *Zoo-TV*, a series based on their 1993 tour, on MTV in the US this summer. It will feature music, home shopping and be interactive.

1995: Freedom FM, London's first gay and lesbian radio station began broadcasting. Boy George is among the first guest DJs.

1993: *Republic,* New Order's seventh album, is released.

1986: Alannah Currie of the Thompson Twins suffers a miscarriage.

1959: They hand out the first Grammy Awards. Henry Mancini and the Kingston Trio are among the winners.

Birthdays: Evan Dando (Lemonheads), 1967. Nicky Turner (Lords Of The New Church/Barracudas), 1959.

May 5th

1994: Courtney Love is to be arraigned for drug possession in Beverly Hills on the day before Kurt's body is found in Seattle, but the charges are dropped when it turns out she was taking a prescription painkiller.

1988: History is made with the first live broadcast from the summit of Mount Everest.

1984: Chrissie Hynde of the Pretenders weds Jim Kerr of Simple Minds in New York's Central Park. It doesn't last.

1979: Fiction Records releases *3 Imaginary Boys*, the Cure's first LP.

1978: One person is killed in a brawl between fans of rival soccer teams during a concert by the Vibrators in Preston, England.

Birthdays: Andrew Sherriff (Chapterhouse), 1969. Kevin Paul Mooney (Adam and the Ants), 1962. Gary Daly (China Crisis), 1962. Ian McCulloch (Echo and the Bunnymen/Electrafixtion), 1959.

May 6th

1994: Beastie Boy Adam Horowitz is put on 2 years probation and told to do 200 hours of community service, after a Los Angeles judge finds him guilty of assaulting a *Hard Copy* cameraman at River Phoenix's funeral.

1984: The fictional band Spinal Tap plays a real concert at CBGB's in New York.

Birthdays: Nick Cash aka Keith Lucas (999), 1950.

May 7th

1994: Verve, rather than face a lawsuit with the American jazz label, changes their name to The Verve.

1983: Paul Weller shows an anti-nuclear benefit in London what he's been doing since leaving the Jam by debuting the Style Council.

1979: Joy Division sign a record deal with Factory.

May 8th

1992: MTV airs *Pearl Jam Unplugged.*

Birthdays: David Rowntree (Blur), 1964. Chris Frantz (Talking Heads/Tom Tom Club), 1951.

May 9th

1990: When comedian Andrew Dice Clay is named as the guest host for *Saturday Night Live,* Sinead O'Connor refuses to appear. The Spanic Boys are brought in as replacement musical guests at the last moment.

Birthdays: Dave Gahan (Depeche Mode), 1962. Paul Heaton (Beautiful South), 1962.

May 10th

1994: Former Crash Test Dummies manager Vince Lambert has decided to sue the band, two years after he says he was dumped without explanation.

1991: Malcolm McLaren debuts his new television commercial in Britain. He directed the dance-oriented spot for a chocolate bar and even makes a split-second cameo appearance.

1989: Bono of U2 gets a nice birthday gift—a brand new daughter named Jordan.

Birthdays: Gary Daley (China Crisis), 1962. Bono aka Paul Hewson (U2), 1960. Sid Vicious aka John Simon Beverly (The Sex Pistols), 1957.

May 11th

1987: Billy Idol storms off stage during a concert in San Francisco, after being hit twice in the face by tennis shoes tossed from the audience.

1983: On the second anniversary of Bob Marley's death, the Jamaican government unveils a statue in his honor. Fans, angry at the poor likeness, pelt it with rocks and fruit. The Jamaican government promises to build a new, more accurate statue.

1981: Bob Marley finally surrenders to brain and lung cancer at a hospital in Miami. He was 36.

1979: The The debuts at the Africa Center in London.

May 12th

1986: Joe Strummer of the Clash is banned from the road for drunk driving.

1984: Echo and the Bunnymen stage an all-day event in their home town of Liverpool. Fans get a tour of the band's favorite restaurant, a hair salon, and enjoy a church organ recital before

Echo and the Bunnymen ➔

THE ALTERNATIVE MUSIC ALMANAC

attending the band's evening concert.

1977: Virgin signs the Sex Pistols after they were fired from A&M.

Birthdays: Billy Duffy (The Cult), 1961.

May 13th

1983: The Smiths release "Hand In Glove," their first single.

Birthdays: Paul Thompson (Roxy Music), 1951.

May 14th

1982: The Clash releases *Combat Rock*.

1982: Bow Wow Wow quit as Queen's opening act after audiences attack them.

Birthdays: David Byrne (Talking Heads), 1952. Ian Astbury aka Ian Lindsay (Cult), 1962.

May 15th

1995: R.E.M. kicks off their American tour in San Francisco. It is their first show since Bill Berry's brain surgery in March.

1983: For the first and only time, Spandau Ballet tops the UK album chart for just a single week with *True*.

1981: A PiL show at the Ritz in New York turns ugly. The band agreed to substitute for Bow Wow Wow knowing full well that they hadn't rehearsed enough. They perform their entire set from behind a video screen and Johnny Lydon exhorts the crowd to throw stuff at the stage. A riot breaks out and a dozen fans are injured. Johnny considers the show a success, since they caught the near riot on film for a movie.

Birthdays: Andrew Eldritch aka Andrew Taylor (Sisters Of Mercy), 1959.

May 16th

1994: KT Records releases a tribute LP to the Wipers, including a Nirvana track and a song Kurt Cobain recorded with William Burroughs, "The Priest They Called Him."

1986: Caitlin O'Riordan of the Pogues marries Elvis Costello in Dublin.

1976: Patti Smith makes her debut in Britain.

Birthdays: Rachel Goswell (Slowdive), 1971. Krist Novoselic (Nirvana), 1965. Glenn Gregory (Heaven 17), 1958.

May 17th

1986: Irish bands, including U2, the Pogues, Elvis Costello and Bob Geldof, play a benefit in Dublin to raise money for efforts to help the young.

1969: Album sales outpace 45s for the first time in the UK.

Birthdays: Dave Abbruzzese (Pearl Jam), 1968. Trent Reznor (Nine Inch Nails), 1965. Tracey Bryn (Voice Of The Beehive), 1962. Enya aka Enya Ni Bhraonain, 1961.

May 18th

1994: John Lydon is sued by a London lawyer over comments made in *Rotten: No Irish, No Blacks, No Dogs.*

1982: Sting causes a stink about the fact his "Don't Stand So Close To Me," is used in a television ad for a deodorant.

1982: Joe Strummer finally turns up. He's been AWOL from the Clash for weeks.

1980: Joy Division's Ian Curtis commits suicide by hanging himself at his Manchester home.

Birthdays: Bruce Gilbert (Wire), 1946.

May 19th

1994: Despite a threatened lawsuit by the soda pop conglomerate, Oasis refuses to remove the lyric "I'd like to buy the world a Coke" when they perform "Shaker Maker."

1987: The Smiths record "I Keep Mine Hidden," their last-ever recording

1984: *Legend* is released on the third anniversary of Bob Marley's death and becomes his first number one hit in the UK.

Birthdays: Martyn Ware (Human League/Heaven 17), 1956. Joey Ramone aka Jeffrey Hyman (The Ramones), 1952.

May 20th

1981: Bob Marley's body lies in state in Kingston, Jamaica.

1977: Blondie makes their live debut in the UK with a show at the Roundhouse in London.

Birthdays: Nasher Nash aka Brian Nash (Frankie Goes To Hollywood), 1963. Nick Heyward (Haircut 100), 1961. Warren Cann (Ultravox), 1952.

May 21st

1993: Former Housemartins drummer Hugh Whitaker is sentenced to six years in jail for attacking former business partner James Hewitt with an axe. The dispute centers around money.

1981: Thousands attend Bob Marley's funeral with full state honors in his home town of St. Ann's, Jamaica.

1980: Joe Strummer is arrested in Hamburg for allegedly assaulting a Clash fan with a guitar.

May 22nd

1994: Leaked reports indicate the Monopolies and Mergers Commission will rule that CDs are not overpriced in Britain, and the industry is not artificially inflating the price by as much as 50%.

1987: The Cure releases *Kiss Me, Kiss Me, Kiss Me,* which features some non-Robert Smith compositions for the first time.

Birthdays: Morrissey aka Stephen Patrick Morrissey (The Smiths), 1959. Jerry Dammers aka Gerald Dankin (The Specials), 1954.

May 23rd

1994: *Never Fade Away*, the first quickie book on Kurt Cobain, hits the bookstores. At the same time, Neil Young announces he will never again sing "Hey Hey, My My (Out Of The Blue)," because Kurt quoted the lyrics in his suicide note.

1987: The Beastie Boys kick off a tour in London.

1984: $17,000 in box office receipts are stolen while the Clash appears at Michigan State University.

1982: A London chapter of the British Musicians Union puts forth a motion that will ban all synthesizers and drum machines from all recording session and live performances. The motion is defeated.

Birthdays: James Mankey (Concrete Blonde), 1952. Robert Moog, 1934.

May 24th

1991: Sony unveils its two-and-a-half inch digital mini disc system, which will be able to record and play up to 74 minutes of music. Sony hopes these will take the place of cassettes.

1982: Topper Headon leaves the Clash. His replacement is Terry Chimes, the band's original drummer.

May 25th

1990: People who attend the premiere of *Back to the Future III* catch a quick cameo performance by Flea of the Red Hot Chili Peppers.

1980: The Cure and their roadies are arrested for indecent exposure while taking a late night swim at a Rotterdam beach.

Birthdays: Paul Weller (The Jam/Style Council), 1958.

May 26th

1990: Angela Bowie, David's ex, sues him for $56 million.

1977: After many delays, much controversy and three record contracts, the Sex Pistols finally release "God Save the Queen" on Virgin. It's promptly banned virtually everywhere in the UK.

Birthdays: Wayne Hussey (Dead Or Alive/Sisters Of Mercy/The Mission), 1959.

May 27th

1982: Robert Smith and Simon Gallup of the Cure get into a fight after a concert in Strasbourg and both leave the band only to return in time for a show a week later in Aix-en-Provence.

1977: D.P. Costello debuts as Elvis at a London nightclub.

Birthdays: Neil Finn (Split Enz/Crowded House), 1958. Siouxsie Sioux aka Susan Dallion (Siouxsie and the Banshees/The Creatures), 1957.

May 28th

1983: David Bowie and Van Halen each receive a million dollars for headlining the US Festival in San Bernadino, California.

1971: David Bowie's son Duncan Zowie Haywood is born.

May 29th

1977: Joy Division debuts as Warsaw at a Manchester club. The Buzzcocks are also on the bill.

Birthdays: Mel Gaynor (Simple Minds), 1959. Danny Elfman (Oingo Boingo), 1953.

May 30th

1990: Midnight Oil sets up a flatbed trailer in front of Exxon World headquarters in New York and gives a free concert to protest the Exxon Valdez oil spill and other black marks on the company's ecological record.

1987: The Beastie Boys' concert in Liverpool is abruptly ended when tear gas floods the auditorium and Adam Horovitz is arrested and charged with hitting a female fan. He's later acquitted of causing bodily harm.

1980: Peter Gabriel releases his third solo LP, again self-titled, featuring "Games Without Frontiers" and "Biko." Kate Bush sings backing vocals on a couple of tracks.

Birthdays: Tim Burgess (Charlatans UK), 1968. Chris Shorrock (Icicle Works), 1964. Nicky "Topper" Headon (Clash), 1955.

May 31st

1977: The BBC refuses to play "God Save the Queen" by the Sex Pistols. Officials say that the single is in "gross bad taste." Other broadcasters are urged not to play the single because it contravenes Section 4:1:A of the Independent Broadcasting Authority Act, which covers material that "offends good taste or decency, or is likely to encourage or incite to crime, or lead to disorder, or to be offensive to public feeling."

Birthdays: Wendy Smith (Prefab Sprout), 1963.

June

June 1st

1982: After leaving the Clash, drummer Topper Headon is arrested in London for stealing a bus stop sign.

1974: Morrissey has his letter to the editor published in *New Music Express*. The fifteen-year-old from Manchester makes it quite clear that he thinks the best band in the world is Sparks.

1959: A report in *Billboard* magazine claims that the decline in record sales is due to teenagers taping their favorite songs off the radio.

Birthdays: Mike Joyce (Smiths), 1963. Simon Gallup (Cure), 1960. Alan Wilder (Depeche Mode), 1959.

June 2nd

1995: Tori Amos is given the 1994 Visionary Award by a Washington,

DC rape crisis clinic and announces the launch of a 24-hour toll-free sex assault hotline. Tori is a rape victim herself.

1986: Jello Biafra, Alternative Tentacles Records and several other people are charged with "trafficking in harmful matter" relating to the H.R. Giger poster that was included with vinyl copies of the Dead Kennedys album *Frankenchrist*. The trial drags on more than 18 months and ends with the jury deadlocked 7-5 for acquittal. The case is dismissed and the charges are dropped.

1896: Guglielmo Marconi is awarded the first radio patent. Five years later he succeeded in send the first trans-Atlantic signal from Newfoundland to Cornwall, England.

Birthdays: Tony Hadley (Spandau Ballet), 1959. Pete Farndon (The Pretenders), 1952.

June 3rd

1977: Major department stores in Britain refuse to carry "God Save the Queen" by the Sex Pistols.

June 4th

1994: Creation Records celebrates its 10th birthday with an "Undrugged" concert in London. Oasis and the Boo Radleys are among the bands on the bill.

1994: Courtney Love surfaces for the first time since Kurt Cobain's suicide, showing up at the MTV Video Awards with R.E.M.'s Michael Stipe.

1991: Stiv Bators of the Dead Boys dies in Paris, two weeks after being hit by a car.

1976: The Sex Pistols play one of the most important concerts of all time at the Lesser Free Trade Hall in Manchester. In the audience that night were future members of the Buzzcocks, Joy Division/New Order, the Pet Shop Boys and a young kid named Stephen Patrick Morrissey. All were so inspired by what they saw and felt that night that they were moved to start bands of their own. Music was never to be the same again.

1942: Capitol Records was born and founder Glenn Wallichs makes history for sending copies of new releases to prominent DJs, a practice that soon became the industry norm.

Birthdays: Steve Grimes (The Farm), 1962.

June 5th

1954: The major record labels announce that from now on, radio stations will be supplied with 45 rpm discs instead of the traditional 78 rpm records. This creates a serious controversy because up until now, radio hasn't been too keen on playing the 7" records.

Birthdays: Richard Butler (Psychedelic Furs), 1956.

June 6th

1987: Simple Minds has their third consecutive number one album in the UK with *Live In The City Of Light*.

1981: Magazine splits up.

1964: David Bowie releases his very first record: a 7" single by Davy Jones and the King Bees.

Birthdays: Terri Nunn (Berlin), 1961.

June 7th

1977: Virgin Records throws a party for the Sex Pistols, hiring a boat called *Queen Elizabeth* to cruise the River Thames. The group sings "Anarchy In The UK" outside the Houses of Parliament and when the boat docks, the party-goers are arrested.

Birthdays: Gordon Gano (Violent Femmes),1963. Paddy McAloon (Prefab Sprout), 1957.

June 8th

1993: Bjork releases "Human Behavior," her first solo single as an adult. (She was a child pop star in Iceland).

1986: The Sugarcubes were formed in Reykjavik, Iceland, the same day Bjork gives birth to her son, Sindri.

1981: No more than 40 people show up for a Cure Show in Freiburg, Germany.

Birthdays: Nick Rhodes (Duran Duran), 1962.

June 9th

1990: While still with the Pixies, Kim Deal forms the Breeders.

1985: The Smiths play their first Canadian gig at the Kingswood Music Theatre north of Toronto. Even though the band had sold only 10,000 albums in Canada, 12,000 fans show up.

Birthdays: Malu Valentine, David Byrne's daughter, 1989. Eddie Lundon (China Crisis), 1962.

June 10th

1993: Sinead O'Connor takes out a full page ad in the *Irish Times* asking people to "stop hurting me, please." O'Connor blames her unhappy life on a history of child abuse.

1989: Someone tosses a firebomb at a McDonalds in London, just two days after Chrissie Hynde of the Pretenders advocated such action during a news conference launching an album supporting Greenpeace.

1986: Bob Geldof of the Boomtown Rats is knighted by the Queen in recognition of his efforts to help feed the hungry in Africa.

1977: Arrested for ignoring a summons, Joe Strummer and Topper Headon of the Clash explain they were in another court at the time, facing another charge. That was for spray-painting "Clash" on the wall of a public building. Both are fined £5 each.

June 11th

1992: Washington State passes a law prohibiting the sale of erotic music to minors. If convicted, retailers face a two month sentence and a $500 fine. The local music community challenges the law in court as a violation of free speech guarantees.

1988: Ziggy Marley and the Melody Makers have their first hit single in the UK with "Tomorrow People." This comes a decade to the day after his dad's *Exodus* hit the British album charts.

1969: David Bowie picks a good time to release "Space Oddity." The single gives his career a nice boost when the BBC decides to use the song as a theme for their coverage of the Apollo 11 moon landing.

June 12th

1988: The Fall provide live accompaniment to a ballet.

1987: U2 packs 'em into Wembley Stadium as part of their world tour promoting *The Joshua Tree*.

1982: Siouxsie Sioux is forced to take time off to rest her damaged vocal chords.

Birthdays: John Linnell (They Might Be Giants), 1959.

June 13th

1994: A fire destroys the pyramid stage at the Glastonbury Festival site, but work begins on a temporary stage so the concert set for June 24th can go ahead as planned.

1993: The Cure debuts as a quartet in London after the departure of guitarist Porl Thompson.

1992: Police in Texas call for a ban of the song "Cop Killer" by Ice-T and Body Count.

June 14th

1989: Echo & The Bunnymen drummer Pete de Freitas is killed in a motorcycle accident.

1982: Pretenders bassist Pete Farndon is fired because of "incompatibility."

1974: David Bowie opens his Diamond Dogs tour in Montreal.

June 15th

1994: Kristen Pfaff, bassist for Hole, dies of a heroin overdose in her bathtub.

1993: The Velvet Underground begins a three night stand at the Olympia in Paris and the shows are recorded for an eventual live double album.

1986: The Amnesty International tour wraps up with a final tour at Giants Stadium in East Rutherford, New Jersey. Fifty thousand people watch U2, Peter Gabriel and Sting. The tour raises three million dollars for human rights.

Birthdays: Neil Arthur (Blancmange), 1958.

June 16th

1987: Angry they couldn't get tickets to a David Bowie concert, fans in Rome go on a rampage, taking on police with bottles and stones. By the end of the three-and-a-half-hour battle, 15 police officers are injured, 48 fans arrested.

1984: Joe Jackson slams rock videos as "a shallow, tasteless and for-mularized way of selling music" and announces he won't make any more of them.

1982: James Honeyman-Scott of the Pretenders dies of a cocaine overdose after a party in London. He was only 25.

Birthdays: Garry Roberts (Boomtown Rats), 1954.

June 17th

1994: Perry Farrell forces Ford to change its Escort ads because they featured the word "lollapalooza." The car company donates money to Farrell's favorite rain forest charity.

1990: Roland Gift of Fine Young Cannibals is playing Shakespeare in London, the lead in *Romeo and Juliet*. The critics save their scant praise for Gift.

Birthdays: Chris Spedding, 1944.

June 18th

1988: Depeche Mode wrap up their world tour at the Rose Bowl in Pasadena. The performance is released on video as *Depeche Mode 101.*

1986: The Cure show up on French television after Robert Smith is assured his appearance won't clash with a World Cup match featuring England.

1977: Johnny Rotten and several friends are attacked outside of a London pub by thugs who object to the sentiments of "God Save the Queen." Johnny is stabbed in the hand and leg with a razor.

Birthdays: Sice (Boo Radleys), 1969. Tom Bailey (Thompson Twins), 1957.

June 19th

1994: WEA announces the theft of the master tapes of an album by Johnny Marr and Ian McCulloch, though insiders say the story was made up to mask a falling out between the two.

1987: At the Glastonbury Festival, the Communards scatter condoms into the crowds.

1977: Paul Cook of the Sex Pistols meets up with some monarchists and gets beaten up with an iron pipe.

Birthdays: Alison Moyet (Yazoo), 1961.

June 20th

1985: Johnny Marr of the Smiths marries girlfriend Angela Brown in San Francisco.

1969: David Bowie signs with Mercury Records.

1964: There are reports that a new dance craze is about to sweep the US. It's a Jamaican creation called "ska."

Birthdays: John Taylor aka Nigel John Taylor (Duran Duran), 1960.

June 21st

1994: MTV is declared illegal in Turkey under a new law designed to regulate private broadcasters, many of whom are airing anti-government material.

1991: UB40, on tour in Europe, appeal for public help back home in finding three men claiming to be members of the band who are in the midst of a crime wave.

1986: Smith Craig Gannon becomes a full fledged member of the Smiths.

1948: Dr. Peter Goldmark demonstrates the first long playing record at CBS Laboratories. The 33 1/3 LP eventually phases out the 78 rpm record.

Birthdays: Mark Brzezicki (Big Country), 1957.

June 22nd

1995: CBS news anchor Dan Rather dons some shades and joins R.E.M. onstage at Madison Square Garden for a rendition of "What's the Frequency, Kenneth?"

1994: A man is arrested outside Courtney Love's Seattle home and charged with trespassing and stalking. He had told his sister he was "the next lead singer for Nirvana."

1991: Sinead O'Connor is a no-show for a concert in Dublin. She's angry that a benefit for a man trying to get a robbery conviction overturned is being promoted as her show.

Birthdays: Mike Edwards (Jesus Jones), 1964. Bobby Gillespie (Primal Scream), 1964. Jimmy Somerville (Communards/Bronski Beat), 1961. Alan Anton aka Alan Alizojvodic (Cowboy Junkies), 1959. Garry Beers (INXS), 1957. Derek Forbes (Simple Minds), 1956.

June 23rd

1994: Curve finally splits up.

Birthdays: Simon Rowe (Chapterhouse), 1969.

June 24th

1995: At a show at the Polo Grounds in San Francisco, an ill Eddie Vedder leaves the stage after seven songs. He's replaced for the rest of the concert by Neil Young.

1990: Roger O'Donnell checks out as keyboardist for the Cure. His replacement is Perry Bamonte, one of the band's roadies.

Birthdays: Curt Smith (Tears for Fears), 1961. Andy McCluskey (OMD), 1959. Astro aka Terence Wilson (UB40), 1957.

June 25th

1992: While Pearl Jam is performing on stage in Stockholm, somebody breaks into their dressing room and steals Eddie Vedder's journal.

Birthdays: Tim Finn (Split Enz/Crowded House), 1952.

June 26th

1992: Still upset over the theft of his journal the night before, Eddie Vedder punches out a security guard at a Denmark concert after stage-diving fans are roughed up by bouncers. Pearl Jam cancels two London shows, saying Eddie is physically exhausted.

1986: Bryan Ferry marries Lucy Helmore in a high society wedding in Sussex.

1976: Roxy Music announces a "trial separation." It doesn't last.

Birthdays: Harriet Wheeler (Sundays), 1963. Mick Jones (The Clash/Big Audio Dynamite), 1955.

June 27th

1978: Peter Gabriel releases his second solo album. It's called *Peter Gabriel*—again.

Birthdays: Margo Timmins (Cowboy Junkies), 1961.

June 28th

1993: Bjork releases *Debut*.

1989: The Pet Shop Boys kick off their first tour in Hong Kong.

1975: David Bowie releases "Fame."

June 29th

1986: Richard Branson, founder of Virgin Records, is part of the crew of Challenger II. The power boat completes a record-breaking Atlantic crossing.

June 30th

1994: Pearl Jam's Stone Gossard and Jeff Ament take their fight against service charges and Ticketmaster to Washington DC and testify before a House sub-committee about the problem of monopolies.

1991: New Order's starts sharing royalties for "Run" with John Denver. He was awarded the royalties the previous fall as part of a copyright infringement suit over his song, "Leaving On A Jet Plane."

1979: Johnny Rotten and actress Joan Collins appear together on the British television show *Juke Box Jury*.

Birthdays: Cammy aka Peter James Camwell (Marshmellow Overcoats/La's), 1967. Adrian Wright (Human League), 1959.

July

July 1st

1984: Music Theatre Network unveils plans for Concert Cinema, which will put rock concert videos in 600 American movie houses.

1975: David Bowie begins work on the movie *The Man Who Fell To Earth*, in New Mexico.

Birthdays: Pol Burton (Transvision Vamp), 1964. Fred Schneider (B-52's), 1951. Tom Robinson, 1950. Debbie Harry (Blondie), 1946.

July 2nd

1994: Courtney Love goes online to slag her father Hank Harrison for appearing on *Geraldo* to talk about the couple and the late Kurt Cobain, even though Harrison had never met his son-in-law.

1993: Pearl Jam opens for U2's *Zooropa* tour in Verona, Italy.

1973: Keyboard wizard Brian Eno quits Roxy Music after fighting with frontman Bryan Ferry.

Birthdays: Roy Boulter (Farm), 1964. Dave Parsons (Transvision Vamp), 1962. Mike Anger (Blow Monkeys), 1957. Pete Briquette (Boomtown Rats), 1957.

July 3rd

1974: Squeeze play their first show.

1973: David Bowie wraps up his UK tour by announcing he plans to retire. It doesn't last. Bowie is back by the following June. The Ziggy Stardust character, however, is toast.

Birthdays: Vince Clarke (Depeche Mode/Yazoo/The Assembly/ Erasure), 1960.

July 4th

1977: Gary Valentine quits as bass player for Blondie, complaining about threats to his "artistic integrity."

1976: The Ramones make their UK debut at the Roundhouse in London. Their performance kicks the English punk movement into high gear.

1973: Davis Bowie is wrapping up his tour at the Hammersmith Odeon in London when Steve Jones and Paul Cook sneak in and make off with much of the gear to use in their own pre-Sex

Pistols act.

Birthdays: Kirk Pengilly (INXS), 1958.

July 5th
1993: U2 releases *Zooropa*.

1983: Bauhaus splits up.

July 6th
1976: The Damned played their first real gig, opening for the Sex Pistols at London's 100 Club.

Birthdays: John Keeble (Spandau Ballet), 1959.

July 7th
1994: Courtney Love and Evan Dando take snapshots of each other in a New York hotel before a Lemonheads gig at the Roseland Ballroom. The *New York Post* publish the photographs three days later and Nirvana fans are upset at seeing Courtney kissing and snuggling with another man so soon after Kurt's death.

1989: For the first time, CDs are outselling vinyl.

1987: One of U2's tour buses is the innocent victim of a bomb blast that tears apart a restaurant in Brussels, Belgium.

July 8th
1984: U2's Bono joins Van Morrison and Bob Dylan on stage at Wembley Stadium.

1980: Jello Biafra of the Dead Kennedys announces he is running for mayor of San Francisco. He doesn't win, but he does finish fourth in a field of ten candidates.

1972: David Bowie tells an audience at a Save the Whales benefit concert in London, "I'm Ziggy." Lou Reed joins him for the set.

Birthdays: Neil Myers (La's), 1971. Andy Fletcher (Depeche Mode), 1961.

July 9th

1993: Concert promoters in the US worry about counterfeit tickets becoming more difficult to spot because of high quality color laser copiers. They announce an ad campaign urging concert goers to only buy their tickets from authorized outlets.

1977: Elvis Costello quits his day job as a computer operator at an Elizabeth Arden cosmetic factory.

Birthdays: Courtney Love (Hole), 1965. Jim Kerr (Simple Minds), 1959. Peter Marc Almond (Soft Cell), 1959.

July 10th

1993: Pearl Jam supports Neil Young at a concert at a 200-year-old castle in Dublin. The crowd breaks through the crash barriers and dozens of semi-conscious fans have to be ferried to the first-aid tent.

1983: The Smiths sign with Rough Trade records.

1974: David Bowie plays a week of live dates in Philadelphia promoting *Diamond Dogs*. Some of the shows were taped, and pieced together for his *David Live* LP later in the year. When they heard that, members of the backing band refuse to play, demanding more money since they were going to be on an album as well.

Birthdays: Neil Tennant (Pet Shop Boys/Electronic), 1954.

July 11th

1984: Music Box, sponsored by Thorn-EMI, Virgin and Yorkshire Television, starts broadcasting music videos from Britain to Europe via satellite.

1969: David Bowie first releases *Space Oddity* but it doesn't generate a lot of initial interest in the UK.

Birthdays: Peter Murphy (Bauhaus/Dali's Car), 1957. Suzanne Vega, 1957.

July 12th

1983: David Bowie opens his Serious Moonlight tour in Montreal.

Birthdays: John Wetton (Roxy Music), 1949.

July 13th

1985: Live Aid begins at 12:01 GMT at Wembley Stadium. Over the next sixteen hours INXS, Bryan Ferry, the Thompson Twins, Spandau Ballet, and many others, perform. The second half of the show takes place in Philadelphia. Seventy million dollars is raised for famine relief and up to two billion watch in 22 countries. Organizer Bob Geldof of the Boomtown Rats is later knighted by the Queen.

July 14th

1980: Bryan Ferry collapses in a French hotel room from a kidney infection. He is flown back home to Britain for treatment.

1977: Despite an earlier ban for cursing during a live interview, the Sex Pistols were back on the BBC, performing "Pretty Vacant" on "Top of the Pops."

1977: Elvis Costello and the Attractions play their first gig together at a club in Cornwall.

Birthdays: Chris Cross aka Christopher St. John aka Christopher Allen (Ultravox), 1952.

July 15th

1994: The Wonder Stuff plays their last show at the Phoenix Festival in Britain.

1993: Midnight Oil stages a concert in a field of tree stumps at Clayoquot Sound on Vancouver Island, to protest the logging of old growth forests.

Birthdays: Ian Curtis (Joy Division), 1956. Johnny Thunders (Heartbreakers), 1952. Trevor Horn (Buggles), 1949.

Peter Garrett of Midnight Oil ➜

July 16th

1993: *Peace Together* is released. Offering cover versions of songs about peace are Blur, Pop Will Eat Itself, U2, Lou Reed and My Bloody Valentine. The proceeds go to help children in Northern Ireland.

Birthdays: Stewart Copeland (Police/Animal Logic), 1952.

July 17th

1977: Even though the punk festival in Birmingham had been aborted by local politicians, the Clash show up to talk to disappointed fans and are threatened with arrest for inciting an unlawful gathering. The band plays an impromptu gig for fans at a nearby club.

July 18th

1991: The first Lollapalooza tour begins in Phoenix. The line-up features headliners Jane's Addiction plus Siouxsie and the Banshees, Living Colour, Nine Inch Nails, Ice-T and Bodycount, the Butthole Surfers and the Rollins Band.

1988: Nico, the one-time fashion model and Warhol confidant who recorded with the Velvet Underground on their first album, dies of a brain hemorrhage. She hit her head while riding her bicycle around the Mediterranean island of Ibiza.

1977: Warsaw records a demo of four songs. By the end of the year, the band renamed itself Joy Division, to avoid confusion with Warsaw Pakt, a London punk band that had just released its first album.

Birthdays: Nigel Twist (Alarm), 1958. Terry Chambers (XTC), 1955.

July 19th

1980: David Bowie makes his stage debut in Denver. He plays the title role of John Merrick in *The Elephant Man*.

Birthdays: Lizzie Borden, 1860.

July 20th

1994: EMF's Derry Brownson is arrested for getting smashed and making crop circles in French corn fields. He's fined £2,000.

1993: Julianna Hatfield releases *Become What You Are.*

1991: EMF's "Unbelievable" is the #1 single in the US.

1974: There is a fundamental change in the Ramones. Joey Ramone stops playing drums and moves out front to be the singer.

Birthdays: Stone Gossard (Pearl Jam), 1965. Michael McNeil (Simple Minds), 1958. Paul Cook (Sex Pistols/Rich Kids), 1956.

July 21st

1973: Ex-Roxy Music member Brian Eno tells the press that his new band will be called Loana and the Little Girls. It doesn't happen.

1969: Apollo 11 lands on the moon. Neil Armstrong becomes sets foot on the surface at 3:56 am GMT.

July 22nd

1984: The Beastie Boys go on tour as the opening act for Madonna.

1977: *My Aim Is True* by Elvis Costello is released in Britain on Stiff Records. The North American release doesn't come until three months later.

Birthdays: Daniel Goodwin (Kitchens of Distinction), 1964.

July 23rd

1994: Green Day never make it onstage at the Buzzard-Palooza free concert in Cleveland because police shut down the show due to overcrowding.

Birthdays: Rob Dickinson (Catherine Wheel), 1965. Martin Gore (Depeche Mode), 1961. Andy Mackay (Roxy Music), 1946.

July 24th

Birthdays: Mick Karn aka Anthony Michaelides (Japan), 1958. Robbie Grey (Modern English), 1957. Lynval Golding (The Specials), 1951.

July 25th

1978: Johnny Lydon announces the formation of his post-Sex Pistols band, Public Image, Ltd.

Birthdays: Elvis Costello, 1955.

July 26th

1993: U2's *Zooropa* became the first album to debut at #1 in *The Record*, the Canadian music industry trade magazine.

1979: Two years after it was released in Britain, the debut album from the Clash finally gets released in North America, after selling one hundred thousand copies as an import. However, there are sharp differences between the import and the domestic version.

1977: Elvis Costello is arrested while performing outside the London Hilton. His explanation was that he was auditioning for CBS Records executives who were attending a meeting at the hotel. He was later signed by the label.

Birthdays: Tom Hooper (Grapes Of Wrath), 1966.

July 27th

1986: During a Cure concert in Los Angeles, a fan named Jon Moreland jumps up on-stage and repeatedly stabs himself with a hunting knife. Thinking it was part of the show, the crowd cheers him on. He later tells police that he was upset over losing his girlfriend.

1973: The New York Dolls release their debut album.

Birthdays: Miles Hunt (Wonder Stuff), 1966.

July 28th

1992: Warner Brothers Records pulls Ice-T's "Cop Killer" from all future copies of his *Body Count* album. Ice-T says he will give away free copies of the song at his concerts.

1958: Esso issues a report explaining that listening to rock and roll while driving costs you money because the rhythm makes the driver jiggle the gas pedal and that wastes fuel.

Birthdays: Dan Warton (Ned's Atomic Dustbin), 1972.

July 29th

1980: New Order debuts at the Beach club in their hometown of Manchester.

July 30th

1983: The English Beat calls it quits.

Birthdays: Sean Moore (Manic Street Preachers), 1970. Louise Wener (Sleeper), 1968. Tex Axile (Transvision Vamp), 1963. Kate

↑ The (English) Beat

Bush (1958). Rat Scabies aka Chris Miller (Damned), 1957.

July 31st

1990: Five members of UB40 are arrested in the Seychelles and deported after drugs are found in their hotel room.

1981: Debbie Harry releases *Koo Koo*, her first solo album since leaving Blondie. There was a controversy about the album cover which features a picture of Harry with long needles penetrating her cheeks.

1969: Reports from Moscow say that more and more telephone booths are being vandalized because the parts are being used to convert acoustic guitars into electrics.

Birthdays: Norman Cook (Housemartins), 1963. Malcolm Ross (Aztec Camera), 1960. Bill Berry (R.E.M.), 1958. Daniel Ash (Bauhaus) 1957.

August

August 1st

1994: Hole takes the stage unannounced at the Lollapalooza stop in Philadelphia, playing two songs and asking for a minute's silence in memory of Kurt Cobain.

1984: Rocshire Records, an indie label, is placed in receivership by a judge in Los Angeles, as the FBI looks into rumors that its funding came from $3 million embezzled from Hughes Aircraft.

1981: MTV makes its debut. The first video aired is "Video Killed the Radio Star" by Buggles.

Birthdays: Nick Christian Sayer (Transvision Vamp), 1964. Michael Dean Wareham (Galaxie 500), 1963.

August 2nd

1991: Perry Farrell announces the imminent demise of Jane's Addiction.

1977: At the Mont DeMarsan festival in France, Captain Sensible of the Damned sets off stink bombs to punctuate a performance by the Clash. A member of the stage crew responds by bashing the Captain in the crotch with a stage barrier.

Birthdays: Lee Myers (La's), 1962. Pete De Freitas (Echo And The Bunnymen), 1961.

August 3rd

1929: Emile Berliner, the inventor of the gramaphone dies. He took out a patent on his machine in 1897 and manufactured gramaphones in Montreal. Berliner sold his firm to the Victor Talking Machine Company in 1924.

Birthdays: Ed Roland (Collective Soul), 1963.

August 4th

1985: The Cure releases *The Head In The Door.*

Birthdays: Paul Reynolds (A Flock Of Seagulls), 1962. Graham Massey (808 State), 1960. Ian Broudie (Lightning Seeds), 1958.

August 5th

1994: The Church play the first of two shows in London.

1991: Hole previews their debut album, releasing "Teenage Whore" as a single.

1966: New York state signs an anti-piracy bill which forbids anyone from reproducing material on phonograph records.

August 6th

1994: Madness plays their last show *ever* in North London. This time, they really mean it.

Birthdays: Pat McDonald (Timbuk 3), 1952. Carol Pope (Rough Trade), 1949.

August 7th

Birthdays: Jacqui O'Sullivan (Bananarama), 1960. Alexei Sayle, 1952.

August 8th

1963: The Great Train Robbery takes place in England. Gang member Ronnie Biggs later records with the Sex Pistols and appears in the film *The Great Rock 'n' Roll Swindle*.

Birthdays: The Edge aka David Evans (U2), 1961. Chris Foreman (Madness), 1958. Ali Score (A Flock Of Seagulls), 1956.

August 9th

1990: A judge in Daytona Beach, Florida, orders Flea and Chad Smith of the Red Hot Chili Peppers to play $5,000 each to a rape crisis center and to apologize to a 20-year-old college student. She complained that Flea and Chad spanked her and tried to take off her bikini bottoms.

1986: To back their demand for more Gary Numan music, fans picket BBC Radio 1.

1969: Roman Polanski's wife, actress Sharon Tate, is one of five people murdered by members of the Manson family. Twenty-four years later, Trent Reznor will record *The Downward Spiral* in the Tate house.

Birthdays: Benjamin Orr (The Cars), 1955.

August 10th

1993: Natalie Merchant announces she's leaving 10,000 Maniacs after twelve years.

1985: A close call for Simon Le Bon of Duran Duran. As he is taking part in a yacht race off the coast of England, his boat, the *Drum* sinks. He has to wait 40 minutes before the navy rescues him from an air pocket inside the boat.

Birthdays: Leo Fender (the famous guitar maker), 1909.

August 11th

1993: Salomon Rushdie shows up on stage at London's Wembley Stadium with U2. The author of *The Satanic Verses* went into hiding in 1989, after the Iranians decided his book was blasphemous and publicly promised to assassinate him.

Birthdays: Paul Gendler (Modern Romance), 1960. Joe Jackson, 1955.

August 12th

1993: The Red Hot Chili Peppers decide Jesse Tobias will replace Arik Marshall, on guitar. Three months later, Jane's Addiction guitarist Dave Navarro is brought in instead.

Birthdays: Bon Harris (Nitzer Ebb), 1965.

August 13th

1994: Trent Reznor has a close call at Woodstock '94 when a live power line breaks loose and falls on the NIN tour bus. They finally had to freeze the line with CO_2 to close the circuit and remove the power line from the bus top.

1981: Echo and The Bunnymen premiere their film, a half hour effort called *Shine So Hard*.

1976: The Clash play their first gig in Camden Town's Rehearsal Studio. Only members of the press are invited.

Birthdays: Mark Nevin (Fairground Attraction), 1959. Feargal Sharkey (Undertones), 1958.

August 14th

1994: A memo from the US Justice Department shows Pearl Jam has accused the Rolling Stones of taking a cut from Ticketmaster service charges. Aerosmith confirms the agency offered them a similar deal, but the band said no.

1994: Green Day has to end their Woodstock set after just 30 minutes because of a mud fight. Bassist Mike Dirnt ends up needing dental work after he's tackled by a member of the security team who wants him to stop throwing hunks of sod. The band ends up missing some Lollapalooza stops.

1976: Stiff Records issues its first single, "So It Goes" by Nick Lowe.

August 15th

1986: Morten Harket of a-ha undergoes emergency surgery to remove a cyst from his throat in Vancouver, BC. He was well enough to sing that night.

1983: Joey Ramone is rushed to hospital for emergency brain surgery after getting into a fight over a woman.

1967: The British government's anti-pirate radio laws go into effect, shutting down the pirates like Radio London and Radio Caroline for not paying taxes. The popularity of the pirates prompted the launch of BBC Radio 1, an official pop station, which hired most of the pirate DJs.

Birthdays: Adam Yauch aka MCA (Beastie Boys), 1967. Marshall Scholfield (The Fall), 1962. Matt Johnson (The The), 1961

August 16th

1991: Erasure has their brains CAT-scanned at a London hospital as part of their search to find a new idea for an upcoming album cover.

1975: Peter Gabriel announces that he is leaving Genesis to pursue a solo career. He states "As an artist, I need to absorb a wide variety of experiences. It's difficult to respond to intuition and impulse within the long-term planning the band needed."

1974: The Ramones play their first show at CBGBs.

Birthdays: Tim Farriss (INXS), 1957.

August 17th

1969: The first Woodstock Music and Arts Festival was held in Bethel, New York—three days of mud and music.

Birthdays: Colin Moulding (XTC), 1955. Kevin Rowland (Dexy's Midnight Runners), 1953.

August 18th

1992: Kurt Cobain and Courtney Love become the proud parents of a baby girl, Frances Bean Cobain.

1984: Nick Rhodes of Duran Duran marries Julie Ann Friedman in London. Both the bride and groom wear pink.

1977: The Police play Rebecca's in Birmingham, their first real gig as a trio, after guitarist Henri Pandovani leaves but not before he recorded their debut single "Fallout."

1976: *Sniffin' Glue*, Britain's infamous punk fanzine, is published for the first time.

Birthdays: Jon Farriss (INXS), 1961. Ron Stryker (Men At Work), 1957.

August 19th

1991: EMF releases "Lies" in the UK after editing out a sample of

Mark Chapman reading John Lennon lyrics. Yoko Ono had threatened to sue.

1977: The Sex Pistols do a show in Wolverhampton as the SPOTS (Sex Pistols on Tour Secretly).

August 20th

1977: Turned away from an Edinburgh club because police said it didn't have a music license, Generation X buses 300 punks to a nearby small town and plays there instead.

1978: Dexy's Midnight Runners are formed.

August 21st

1984: The *Wall Street Journal* asks the question in print "Is Hollywood Ready for Frankie?" as in Frankie Goes To Hollywood, which the paper calls "the hottest UK pop group since the Beatles."

Birthdays: Budgie (Siouxsie and the Banshees), 1957. Joe Strummer aka John Graham Mellor (The Clash), 1952.

August 22nd

1992: Sting finally marries his long time love, Trudy Skyler.

Birthdays: Roland Orzabal aka Roland Orzabal de la Quintana (Tears for Fears), 1961.

August 23rd

1994: Suede puts an ad in *Melody Maker* for a new guitarist to replace Bernard Butler.

1993: Duran Duran gets a star on the Hollywood Walk of Fame near the Capitol Records building.

1980: Billed as a new wave Woodstock, the Heatwave festival was held at Mosport, Ontario, north of Toronto. For a mere 20 dollars a head, fans got to see Talking Heads, the Pretenders and Elvis Costello. Since only 50 thousand people showed up, Heatwave

← Joey Ramone of the Ramones

lost a million dollars. By the way, this featured the debut of Talking Heads as a nine piece band. Most of their other appearances were as a quartet.

1970: After a gig at Max's Kansas City, Lou Reed leaves Velvet Underground.

Birthdays: Shaun Ryder (Happy Mondays), 1962. Graham Cunnington (Test Department), 1960.

August 24th

1993: Cracker releases *Kerosene Hat* which was recorded in an abandoned sound stage in the Mojave desert.

1990: Sinead O'Connor demands "The Star Spangled Banner" not be played before her show in New Jersey. The Garden State Arts Center in Holmdel responds by banning any further appearances by O'Connor. Several radio stations in the greater New York area stop playing her records in protest.

1979: The Cars play for a half million fans in New York's Central Park.

Birthdays: Mark Bedford (Madness), 1961.

August 25th

1994: Soundgarden cancels their European tour because Chris Cornell is ordered by his doctor to rest his voice. He has nodules on his vocal chords.

1989: Simon Le Bon gets a brand new baby daughter, Amber Rose.

1979: Gary Numan released "Cars."

Birthdays: Elvis Costello aka Declan McManus, 1954.

August 26th

1994: At the Reading Festival, Hole's Courtney Love tells the crowd that contrary to press reports, she has not been playing "hide the sausage" with Evan Dando.

1977: Ian Dury releases "Sex and Drugs and Rock 'n' Roll."

Birthdays: Jet Black aka Brian Duffy (The Stranglers), 1943.

August 27th

1994: Hole names Melissa Auf Der Maur as the new bassist to replace the late Kristin Pfaff.

1992: *The Sun* newspaper alleges Frances Bean Cobain, daughter of Courtney and Kurt, was born a drug addict. Courtney files suit.

Birthdays: Glen Matlock (Sex Pistols), 1956.

August 28th

1978: Television announces that they're breaking up.

Birthdays: Eddi Reader (Fairground Attraction), 1959. Hugh Cornwell (Stranglers), 1949.

August 29th

1990: A disguised Sinead O'Connor joins an anti-Sinead rally prior to her own concert in Sarasota Springs, New York. The rally was in protest of her trying to prevent the American national anthem from being played at the start of her concerts.

Birthdays: Alex Griffin (Ned's Atomic Dustbin), 1971.

August 30th

1983: The Smiths played Dingwall's in London supported by Easterhouse and a drum machine.

August 31st

1986: Ex-Boomtown Rat Sir Bob Geldof marries long time girlfriend Paula Yates in Las Vegas. Dave Stewart and Annie Lennox act as witnesses.

1983: MuchMusic, Canada's music video channel, goes on the air from Toronto.

Birthdays: Glenn Tillbrook (Squeeze), 1957.

September

September 1st

1994: Alan Wilder of Depeche Mode has a close call when a RAF plane on a training flight crashes into a Scottish hillside and rains debris on his convertible.

1990: The Cure launches their new album, *Mixed Up*, via a pirate radio show. The four hours feature unreleased recordings, interviews, news and traffic, all done in the band's style.

1989: Adam Clayton of U2 has charges of marijuana possession dropped when a Dublin judge offers him the option of donating money to a local women's center.

1983: Accused of "drifting apart from the original idea of the band," Mick Jones is fired from the Clash.

1977: Blondie signs a major deal with Chrysalis.

Birthdays: Bruce Foxton (The Jam), 1955.

September 2nd

1993: At the tenth annual MTV awards, Pearl Jam performs "Animal" live, providing MTV with the only video clip from the *Vs.* album since the band won't do a video.

1989: Ric Ocasek of the Cars marries supermodel Paulina Porizkova.

September 3rd

1982: The first US festival begins in San Bernadino, California. Financed by Apple Computer's founder Steve Wozniak, 400,000 fans enjoy bands like Talking Heads, the Cars and the Police.

September 4th

1986: After seven years, and 23 UK hit singles, Madness splits up. Six years later they get back together after a compilation LP tops the UK album charts.

1976: The Sex Pistols make their first television appearance on the British show "So It Goes."

Birthdays: Martin Chambers (The Pretenders), 1951.

September 5th

1993: Halfway through a Pearl Jam concert at The Gorge in Grant County (in Washington state), hundreds of ticketless fans crash through two metal fences, slide down a 25 foot drop and try to rush the stage. More than 100 are treated for minor injuries.

1991: R.E.M.'s "Losing My Religion" wins MTV's Best Video award.

September 6th

1990: "Nothing Compares 2 U" is named the Best Video at the MTV Music Awards.

1988: INXS's "Need You Tonight" wins MTV's Best Video award.

Birthdays: Pal Gamst Waaktaar (a-ha), 1961. Buster Bloodvessel aka Douglas Trendle (Bad Manners), 1958.

September 7th

1978: Sid Vicious plays a solo show at Max's Kansas City in New York. His back-up band features Mick Jones of the Clash on guitar along with Jerry Nolan and Arthur Kane of the New York Dolls on drums and bass.

1974: Joe Strummer plays his first show with the 101ers, the band he was in before the Clash.

September 8th

1993: Depeche Mode kicks off their North American tour in support of *Songs Of Faith And Devotion* in Montreal. The The is their opening act.

1980: Kate Bush releases *Never For Ever*, her third album.

1978: Public Image, Ltd. release their first single, "Public Image."

Birthdays: David Steele (English Beat/Fine Young Cannibals), 1960.

September 9th

1977: David Bowie appears on Marc Bolan's television show in Britain. They tape a demo, but nothing comes of it because Bolan dies a week later.

Birthdays: Tony Cudlip (Test Department), 1959. Dave Stewart (Eurythmics), 1952.

September 10th

1974: The New York Dolls break up.

Birthdays: Johnnie Fingers aka John Moylett (Boomtown Rats), 1956.

September 11th

1987: "Sledgehammer" by Peter Gabriel wins MTV's Best Video award.

1987: Peter Tosh, guitarist and co-founder of the Wailers, is killed during a robbery at his home in Jamaica.

1977: David Bowie tapes an appearance on a Bing Crosby Christmas special, duetting with Der Bingle on "The Little Drummer Boy."

Birthdays: Mick Talbot (Style Council), 1958.

September 12th

1993: U2's Adam Clayton and model Naomi Campbell are supposed to be married in Ireland. They aren't.

1987: Morrissey splits from the Smiths, just before the group was about to sign a deal with EMI Records. Morrissey later signed with the label as a solo artist.

1979: 2 Tone Records releases its first single: "Gangsters" by the Specials.

Birthdays: Jonathan Stewart (Sleeper), 1967. Barry Andrews (XTC/Shriekback), 1956.

September 13th

1994: A male-only Roadie of the Year contest was canceled after complaints it was sexist. The rules are changed and women are allowed to compete, including a roadie for New Order and Carter USM.

1993: Kate Bush releases *The Red Shoes.*

1989: Sting makes his stage debut in *The Threepenny Opera* in Washington, DC. The reviews were not good. One critic called Sting's singing voice "surprisingly thin."

1982: Kate Bush releases *The Dreaming*.

September 14th

1994: Nic Dalton leaves The Lemonheads to concentrate on his own band, Godstar.

1991: Nirvana releases *Nevermind.*

Birthdays: John Power (La's), 1967. Morton Harket (a-ha), 1959.

September 15th

1990: The Stone Roses sign a *thirty-five year* deal with Silvertone, prompting the band to joke, "We would have only got ten for armed robbery."

1984: "Relax" by Frankie Goes to Hollywood makes the British charts for the 43rd consecutive week. This is the longest streak of any song since "Release Me" by Englebert Humperdinck managed to chart for 56 weeks in 1967-68.

1980: *The Elephant Man,* starring David Bowie as John Merrick, opens on Broadway after a reasonably successful run in Denver.

September 16th

1994: The Cure win their legal fight with founding member Lol Tolhurst who had sued for more of the band's royalties. Tolhurst won't appeal the ruling and is now facing a £1 million legal bill.

1994: Lollapalooza '94 wraps up. The tour generates some interesting numbers: 970,000 attended (90% of tickets sold); trash cans were emptied 154,000 times; 15,000 miles traveled; 6,500 crowd surfers made it to the stage; 215,000 smart drinks consumed; $856,000 raised for charities.

1985: Kate Bush releases *The Hounds Of Love* in the UK.

Birthdays: Colin Newman (Wire), 1954.

September 17th

1994: Scott Weiland (Stone Temple Pilots) marries his longtime girlfriend, Jannaina Castenada.

1993: Because she is such a fan of the band, Chryssie Hynde mans the T-shirt concession booth at an Urge Overkill show in San Francisco.

1992: Hole's first album *Pretty On The Inside* is released in the US.

1976: The Sex Pistols serenade the inmates at Chelmsford prison.

Birthdays: John Penney (Ned's Atomic Dustbin), 1968. Chrissie Hynde (The Pretenders), 1951. Fee Waybill aka John Waldo (The Tubes), 1950.

September 18th

1986: Wayne Hussey of the Mission is banned from the Warehouse Club in Leeds England, after he gets into an argument in the women's bathroom.

Birthdays: Joanne Catherall (Human League), 1962. Dee Dee Ramone aka Douglas Colvin, 1952

September 19th

1984: The Discovery Music Network files a lawsuit against rival MTV alleging unfair competition and anti-trust violations. They claim MTV has exclusivity arrangements with a number of record labels.

1976: Marco Pirroni joins Siouxsie and the Banshees on guitar. Sid Vicious is added on drums, although he refuses to use cymbals or sing.

1975: The Ramones record another series of demos, including "Judy is a Punk." This tape finds its way to Seymour Stein of Sire Records who signs them to a deal.

September 20th

1992: Pearl Jam finally holds its free concert in Seattle in support of voter registration.

1976: The 100 Club Punk Rock Festival begins in London. The event features the Sex Pistols and the debut of Siouxsie and the Banshees with Sid Vicious on drums. A member of the audience loses an eye when she is hit in the face with a beer bottle and Sid is accused of doing the tossing.

Birthdays: David Hemmingway (Housemartins/Beautiful South), 1960. Alannah Currie (Thompson Twins), 1959.

September 21st

1994: Elvis Costello splits with Jake Riviera, his manager of 17 years , and the man who came up with the singer's stage name.

1984: David Bowie releases *Tonight*.

September 22nd

1986: The Smiths sign a deal with EMI for almost £1 million.

1981: *The Catherine Wheel* premieres in New York. Twyla Tharp choreographed the ballet to music written by David Byrne.

1979: The New/No/Now Wave Festival at the University of Minneapolis attracts 5,000 people to see bands like Devo and the Monochrome Set.

Birthdays: Johnette Napolitano (Concrete Blonde), 1957.

September 23rd

1848: John Curtis introduces chewing gum.

Birthdays: James Joyce (La's), 1970.

September 24th

1990: Jesus Jones releases "Right Here, Right Now."

1983: Annabella Lwin leaves as vocalist for Bow Wow Wow. She had joined the group when she was only fourteen after meeting Malcolm McLaren in a laundromat.

September 25th

1818: The first blood transfusion using human blood (instead of the standard animal blood) takes place in Guy's Hospital in London.

Birthdays: Steve Severin aka Steven Bailey (Siouxsie And The Banshees), 1955.

September 26th

1980: A show by the Dead Kennedys is banned because of the group's name.

1979: The Clash release "I Fought The Law," their first US single.

Birthdays: Bryan Ferry (Roxy Music), 1945.

September 27th

1990: Dee Dee Ramone is picked up for pot possession in Greenwich Village.

1980: Martha Ladley, one of the two "Marthas" in Martha and the

Muffins, leaves the group, presumably for Echo Beach.

September 28th

1987: The Smiths final LP, *Strangeways, Here We Come,* is released.

Birthdays: Peter Hooton (The Farm), 1962.

September 29th

1950: Bell Telephone tests the first automatic phone answering machine.

Birthdays: Barry D aka Iain Richard Foxwell Baker (Jesus Jones), 1965.

September 30th

1994: Michael Stipe inks a movie development deal with New Line Cinema.

1993: Kate Pierson of the B-52's is arrested during a sit-in at *Vogue* magazine's offices in New York City. The protest was over the magazine's ads for fur coats.

1985: Kate Bush scores a number one album in Britain, *Hounds of Love,* five years to the week after hitting the top for the first time with her third album, *Never For Ever.*

1967: BBC Radio 1, the government response to pirate radio, goes on the air offering pop music to the masses.

Birthdays: Steve Jones (Sex Pistols), 1955.

October

October 1st

1984: U2 begins a European tour in Rotterdam, the day *The Unforgettable Fire* is released.

1981: The Pretenders are forced to cancel the rest of their American tour after drummer Martin Chambers cuts himself up while trying to break a window.

Birthdays: Richard Oakes (Suede), 1976. Larry Mullen (U2), 1960.

October 2nd

1990: Sinead O'Connor is serenaded with the American national anthem while shopping in a natural food store in Beverly Hills. The employee who broke into impromptu song was fired.

1982: A reunion of sorts. Peter Gabriel and Genesis play together at a WOMAD benefit in London.

Birthdays: Phil Oakey (Human League), 1955. Sting aka Gordon Sumner (The Police), 1951. Richard Hell aka Richard Myers (Television/Voidoids), 1949.

October 3rd

1992: During a performance of Bob Marley's "War" for her guest spot on *Saturday Night Live*, Sinead O'Connor tears up a picture of Pope John Paul II, calling him "the real enemy." The studio audience is stunned and the NBC switchboard logs 500 complaint calls.

1977: The Live Stiffs tour begins. It features Elvis Costello, Nick Lowe and Ian Dury.

Birthdays: Robbie Jaymes (Modern Romance), 1961. Adam Ant, 1954.

October 4th

1994: After hearing a woman complain she didn't want any more kids and she couldn't afford to pay for her husband's operation, U2's Bono appears on an Irish radio show and donates a vasectomy his wife had bought him at an auction two weeks before.

1982: The Smiths make their debut playing just three songs at The Ritz in Manchester.

1980: Stiff Records loses its fight to have a £50 fine and a like amount for court costs reversed. The indecent exhibition charges are because the label displayed a t-shirt with the slogan "If it ain't stiff it ain't worth a fuck."

Birthdays: Neil Sims (Catherine Wheel), 1965. Chris Lowe (Pet Shop Boys), 1959. Barbara Kooyman (Timbuk 3), 1959.

October 5th

1990: The Stone Roses plead guilty to wrecking the officers of FM/Revolver, and are fined £5,000 each.

1969: "Monty Python's Flying Circus" debuts on British TV.

Birthdays: Alistair Adams (Test Department), 1960. Lee Thompson (Madness), 1957. Leo Barnes (Hothouse Flowers), 1955. Bob Geldof aka Robert Frederick Zenon Geldoff (Boomtown Rats), 1951.

October 6th

1980: Johnny Lydon is arrested after a brawl at a club in Dublin, Ireland. He's initially sentenced to three years in jail but is later acquitted by an appeals court.

Birthdays: Tommy Stinson (The Replacements). 1966.

October 7th

1994: Suede shows off new guitarist Richard Oakes at a record company showcase in Paris.

1977: David Bowie releases *Heroes*. The title track is issued as a single in three languages: English, French and German.

Birthdays: Neil Halstead (Slowdive), 1970.

October 8th

1994: The Cult's Ian Astbury tells *Melody Maker* he was sexually abused at the age of 15 by the manager of a restaurant where he worked.

1991: Soundgarden releases *Badmotorfinger* a little behind schedule because of delays over the cover art.

1980: Bob Marley gives his last performance. During a show in Pittsburgh, he collapses on stage. He is flown to New York where doctors discover he has brain and lung cancer. Despite intense treatment, Marley dies the following May at age 36.

Birthdays: Johnny Ramone aka John Cummings (Ramones), 1951.

October 9th

1994: Primal Scream's Bobbie Gillespie speaks out against the Criminal Justice Bill, claiming it will crack down on British concert goers. An anti-bill demonstration in London erupts in violence.

1983: Aztec Camera signs with WEA.

Birthdays: Peter Tosh aka Winston Hubert MacIntosh (Wailers), 1944.

October 10th

1994: Suede releases *Dog Man Star.*

1994: Primal Scream's Bobbie Gillespie claims he was roughed up by police when they came to look into complaints about loud music at a London flat.

1993: Eddie Vedder goes on radio with Howard Stern and gives out his home phone number and tells fans to call him with questions. They do, and the line is jammed for weeks.

1976: EMI outbids Polydor and signs the Sex Pistols for £40,000. They regret the decision by the end of the year.

Birthdays: Martin Kemp (Spandau Ballet), 1961. Kirsty MacColl, 1959. Midge Ure aka James Ure (Rich Kids/Ultravox), 1953.

October 11th

1993: Pearl Jam releases *Vs.* For the first week, it's only available on vinyl.

1977: The Cure go into the studio to make their first proper demos.

Birthdays: Wesley Magoogan (Madness), 1951.

October 12th

1982: The Clash play Shea Stadium in New York as the opening act for the Who.

1981: U2 releases *October.*

1978: Orchestral Manoeuvres in the Dark makes their debut at a club in Liverpool.

Birthdays: Dave Vanian aka David Letts (Damned), 1956.

October 13th

1986: Australia's Nick Cave is picked up by New York City's finest and jailed for two days on vagrancy charges.

1985: B-52's guitarist Ricky Wilson dies from complications resulting from AIDS.

1978: Nancy Spungen is found dead of stab wounds in room 100 of the Chelsea Hotel in Manhattan. Sid Vicious is charged with murdering his girlfriend.

October 14th

1994: Scotland Yard raids A&M offices in London, confiscating artwork for the Dodgy album *Homegrown*, after the band sent out promotional copies complete with cannabis seeds. Police were investigating whether or not the album incited people to take drugs.

1986: Close but no cigar for Bob Geldof, who was in the running for the Nobel Peace Prize.

Birthdays: Meriel Barham (Pale Saints), 1964. Thomas Dolby aka Thomas Morgan Robertson, 1958.

October 15th

1993: Leonard Cohen and Nick Cave are asked to supply music for the film *Natural Born Killers.* Oliver Stone gets Trent Reznor to compile and manipulate the soundtrack.

October 16th

1987: Dave Robinson quits as Managing Director of Stiff Records, the label he started 11 years earlier with Elvis Costello's manager Jake Riviera.

Birthdays: Flea aka Michael Balzary (Red Hot Chili Peppers), 1962. Gary Kemp (Spandau Ballet), 1960.

October 17th

1990: For the first time in history, the number one album in the US is available on CD and cassette but not on vinyl. The album in question was less historic, *Extreme* by Vanilla Ice.

1986: *Sid and Nancy*, the biopic based on the lives of Sid Vicious and Nancy Spungen, has its premiere.

1919: RCA (The Radio Corporation of America) is born.

Birthdays: Ziggy Marley, 1968.

October 18th

1931: Thomas Edison, the father of the phonograph, dies.

1922: The BBC is officially formed.

October 19th

1993: Pearl Jam celebrates the full release of *Vs.* It sells a million copies in just five days.

1991: Oasis play their first proper gig at the Boardwalk in Manchester.

1984: Billy Bragg is arrested taking part in an anti-apartheid sit-in outside the South African embassy in London.

1979: A forty day ska revival tour opens in Britain and features bands like Madness and the Specials.

1973: David Bowie releases *Pin Ups.*

Birthdays: Dan Woodgate (Madness), 1960. Karl Wallinger (World Party), 1957.

October 20th

Birthdays: Norman Blake (Teenage Fanclub), 1965. Tad Winklarz (Chalk Circle), 1965. Mark King (Level 42), 1958.

October 21st

1994: Sarah McLachlan is sued by an Ottawa man who claims her "Possession" is really all about him and is based on private letters he wrote to the singer. The song is about an obsessed fan.

1978: The Clash fire manager Bernie Rhodes.

Birthdays: Julian Cope, 1957.

October 22nd

1993: A Mighty Mighty Bosstones show in Rochester had to be cut short when the floor of the concert hall started giving way because enthusiastic fans pogoed it out of place.

1976: The Damned release "New Rose," considered by most to be the first punk single.

Birthdays: Stiv Bators (Dead Boys/Lords Of The New Church), 1956.

October 23rd

1978: Sid Vicious attempts suicide while being held at Riker's Island Detention Center following the death of Nancy Spungen.

October 24th

1979: The Boomtown Rats release *The Fine Art of Surfacing* which

contains the monster single, "I Don't Like Mondays."

October 25th

Birthdays: Victor De Lorenzo (Violent Femmes), 1954.

October 26th

1982: On the eve of their *Know Your Rights* Tour, Joe Strummer of the Clash disappears. It turns out to be a publicity stunt.

Birthdays: Keith Strickland (B-52's), 1953.

October 27th

1986: After Morrissey is hit in the head by something thrown from the audience, the Smiths bring the curtain down after playing a single song at a concert in Preston, England. Witnesses disagree over whether the object which bopped Morrissey was a coin or a drumstick.

1972: The New York Dolls wander into Malcolm McLaren's "Let It Rock" shop in Chelsea. He was so impressed with their look and attitude, he eventually became their manager.

Birthdays: Simon Le Bon (Duran Duran), 1958.

October 28th

1992: After fighting with her record company over whether her version of "Don't Cry for Me, Argentina" needs a video, Sinead O'Connor announces that she is retiring to study opera.

1977: The Sex Pistols' *Never Mind the Bollocks* is released in the US. It eventually sells a million copies—but it takes more than ten years.

1966: The British Musicians Union announces that they are against allowing BBC Radio to play continuous pop music.

Birthdays: Neville Henry (Blow Monkeys), 1959. Stephen Morris (Joy Division/New Order), 1957.

← Sarah McLachlan

October 29th

1992: Seattle bands rejoice after a state law prohibiting the sale of "erotic" music to minors is struck down as unconstitutional.

1988: R.E.M.'s *Eponymous* hits the UK album charts, but drops off after three weeks.

Birthdays: Peter Timmins (Cowboy Junkies), 1965. Steven Luscombe (Blancmange), 1954.

October 30th

1982: Paul Weller announces that the Jam is disbanding.

Birthdays: Jerry De Borg (Jesus Jones), 1963.

October 31st

1993: Shannon Hoon of Blind Melon strips naked and urinates off the stage during a show in Vancouver. When the police arrived, he climbs on top of the band's tour bus and screams obscenities at them. He is charged with public nudity and committing an indecent act. The charges are eventually dropped.

1983: Everybody is wearing "Frankie Says" T-shirts, marking the release of Frankie Goes To Hollywood's "Relax."

1968: The MC5 release *Kick Out the Jams.*

1967: Iggy Pop & The Stooges debut at a Halloween party in Ann Arbor, Michigan.

Birthdays: Adam Horowitz aka King Ad-Rock (Beastie Boys), 1966. Annabella Lwin aka Myant Myant Aye (Bow Wow Wow), 1965. Johnny Marr aka John Maher (Smiths/Electronic), 1963.

November

November 1st

1986: Virgin Records goes public, offering stock for sale in Britain.

1980: The Pretenders release their self-titled debut LP.

Birthdays: Anthony Kiedis (Red Hot Chili Peppers), 1962. Eddie MacDonald (Alarm), 1959.

November 2nd

1986: Billy Bragg is arrested for cutting through a fence surrounding a US Air Force base in Norfolk, England.

1981: The Specials announce that they're breaking up.

Birthdays: Ashley Bates (Chapterhouse), 1971.

November 3rd

1993: Leon Theremin dies in Moscow at the age of 97. He invented the predecessor to the synthesizer in the early 1920s, and the invention was used in *The Bride of Frankenstein* and *The Day the Earth Stood Still.*

1988: The U2 concert film *Rattle and Hum* has its North American premiere.

Birthdays: Ian McNabb (Icicle Works), 1962. Stuart Goddard (Adam of Adam and the Ants), 1954.

November 4th

1982: Chris Frantz and Tina Weymouth of the Talking Heads have a baby boy while recording an album in the Bahamas.

Birthdays: James Honeyman-Scott (The Pretenders), 1956. Chris Difford (Squeeze), 1954.

November 5th

1994: Fred "Sonic" Smith, husband of Patti Smith and legendary MC5 guitarist, dies of a heart attack in Detroit. He was 47.

Birthdays: Mike Score (A Flock Of Seagulls), 1957.

November 6th

1982: Cait O'Riordan leaves the Pogues.

1975: The Sex Pistols play their first gig at Saint Martin's College of Art in London. They were determined to be so awful and offensive that they had their power cut after about ten minutes.

1972: Billy Murica, drummer for the New York Dolls, dies in a freak accident. He passes out at a party in London after spending the day taking barbiturates. His girlfriend panics and pours hot coffee down his throat. He aspirates the coffee and dies.

Birthdays: Paul Brindley (Sundays), 1963.

November 7th

1980: Dexy's Midnight Runners split up.

1977: Displays featuring *Never Mind the Bollocks* by the Sex Pistols are removed from many record store windows. It all starts when a police sergeant sees a 6'x9' poster in the window of Virgin Records in the Kings Road and declares it in violation of the 1889 Indecent Advertisements Act. The offending word is "bollocks."

1975: The Sex Pistols *finish* their first gig. They play a rough and loose 30 minute set at the Central School of Art and Design in London.

November 8th

1985: Sting's concert film *Bring on the Night* debuts in North America.

1980: Craig Marsh and Martyn Ware leave the Human League and form a new band called Heaven 17.

1980: The British Photographic Industry cracks down on chart fixing with new rules.

Birthdays: Rat (Ned's Atomic Dustbin), 1970. Stephen Patman (Chapterhouse), 1968. Terry Lee Miall (Adam and The Ants), 1958.

November 9th

1994: Courtney Love chases Mary Lou Lord down Sunset Blvd. shouting "You killed my husband and I'm going to kill you." The two are feuding because Lord claimed to have an affair with Kurt Cobain before his death.

1967: The first issue of *Rolling Stone* appears.

November 10th

1994: Factory Records re-opens under the name Factory Too. The label went under in 1992. As he had done with the original company. Tony Wilson chooses the Duritti Column to be the first group with a release on the label.

1984: The Smiths release *Hatful Of Hollow.*

1984: Frankie Goes To Hollywood releases their album. *Welcome To The Pleasuredome* hits the top of the charts in the UK, which is no surprise since there were advance orders for more than a million copies.

1978: The Clash release their second album, *Give 'Em Enough Rope.*

1973: CBGBs opens in New York. In less than two years, it will become the center of the New York punk and new wave scene.

Birthdays: David Hawes (Catherine Wheel), 1965. Frank Maudsley (A Flock of Seagulls), 1959.

November 11th

1986: Johnny Marr of the Smiths is hospitalized following a car crash.

1965: The Velvet Underground debuts at a high school dance in Summit, New Jersey.

1954: *Billboard* magazine predicts that 78 rpm records will soon be totally replaced by the 7" 45 rpm format. Music fans start complaining about how they're being forced to abandon the old technology for the new.

Birthdays: Craig Marsh (Human League/Heaven 17), 1956.

November 12th

1994: Boris Williams quits drumming for the Cure to work with Peter Gabriel and his girlfriend, ex of Shellyan Orphan.

1987: *The Cure Live In Orange* video is released and Barry Gibb of the Bee Gees admits he's a big fan.

November 13th

1993: *The Line, the Cross and the Curve* premieres in London. Kate Bush not only stars in the movie inspired by music from *The Red Shoes* album, but also wrote the screenplay and directed the movie as well.

1987: U2 startle people in San Francisco by playing an impromptu concert in the downtown. It later shows up on the video for "Where The Streets Have No Name."

1978: *Lionheart*, Kate Bush's second album, is released.

November 14th

1942: The *NME* publishes its first issue.

1922: The BBC began airing its first daily radio program from a studio at Alexandra Palace in London.

Birthdays: Joe Leeway (Thompson Twins), 1949.

November 15th

1991: The 500,000th copy of Nirvana's *Nevermind* is sold.

1987: After two members of the audience are bopped with a mike stand during a concert in Toronto, Jim Reid of the Jesus and Mary Chain is arrested and charged with assault. The confrontation comes after some people in the crowd shouted that the show was boring. The following February, Reid pleads guilty but is let off with a conditional discharge after making a donation to the Salvation Army.

1926: NBC goes on the air, broadcasting its first radio program from the Waldorf Astoria hotel in New York City.

November 16th

1985: U2 launch their own label, Mother Records.

1973: The movie *Just a Gigolo* debuts in Berlin. One of the stars is David Bowie. That night, Bowie's first TV special airs on NBC's *Midnight Special*.

Birthdays: Gary "Mani" Mounfield (The Stone Roses), 1962. Harry Rushakoff (Concrete Blonde), 1958.

November 17th

1991: Fox becomes the first American television network to air a commercial for condoms.

1987: During a U2 show in Los Angeles, Bono pulls a member of the audience up on stage to help out with a version of "People Get Ready." Once the song is over, the guy hands Bono his demo tape.

1968: David Bowie makes a silent debut as the leader of Feathers, a small mime troupe at the Country Club in Belsize Park, Hampstead.

Birthdays: Jimmy Marinos (The Romantics), 1953

November 18th

1993: Pearl Jam's Eddie Vedder is booked for disturbing the peace and public drunkenness in New Orleans. He and Chicago White Sox pitcher Jack McDowell got into a barroom brawl with a waiter. McDowell was knocked cold during the fight. Vedder was accused of spitting in the waiter's face, and was arrested. He was finally released on $600.

1991: U2 releases *Achtung Baby*, their seventh album.

1987: U2 opens for themselves at a Los Angeles concert. Wearing wigs and cowboy hats, they pretend to be the Dalton Brothers and fool the audience.

1979: The B-52's self-titled debut album goes gold.

November 19th

1988: Mother Love Bone signs a seven album contract with Polygram, and is handed a $250,000 advance, a record for the Seattle music scene.

Birthdays: Sonic Boom aka Pete Kember (Spacemen 3), 1965. Jason Pierce (Spacemen 3), 1965.

November 20th

1992: Grunge becomes high fashion with a feature in the December issue of *Vogue.*

Birthdays: Mike D aka Mike Diamond (Beastie Boys), 1965.

November 21st

1994: Lol Tolhurst, ex of the Cure, is back in a London court trying to have his £1 million legal bill reduced. He had sued the band for increased royalties.

1877: Thomas Edison invents the "talking machine." He later calls it the "phonograph."

Birthdays: Alex James (Blur), 1968. Fiachna O'Braonain (Hothouse Flowers), 1965. Brian Ritchie (Violent Femmes), 1960. Jim Brown (UB40), 1957.

November 22nd

1994: Pearl Jam releases *Vitalogy*—but first on limited-edition vinyl.

1982: Japan plays their final British concert at London's Hammersmith Theater.

Birthdays: Jimbob aka James Morrison (Carter The Unstoppable Sex Machine), 1960. Tina Weymouth (Talking Heads/Tom Tom Club), 1950.

November 23rd

1889: The world's first jukebox is installed in San Francisco's Palais Royal Hotel. It is an Edison cylinder phonograph which plays a single song for a nickel.

November 24th

1964: Radio Manx becomes Britain's first land-based commercial radio station.

Birthdays: Derrick Murphy (Chalk Circle), 1962. John Squire (The Stone Roses), 1962. Clem Burke (Blondie), 1955.

November 25th

1984: Band-Aid records "Do They Know It's Christmas" at SARM studios in London. Thirty-six artists, including Bob Geldof, Sting, U2 and Heaven 17, took part in the session. Geldof wrote the song with Midge Ure of Ultravox after seeing a BBC special on the famine in Ethiopia.

November 26th

1983: David Bowie entertains 80,000 at a concert in Auckland, New Zealand.

1976: "Anarchy In The UK," the Sex Pistols' debut single is released.

November 27th

1987: The Cowboy Junkies record their second album, *The Trinity Session*, in a Toronto Church for a whopping $162.

Birthdays: Charlie Burchill (Simple Minds), 1959.

November 28th

1987: R.E.M. hits the UK singles chart with "The One I Love."

Birthdays: Matt Cheslin (Ned's Atomic Dustbin), 1970. David Jaymes (Modern Romance), 1954.

November 29th

1992: U2's first television special, *U2's Zoo TV Outside Broadcast*, airs

THE ALTERNATIVE MUSIC ALMANAC

on Fox in the US.

Birthdays: Martin Carr (The Boo Radleys), 1968.

November 30th

1994: Kelley Deal of the Breeders is arrested for drug trafficking in Ohio after accepting delivery of a package of heroin.

1985: The Dead Kennedys release *Frankenchrist* which includes a poster that was later alleged to be obscene.

Birthdays: Paul Wheeler (Icehouse), 1965. Richard Barbieri (Japan), 1958. Billy Idol aka William Broad (Generation X), 1955.

December

December 1st

1981: Vince Clarke quits Depeche Mode to form Yazoo with Alison Moyet.

1980: The Talking Heads start a brief tour of the UK. The opening act is an obscure Irish group called U2.

1978: Ian Dury releases "Hit Me With Your Rhythm Stick." The single ends up selling more than two million copies.

1976: Taunted by host Bill Grundy, the Sex Pistols let loose with a four letter word attack during a two minute live interview on a BBC-TV show called *Today*. The controversy leads to the cancellation of all but five dates on the band's first national tour. EMI, the band's label, later withdraws their first single "Anarchy in the UK" and cancels their contract.

Birthdays: Steve Jansen aka Steve Batt (Japan), 1959.

December 2nd

1986: While singing "Missionary Man" in concert, Annie Lennox gives them more than their money's worth by ripping off her bra in mid-song.

December 3rd

1976: Bob Marley, his wife, manager, and a houseguest, are shot and wounded by gunmen who break into his Jamaican home. The seven suspects get away. Thinking the assassination attempt was politically motivated, Marley moves to Miami for a year-and-a-half.

1976: The Sex Pistols' opening date on their first British tour is canceled because of the flack from Glen Matlock swearing on a live BBC chat show.

Birthdays: John Cale (Velvet Underground), 1940.

December 4th

1986: a-ha fans stop traffic in downtown London when they line up to see the band at a record store.

1979: Billed as "The V2's," the band plays a concert in Islington but only nine people show up. When the Edge breaks a guitar string halfway through the concert, the band is so upset that they quit playing for the night.

December 5th

1994: More than 2,000 days after the released of their debut album, the Stone Roses finally release their second. They call it *Second Coming.*

1986: Mark E. Smith of the Fall turns playwright and his first effort, *Hey Luciani*, premieres in London.

1971: Ian Dury's Kilburn And The High Roads make their debut at Canterbury Art College and get paid a whopping 20 pounds.

December 6th

1994: Pearl Jam's *Vitalogy* is released on CD and cassette.

1993: Depeche Mode releases *Songs of Faith and Devotion Live.*

1980: U2 get to make their American debut at The Ritz in New York City after their gig planned for Rochester the night before is

canceled.

1978: Out on bail for the murder of girlfriend Nancy Spungen, Sid Vicious is arrested in a Manhattan night club for assaulting Patti Smith's brother.

1877: Thomas Edison makes the first sound recording. He records himself reciting "Mary Had a Little Lamb."

Birthdays: Brook Christian Savill (Slowdive), 1970. Claudia Brucken (Propaganda), 1963. Ben Watt (Everything But the Girl), 1962. Peter Buck (R.E.M.), 1956. Rick Buckler aka Paul Richard Buckler (The Jam), 1955.

December 7th

1994: Liam Gallagher walks off-stage during an Oasis concert in Glasgow after losing his voice. Noel Gallagher tries to carry on by himself, but was faced with boos and catcalls. The band reschedules the show and denies rumors they are splitting up.

Birthdays: Brian Futter (Catherine Wheel), 1965. Tom Waits, 1949.

December 8th

1984: "The Power of Love" is Frankie Goes To Hollywood's third straight number one single in the UK.

Birthdays: Sinead O'Connor, 1967. Paul Rutherford (Frankie Goes To Hollywood), 1959.

December 9th

1991: Rita Marley, Bob Marley's widow, wins her long court battle over the singer's estate. She and the kids will share in $11.5 million. Ziggy's daughter is born the same day the verdict comes down and he names her Justice.

1980: U2 plays The El Mocambo in Toronto and it's an angry performance, because the band is still upset over the murder of John Lennon in New York the night before.

December 10th

1993: Killing Joke re-forms.

1984: Band Aid's "Do They Know It's Christmas" debuts at number one on the UK chart, and goes on to become the biggest selling record of all time in Britain.

1976: Billy Idol's Generation X played their first show at London's Central Art School.

Birthdays: Geoff Deane (Modern Romance), 1954. Jack Hues (Wang Chung), 1954.

December 11th

1982: The Jam play their last show in Brighton.

Birthdays: Andy Partridge (XTC), 1953.

December 12th

1987: The first picture disc CDs are released.

1986: The Smiths play the Anti-Apartheid Movement concert at Brixton's Academy Theatre in London. It turns out to be their last concert in the UK and their last song is "Hand In Glove."

1977: The B-52's play their first show at Max's Kansas City, a new wave bar in New York City. Only 17 people are in the audience, but the band is invited back again and again, and quickly develop a cult following.

1901: Guglielmo Marconi receives the first transatlantic wireless signal at St. John's, Newfoundland. The inventor of wireless telegraphy uses a box-kite with a tail of copper wire to pick up faint clicking sounds from a station at Cornwall, England. Today, they call the spot where this bit of history was made Signal Hill.

December 13th

1985: Sigue Sigue Sputnik plays a concert at EMI's Abbey Road Studios.

1980: The Clash release *Sandinista!*

Birthdays: Tom Verlaine aka Thomas Miller (Television), 1949.

December 14th

1979: The Clash release *London Calling.*

Birthdays: Mike Scott (The Waterboys), 1958.

December 15th

1994: A private eye hired by Courtney Love and Geffen Records to find Kurt Cobain in the days before his death, now says the singer did not commit suicide. Seattle police deny rumors that other fingerprints were found on the gun.

1992: Nirvana issues *Incesticide*, a rarities collection. Kurt Cobain's liner notes are omitted for legal reasons.

1977: The Sex Pistols are denied visas to enter the US, just two days before they are supposed to appear on *Saturday Night Live* to kick off their first American tour.

Birthdays: Paul Simonon (The Clash), 1956.

December 16th

1982: Japan plays their final concert in Nagoya, Japan.

December 17th

1977: Elvis Costello is booked on *Saturday Night Live* as a replacement for the Sex Pistols. Producer Lorne Michaels makes Elvis promise not to do anything controversial—but instead of performing "Less Than Zero," Elvis stops the song after a few bars and launches into "Radio Radio." NBC, which owns a large number of radio stations, is not amused.

1971: David Bowie releases his *Hunky Dory* album, a tribute to the New York City music scene.

Birthdays: Bob Stinson (The Replacements), 1959. Mark Gane (Martha and The Muffins), 1958. Mike Mills (R.E.M.), 1956. Carlie Barrett (Wailers), 1950.

December 18th

Birthdays: Martha Johnson (Martha and The Muffins), 1950.

December 19th

1991: On their way home from the store, Henry Rollins and his friend Joe Cole are held up by a gang in Venice Beach, California. They are ordered back to the house where the gang forces them to lie on the floor while they tear the place apart. However, there is a struggle and Joe is shot dead.

1987: The Pet Shop Boys cover of Presley's "Always On My Mind" shoots to the top of the singles chart in the UK.

December 20th

1987: U2 ends their eight month world tour in Arizona with two sold-out shows. Both are recorded for their documentary film, *Rattle and Hum.*

1986: Soviet rocker Stas Namin joins stars like Peter Gabriel at a two-day benefit concert in Tokyo to raise money for UNICEF.

Birthdays: Billy Bragg aka Steven William Bragg, 1957.

December 21st

1983: Keyboard player and songwriter Mike Barson leaves Madness.

December 22nd

1992: Morrissey records material for a live album at the Zenith in Paris. The result is called *Beethoven Was Deaf.*

1990: Mookie Blaylock play their first gig, opening for Alice In Chains in Seattle. The group later adopts the name Pearl Jam.

1988: Morrissey plays his first solo concert at Wolverhampton Civic Hall. In his band are three former members of the Smiths: Andy Rourke, Mike Joyce and Craig Gannon. More than 1,700 people show up and all those wearing a Smiths T-shirt get in for free. The event is captured on film and released as a video entitled *Hulmerist.* The first song in the set is "Stop Me If You Think You've Heard This One Before."

1980: Stiff Records releases *The Wit And Wisdom Of Ronald Reagan.* It's forty minutes of silence.

1978: The Cure release their first single "Killing An Arab" b/w "10.15 Saturday Night."

December 23rd

1966: *Ready Steady Go* airs for the last time in Britain. Among the young performers featured on the television show were David Bowie.

1928: NBC sets up a permanent coast-to-coast radio network in the US.

Birthdays: Eddie Vedder aka Edward Louis Severson Junior (Pearl Jam), 1966. Nicholas Chaplin (Slowdive), 1970.

December 24th

1906: Reginald Fessenden of Canada presides over the first advertised radio broadcast from Brant Rock, MA. As well as reading a poem, he plays "O Holy Night" on his violin.

Birthdays: Ian Burden (Human League), 1957.

December 25th

1992: Members of the Pearl Jam fan club get a great Christmas present from the band: a 45 called "Who Killed Rudolph."

1978: Public Image, Ltd. play their first concert at the Rainbow Theatre in London.

1977: The Sex Pistols play a children's Christmas party at Ivanhoe's in Huddlersfield. It's a benefit for the families of local firemen, laid-off workers and single parent families.

Birthdays: Annie Lennox (Eurythmics), 1954. Robin Campbell (UB40), 1954. Shane McGowan (The Pogues), 1957.

December 26th

1988: The Pogues' Shane McGowan is arrested for kicking in a shop window after spending the day drinking. He is fined £250.

December 27th

1985: Simon Le Bon of Duran Duran marries model Yasmin Parvanah.

1978: On his way home from the band's first London show, Ian Curtis of Joy Division suffers his first attack of epilepsy.

1978: The Cars make their live debut in Boston.

Birthdays: Richey Edwards (Manic Street Preachers), 1969. Youth aka Martin Glover (Killing Joke), 1960.

December 28th

1967: David Bowie keeps his mouth shut during his debut as a mime artist at Oxford's New Theatre.

December 29th

1989: Andrew Wood performs with Mother Love Bone for the first time after getting out of detox.

1982: Jamaica issues a postage stamp featuring Bob Marley.

1939: Radio Luxembourg is given government permission to broadcast. The only commercial radio station to broadcast in English during the 1950s and 1960s, it was also the only European station to play rock and roll.

Birthdays: Mark "Cow" Day (Happy Mondays), 1961.

December 30th

1992: Courtney Love sues her doctor and a Los Angeles hospital for a million dollars, accusing them of leaking word that she was treated for a heroin addiction while pregnant. Four months later, Love and husband Kurt Cobain have a healthy baby girl.

1981: XTC play their first American date in Philadelphia.

1977: What would have been the Sex Pistols first US concert is canceled when the band runs into visa problems.

December 31st

1982: Max's Kansas City, the famous New York punk club, closes after a New Year's party.

1978: After trying out the names the Submerged Tenth, and the Craze, Bauhaus is born and plays its first live performance in a Wellingborough pub using the name "Bauhaus 1919."

Birthdays: Paul Westerberg (The Replacements), 1960. Patti Smith, 1946. Andy Summers aka Andrew Somers (The Police), 1942.

Section 3

By Any Other Name: Band Names

Finding a name for your band is tough. In fact, it's one of the biggest hassles every group faces. Think about it: You have to come up with something that is new and unique that captures the essence of what you're all about. It can't sound stupid or pretentious. The name has to be catchy, easy to remember and easy to spell. And if you're really thinking ahead, you have to consider if the name you choose lends itself to graphic design so you can come up with a proper logo. And when you've finally thought of something, you have to make sure that someone else hasn't thought of the same name at some point over the last forty years. It is a truly torturous exercise.

What follows is a list of bands and their inspirations. If you're in a group (or want to be), you might want read this section carefully and perhaps follow a few of the same thought processes.

ABC
Other Names Considered/Used: Vice-Versa
The Story: Singer Martin Fry wanted a name that would be listed at the beginning of the phone book.

THE ALARM
Other Names Considered/Used: The Toilets, Seventeen, Alarm Alarm
The Story: "The Toilets" was picked as a joke. After the Sex Pistols released *Never Mind the Bollocks*, they took the name "Seventeen" after one of the songs on the album. When that got tired, they thought up "Alarm Alarm," which they thought conveyed more urgency. But when BBC DJ John Peel made fun of the fact that the band was right up there with Duran Duran and Talk Talk, they dropped the second "alarm."

ALICE IN CHAINS
Other Names Considered/Used: The Fucks, Alice 'N Chains
The Story: Layne Stanley came up with the name while contemplating the formation of a glam-punk S&M band. That didn't happen so he kept the name for his new group (which eventually underwent a minor spelling change).

ALL ABOUT EVE
Other Names Considered/Used: ?
The Story: *All About Eve* is a Bette Davis film.

TORI AMOS
Other Names Considered/Used: Myra Ellen Amos (her real name), Y Kant Tori Read
The Story: After Myra Ellen Amos moved to pursue a music career in L.A., she re-named herself "Tori" after a tree. Y Kant Tori Read was the name of the bad bimbo rock band she fronted before going solo.

THE ART OF NOISE
Other Names Considered/Used: None
The Story: The group named themselves after a treatise published in 1913 by Italian futurist Luigi Russolo.

BABES IN TOYLAND
Other Names Considered/Used: ?
The Story: *Babes in Toyland* was a 1934 Laurel and Hardy musical.

BANANARAMA
Other Names Considered/Used: ?
The Story: The name was derived by combining the TV show *The Banana Splits* with the Roxy Music song "Pajamarama."

BAUHAUS
Other Names Considered/Used: Bauhaus 1919
The Story: "Bauhaus" was the architectural school of Walter Gropius that was founded in Germany, 1919. It was a school of thought that incorporated painting, sculpture, architecture, science and technology.

BEASTIE BOYS
Other Names Considered/Used: Young Aborigines, Young and the Useless.
The Story: There is no story. MCA was just goofing around with words one day and came up with the name.
More Stuff: MCA is really Adam Yauch. King Ad-Rock's real name is Adam Horovitz. Mike D's mom knows him as Michael Diamond.

BELLY
Other Names Considered/Used: None
The Story: It's Tanya Donnelly's favorite word "because it's pretty and it's ugly."

Tanya Donnelly of Belly ➜

BETTIE SERVEERT
Other Names Considered/Used: ?
The Story: This is a phrase found in a tennis instructional manual written by 1977 Wimbledon finalist Betty Stove. If you translate the name from Dutch, you literally end up with "service to Betty."

BIG AUDIO DYNAMITE
Other Names Considered: See below.
The Story: When Mick Jones formed the group, he wanted to use the initials B.A.D. Problem was, he didn't have a clue what they should stand for. After considering possibilities such as Black And Decker and Before Alien Domination, he settled on Big Audio Dynamite. Since then, the group was been re-dubbed Big Audio Dynamite II and Big Audio. At last word, Mick has gone back to using Big Audio Dynamite.

BLACK FLAG
Other Names Considered/Used: None
The Story: They guys were inspired by the bug spray of the same name. A black flag is also a symbol of anarchy.

THE BLAKE BABIES
Other Names Considered/Used: None.
The Story: After a reading of William Blake by poet Allen Ginsberg at Harvard, John Stroehm and Freda Boner asked him what they should call their new group. Ginsberg thought for a moment and then said "Blake Babies."

BLONDIE
Other Names Considered/Used: The band that immediately preceded the Blondie we know was called Blondie and the Bonzai Babies.
The Story: Just look at Deborah Harry's head. Strangers were always referring to her as Blondie.

B-52'S
Other Names Considered/Used: None
The Story: It came to Keith Strickland in a dream. It was a vision of a lounge group featuring a woman with a large hairdo playing the organ. The name of her group was the B-52's. When Keith first suggested this name to the rest of the band, they were apprehensive. They were con-

cerned that it would conjure up visions of B-52 bombers and nuclear war. That's when they came up with the idea of outfitting Cindy Wilson and Kate Pierson in big bouffant hairdos, which (in the local slang), were known as B-52's.

BLUR
Other Names Considered/Used: Seymour, Sub, The Shining Path, Whirlpool
The Story: When the band was looking for a record deal, Food Records said they would sign the band if they changed their name to something other than "Seymour." They were then presented with a list of possible monikers with the instructions to pick on. The band agreed on Blur.

BOO RADLEYS
Other Names Considered/Used: None
The Story: Boo Radley is a character in the classic Harper Lee novel, *To Kill a Mockingbird*. In the 1962 film adaptation, Boo Radley is played by Robert Duvall, in his movie debut.

THE BOOMTOWN RATS
Other Names Considered/Used: Mark Skid and the Y-Fronts, Traction, Darker Days, The Nightlife Thugs
The Story: "The Boomtown Rats" was the name given to a group of kids in an Oklahoma oil town. Bob Geldof came across the term in *Bound for Glory*, the biography of folk legend Woody Guthrie.

DAVID BOWIE
Other Names Considered/Used: David Robert Hayward-Jones (his real name).
The Story: David was forced to change his name in 1965 to avoid being confused with David Jones of the Monkees. "Bowie" was inspired by the knife he was always hearing about in American westerns.

BOW WOW WOW
Other Names Considered/Used: Adam and the Ants
The Story: When Malcolm McLaren fired Adam Ant, the rest of the group was reorganized under a new name. His inspiration for the name was a picture of the old "Little Nipper" logo used by HMV and RCA.
More Stuff: Annabella Lwin was born in Burma with the name Myant

Myant Aye.

THE BREEDERS
Other Names Considered/Used: None
The Story: "Breeders" is derogatory homosexual slang for "heterosexuals."

BUSH (OR BUSH-X)
Other Names Considered/Used: ?
The Story: Frontman Gavin Rossdale says a number of things came together with the word "bush." First of all, he lived near Shepherd's Bush in London. Second, "bush" is slang for pot in Britain. And third, there's the connection to pubic regions. "Bush is a very powerful word," he says. "I knew it was just right."
More Stuff: The "Bush-X" handle is for use in Canada where a '70s rock band had first dibs on the name.

THE BUTTHOLE SURFERS
Other Names Considered/Used: Ashtray Baby Heads, Vodka Family Winstons, Abe Lincoln's Bush, Nine Foot Worm Makes Own Food, Ed Asner Is Gay, Dick Gas Five, Independent Worm Saloon, the Inalienable Right to Eat Fred Astaire's Asshole, among others.
The Story: In the early days, the band used to use a different name for every gig they played. When they finally got a gig for which they actually got paid, they decided to stick with that name that had brought them such good luck.

THE BUZZCOCKS
Other Names Considered/Used: None
The Story: "Buzzcocks" was derived from a sentence in a review in *Time Out*, a British magazine. The article ended with the phrase "...it's getting a buzz, cocks!"
More Stuff: Howard Devoto's real name is Howard Trafford. Pete Shelley is really Pete McNeish.

CABARET VOLTAIRE
Other Names Considered/Used: None.
The Story: In 1916, adherents of Dada philosophy used to hang out at a Zurich cafe called Cabaret Voltaire.

Rob Dickinson of Catherine Wheel ➔

More Stuff: See also "dada."

CAPTAIN BEEFHEART
Other Names Considered/Used: Don Van Vliet (his real name)
The Story: The name was taken from the title of screenplay he had written: *Captain Beefheart Meets the Grunte People.*

THE CARS
Other Names Considered/Used: Cap'n Swing.
The Story: Ric Ocasek liked it because it was easy to spell.
More Stuff: Elliot Easton's real name is Elliot Shapiro. Ben Orr shortened his name from Benjamin Orzechowski.

CARTER USM
Other Names Considered/Used: Jamie Wednesday
The Story: The guys were inspired by a newspaper headline—and considering the name of one of the band members, it seemed appropriate (see below).
More Stuff: Jimbob's legal name is James Morrison. Fruitbat is actually Leslie Carter.

CATHERINE WHEEL
Other Names Considered/Used: ?
The Story: St. Catherine was martyred when she refused to renounce her Christianity and marry the Roman emperor Maxentius in about AD 310. He was so peeved that he ordered that she be ripped to death using a device featuring two spiked wheels. But at the crucial moment, a miracle occurred. Lightning struck the wheels and destroyed them, interrupting the execution. From them on, the execution machine was known as a "catherine wheel." Catherine herself survived until Maxentius found out what happened. Then he had her beheaded.
More Stuff: A Vancouver band called Slowburn was also once called Catherine Wheel—until they found out that the Irish band got there first.

CHARLATANS UK
Other Names Considered/Used: ?
The Story: This is one of those names that was just grabbed out of a dictionary. The "UK" was added to avoid being confused with a '60s

group from California.

CIRCLE JERKS
Other Names Considered/Used: Plastic Hippies, The Runs
The Story: Raymond Pettibone found the term in a dictionary of American slang.

THE CLASH
Other Names Considered/Used: The Psycho Negatives, The Weak Heartdrops, The Outsiders, The Phones, The Negatives
The Story: Paul Simonon noticed the word in a newspaper headline. It described "a clash with police."
More stuff: Joe Strummer's real name is John Graham Mellors. "Strummer" is a nickname based on the way he strummed his guitar. Topper Headon's proper first name is Nicky.

THE COCTEAU TWINS
Other Names Considered/Used: ?
The Story: Liz and Robin were big fans of French artist Jean Cocteau. There is also an outside chance that the group co-opted the title of a song recorded by fellow Scotsmen Simple Minds in 1978. Or it may just be a coincidence.

THE COMMUNARDS
Other Names Considered/Used: ?
The Story: Jimmy Somerville borrowed the name after a group of French revolutionaries who took over Paris in the spring of 1871.

CONCRETE BLONDE
Other Names Considered/Used: Dream 6
The Story: Michael Stipe of R.E.M. thought this one up—but even he doesn't know what it means.

ELVIS COSTELLO
Other Names Considered/Used: Declan Patrick McManus (his real name), Declan Costello, D.P. Costello
The Story: Jack Riviera, the head of Stiff Records, dubbed Declan "Elvis." The "Costello" part was derived from the maiden name of Declan's mother.

More stuff: When Elvis recorded his 1977 debut album, *My Aim is True*, he hired an American group called Clover to be his back-up band. After the record was done, they moved back to the States—John McFee joined The Doobie Brothers, while Huey Lewis and Sean Hopper formed Huey Lewis and the News.

COWBOY JUNKIES
Other Names Considered/Used: Germinal
The Story: Their twangy music is so mellow, it sounds like they're all on smack.
More Stuff: Bassist Alan Anton was born Alan Alizojvodic.

THE CRANBERRIES
Other Names Considered/Used: The Cranberry Saw Us
The Story: The original name was a bad pun (Get it? Cranberry Saw Us—Cranberry Sauce?). The name was shortened for convenience and good taste.

THE CULT
Other Names Considered/Used: Southern Death Cult, Death Cult
The Story: "Southern Death Cult" was part of a newspaper headline spotted by singer Ian Astbury. The name was shortened over the years for convenience sake.
More Stuff: Ian Astbury was born Ian Lindsay.

THE CURE
Other Names Considered/Used: The Obelisks, Goat Band, Malice, The Easy Cure
The Story: "The Easy Cure" was one of the first songs Lol Tolhurst ever wrote. The "Easy" was dropped in May 1978 because, according to Robert Smith, it sounded "too hippyish."

DADA
Other Names Considered/Used: None
The Story: "Dada" was a cult founded by Tristan Tzara in 1916 that was based on the rejection of all accepted conventions. These people were into meaningless babble in their art, literature and sculpture.

THE DAMNED

Other Names Considered/Used: The Doomed.

The Story: "The Damned" sound so much more *punk* than "The Doomed."

More Stuff: Just about everyone in the band worked under a pseudonym. Dave Vanian's real name is David Letts. Captain Sensible has Ray Burns on his birth certificate. Lu was actually Robert Evans. For some reason, Brian Robertson found it necessary to rename himself Brian James. And finally, Rat Scabies was born Chris Miller.

DEAD KENNEDYS

Other Names Considered/Used: Thalidomide, The Sharks.

The Story: Jello Biafra wanted something shocking. Good choice.

More Stuff: Jello's given name is Eric Boucher.

DEAD MILKMEN

Other Names Considered/Used: None

The Story: Guitarist Joe Jack Talcum made up the name for a fake newsletter. He needed a name for a fictitious band and got to thinking about the Dead Boys. One thing led to another and suddenly, he had the Dead Milkmen.

↑ Dolores O'Riordan of the Cranberries

DEPECHE MODE
Other Names Considered/Used: Composition of Sound, Peter Bonetti's Boots, The Lemon Peels, The Runny Smiles, The Scamps, The Glow Worms
The Story: Dave Gahan noticed the phrase "depeche mode" while flipping through a French fashion magazine. Translated, the phrase means "fast fashion."

DEVO
Other Names Considered/Used: None.
The Story: According to Mark Mothersbaugh, "Devo" is short for "devolution," which is the opposite of "evolution."

DEXY'S MIDNIGHT RUNNERS
Other Names Considered/Used: None
The Story: The name is a tribute to an amphetamine called Dexedrine. Take enough Dexedrine and you'll be running all night.

DRAMARAMA
Other Names Considered/Used: None.
The Story: "Dramarama" is apparently theater slang for actors who take their roles home with them. Plus it sounded a lot like "Bananarama," which was cool.

DURAN DURAN
Other Names Considered/Used: None
The Story: In the 1968 movie *Barbarella*, Jane Fonda is instructed by her president to find the evil villain, Duran Duran. Milo O'Shea played the character.
More Stuff: Nick Rhodes is actually Nicholas Bates.

DURITTI COLUMN
Other Names Considered/Used: ?
The Story: The Duritti Column was a gang of anarchists who fought in the Spanish civil war.

ECHO AND THE BUNNYMEN
Other Names Considered/Used: Glycerol and the Fan Extractors, Mona Lisa and the Grease Buns, Something and the Daz Man

The Story: In the beginning, there were just two Bunnymen: Will Sergent and Ian McCulloch. Echo was the name they gave their drum machine. This is one of the very few examples in alternative music where a machine got higher billing than the humans in the band.

808 STATE
Other Names Considered/Used: None
The Story: Here's another band named after a piece of machinery. In this case, it's the Roland 808 drum machine.

EINSTURZENDE NEUBAUTEN
Other Names Considered/Used: None
The Story: Translated from German, the name means "collapsing new buildings." Makes sense when you hear how the band sounds.

ELASTICA
Other Names Considered/Used: Spastica, Spastics Society, Kirby Grip, Dad
The Story: The name was chosen in a hurry. "I liked the idea of elasticity," says Justine, "and that it sounded like a girl's name or a cartoon character that can change shape." "Elastica" evolved out of "Spastica."

THE ENGLISH BEAT
Other Names Considered/Used: None
The Story: Dave Wakeling was flipping through *Roget's Thesaurus* looking for a name and the word "beat" struck him as interesting. The "English" part was added later when they realized that there was already an American band using "The Beat."
More Stuff: Ranking Roger's full name is Roger Charlery. See also General Public.

EUGENIUS
Other Names Considered/Used: The Vaselines, Captain America
The Story: Leader Eugene Kelly went for "Eugenius" after he found out that Marvel Comics was thinking about suing for stealing the name of one of their most popular characters.
More Stuff: The Vaselines were one of Kurt Cobain's favorite groups.

EURYTHMICS

Other Names Considered/Used: Annie Lennox and David Stewart worked together in the Catch and the Tourists.

The Story: "Eurythmics" was a form of dance and mime based on Greek traditions developed by Emil Jacques-Dalcrose. It was designed to teach music to children through movement.

FAITH NO MORE

Other Names Considered/Used: ?

The Story: According to legend, the band was almost broke and in desperation went to the dog track to try and win some money. They pooled all their cash and placed a bet on a greyhound named Faith No More. Naturally, the dog came in first and the band was so grateful that they named their group after him.

THE FALL

Other Names Considered/Used: ?

The Story: *The Fall* is the title of a novel by Albert Camus.

FIELDS OF THE NEPHILIM

Other Names Considered/Used: ?

The Story: The Fields of the Nephilim were a race of super-tall men mentioned in the Bible.

54-40

Other Names Considered/Used: ?

The Story: "54-40 or Fight" was the campaign slogan of James Polk in the US presidential election of 1844. It referred to his ambition to annex all the territory from the 40th parallel up to the 54th. He won the election but was convinced to compromise on a border at the 49th parallel.

FINE YOUNG CANNIBALS

Other Names Considered/Used: None

The Story: Look no further than the 1960 film *All the Fine Young Cannibals*. It starred Natalie Wood, Robert Wagner and Pearl Bailey and told the life story of jazz trumpeter Chet Baker.

THE FIXX
Other Names Considered/Used: The Portraits
The Story: The group was originally going to go under the name "The Fix" (as in a heroin fix). Unfortunately, their record company wasn't comfortable with the drug reference so the band was obliged to compromise by adding the extra "X."

FLESH FOR LULU
Other Names Considered/Used: ?
The Story: There are two parts to this story. First, the entire group was vegetarian. Secondly, they were enamored with Lulu, the Scottish pop singer. When they saw her buying a burger at McDonald's one day, one of them made a remark that the burger was "flesh for Lulu." The name stuck.

A FLOCK OF SEAGULLS
Other Names Considered/Used: None
The Story: The band found so much inspiration in the book *Jonathan Livingston Seagull* that they designed a name around it.

FRANKIE GOES TO HOLLYWOOD
Other Names Considered/Used: None
The Story: "Frankie Goes to Hollywood" was the caption on a poster for one of Frank Sinatra's movies.
More Stuff: Holly Johnson's real first name is William. He got the "Holly" part from the transvestite character in Lou Reed's "Walk on the Wild Side." Nasher Nash is really Brian Nash.

GANG OF FOUR
Other Names Considered/Used: ?
The Story: The original "Gang of 4" were the people who seized power in China in 1976.

GENE
Other Names Considered/Used: ?
The Story: Singer Martin Rossiter named the band after a friend who died in 1992.

GENE LOVES JEZEBEL
Other Names Considered/Used: None
The Story: When they were just starting out, the group wanted somthing arty and gothic that involved a phrase—like Alien Sex Fiend or Sisters of Mercy. Eventually, they pieced together a name. "Gene" was Michael Ashton's nickname. "Jezebel" was inspired by the name of a homemade film. The two were linked together by "loves" in order to demonstrate a masculine/feminine relationship.

GENERAL PUBLIC
Other Names Considered/Used: None
The Story: Dave Wakeling was always hearing news reports that referred to "the general public." Then he realized that if he used this name for a band, it would *always* be mentioned in the news. Figuring that this was a chance at free unlimited advertising, he jumped on it.
More Stuff: See also the English Beat.

GENERATION X
Other Names Considered/Used: Chelsea
The Story: Generation X was the title of a book on the mods and rockers in England in the '60s. Billy Idol found it lying around at his mother's house.
More stuff: Billy Idol's real name is William Broad.

THE GLOVE
Other Names Considered/Used: None
The Story: This Robert Smith-Steve Severin side project was inspired by the jet-propelled glove that appears in the Beatles movie *Yellow Submarine*.

THE GO-BETWEENS
Other Names Considered/Used: ?
The Story: The members of the band were big fans of an obscure 1970 film of the same name that starred Julie Christie and Alan Bates.

THE GODFATHERS
Other Names Considered/Used: The Sid Presley Experience
The Story: All the guys were big fans of Marlon Brando in *The Godfather.*

THE GRAPES OF WRATH
Other Names Considered/Used: None
The Story: A couple of members were big fans of the classic 1940 John Ford film that starred Henry Fonda, based on the novel by John Steinbeck.

GREEN DAY
Other Names Considered/Used: Sweet Children
The Story: A "green day" is the band's idea of heaven: a day spent sitting around smoking pot.
More Stuff: Mike Dirnt's original name is Mike Pritchard. Tre Cool is really Frank Edwin Wright III.

GREEN RIVER
Other Names Considered/Used: ?
The Story: The Green River Killer was a serial killer who patrolled Seattle's Green River district between 1982 and 1984. He may have taken as many as 49 lives and was never caught. Being a Seattle band in search of a notorious name, the guys thought that going by "Green River" was appropriate.

HAPPY MONDAYS
Other Names Considered/Used: ?
The Story: "Happy Mondays" are supposed to be the opposite of "Blue Monday," the song from fellow Mancunians, New Order.
More Stuff: Bez is the nickname of Mark Berry.

HEAVEN 17
Other Names Considered/Used: None.
The Story: "Heaven 17" is one of the names dropped by Alex when he visits the record store in the 1971 Stanley Kubrick film, *A Clockwork Orange.*

HELMET
Other Names Considered/Used: Helmut
The Story: Guitarist Page Hamilton used to live in Germany. He and a friend were joking around about this one day and decided that Helmut would be a perfect name for Page's new band. That eventually evolved into Helmet.

HOLE
Other Names Considered/Used: ?
The Story: Get your mind out of the gutter. "Hole" refers to a line spoken by Midea, a character in an ancient Greek tragedy written by Euripides.
More Stuff: Courtney was born Love Michelle Harrison. When he parents split up when she was three, she stayed with her mother and was renamed Courtney Michelle Harrison. From there, she became Courtney Michelle Rodriguez, Courtney Michelle Manely and then finally just plain Courtney Love.

THE HOODOO GURUS
Other Names Considered/Used: Le Hoodoo Gurus.
The Story: The band liked the name The Gurus. "Hoodoo" was added because it rhymed.

THE HOTHOUSE FLOWERS
Other Names Considered/Used: ?
The Story: The band copped the title of a Wynton Marsalis album.

HUMAN LEAGUE
Other Names Considered/Used: The Dead Daughters, The Future
The Story: "The Human League" taken from of a science fiction computer war game called "Strike Force." When founding members Martyn Ware and Ian Craig Marsh left the group in 1980, they gave Phil Oakley permission to use the name in exchange for one percent of all future royalties. Smart move.

HÜSKER DÜ
Other Names Considered/Used: None
The Story: Hüsker dü is Swedish for "Do you remember?" It's also the name of a board game that was big in Minneapolis.

ICEHOUSE
Other Names Considered/Used: Flowers
The Story: An "icehouse" is Australian slang for an insane asylum.

ICE-T
Other Names Considered/Used: Tracy Marrow (his real name)

The Story: Tracy dubbed himself Ice-T in honor of a black author of the same name.

THE ICICLE WORKS
Other Names Considered/Used: None.
The Story: This name was adapted from the title of a sci-fi novel entitled *The Day the Icicle Works Closed Down*.

INXS
Other Names Considered/Used: The Farris Brothers (after the band's real-life brothers Tim, Andrew and Jon).
The Story: They figured "Hey, if XTC can do it, so can we!"

JALE
Other Names Considered/Used: ?
The Story: This one is real simple. Just take the first initial of all the members of the band: Jennifer, Alyson, Laura and Eve.

THE JAM
Other Names Considered/Used: None
The Story: The band's name came about after they developed the habit

↑ Husker Du board game

of rehearsing during lunch hour at school. The guys would just get together and "jam."

JAMES

Other Names Considered/Used: Venereal and the Diseases, Volume Distortion, Model Team.

The Story: We're not really sure. It could be because the band features two guys names James and it was a case of majority rules.

JANE'S ADDICTION

Other Names Considered/Used: None

The Story: After Perry Farrell bailed out of Psi-Com in 1985 (because the other guys in the band wanted him to join the Hare Krishnas), he turned his attention to forming a new band. Legend has it that a certain hooker named Jane was so impressed with the band that she underwrote a lot of their start-up costs. As a tribute to her faith and trust, the group chose a name that acknowledged Jane's fascination with them.

More Stuff: "Perry Farrell" is a play on the word "peripheral." His real name is Simon Bernstein.

JAPAN

Other Names Considered/Used: ?

The Story: The name is taken from a guidebook entitled *A Tourist's Guide to Japan.*

More Stuff: Mick Karn is Greek. His proper name is Anthony Michaelides. David Sylvian and Steve Jansen are brothers. Their actual last name is Batt.

THE JESUS AND MARY CHAIN

Other Names Considered/Used: The Daisy Chain

The Story: There is no story. William Reid just made it up one day.

JESUS JONES

Other Names Considered/Used: Farewell Camouflage.

The Story: Mike Edwards thought of the name while in Spain. All he did was take a very common Spanish name and mate it with a very common English name.

JOY DIVISION
Other Names Considered/Used: The Stiff Kittens, Warsaw
The Story: Pete Shelley of the Buzzcocks was the one who suggested "The Stiff Kittens." But after David Bowie released his *Low* album in 1978, the band decided to name themselves after the song "Warsaw." Unfortunately, that created confusion because there was already a London metal band called Warsaw Pakt. That's when they shifted to Joy Division. The name comes from a novel by Karol Cetinsky called *House of Dolls.* In the book, the "joy division" is a special group of huts in a WW II concentration camp where women were forced into prostitution for the benefit of Nazi officers on leave.
More Stuff: Bernard Sumner has also gone by the name "Bernard Albrecht." The name on his birth certificate is "Bernard Dicken."

KILLDOZER
Other Names Considered/Used: ?
The Story: *Killdozer* was the name of a 1974 horror movie featuring a bulldozer transformed into a killing machine by an alien presence.

KILLING JOKE
Other Names Considered/Used: ?
The Story: Remember the Monty Python skit about the joke that was so lethally funny that it was used as an offensive weapon in the war?
More Stuff: Youth is actually named Martin Glover. Geordie's signs official documents as K. Walker. Jaz Coleman's first name is Jeremy.

KING MISSILE
Other Names Considered/Used: ?
The Story: King Missile is the name of a Japanese comic book character.

THE KLF
Other Names Considered/Used: The Justified Ancients of Mu-Mu (JAMMs), The Timelords
The Story: There are two possibilities: Kylie Lives Forever (a tribute to pop-tart Kylie Minogue) or Kopyright Liberation Front (a statement on their attitude regarding sampling).

KMFDM

Other Names Considered/Used: ?

The Story: Unofficially, KMFDM stands for the German phrase that translates as "no pity for the majority" ("Kein Mehrheit Fur Die Mitleid). Others insist it stands for Killing Madonna Frees Desperate Minds, Kill Moshers For Doc Martens or Kill Mother Fucking Depeche Mode. However, one of the bandmembers says "there's no actual official meaning. It's just serving the public's need to fill a void."

KRAFTWERK

Other Names Considered/Used: Organisation

The Story: "Kraftwerk" is German for "powerplant."

LEVEL 42

Other Names Considered/Used: ?

The Story: If you read Douglas Adams' *The Hitchiker's Guide to the Galaxy* series, you'll find that Deep Thought, the great computer, says that the answer to "life, the universe and everything" is exactly "42." Unfortunately, no one seems to know what the question was. But at least it was an answer for Mark King's problems with naming his new band.

THE LIGHTNING SEEDS

Other Names Considered/Used: ?

The Story: Ian Broudie misunderstood a Prince lyric. He thought he was singing "The thunder drowns out what the lightning sees." Ian thought he said *seeds.*

LIVE

Other Names Considered/Used: ?

The Story: The band wanted a name which conveyed their intense playing style. For them, the word "live," with its connotations of seeing a band in their rawest form, captured that.

LOVE AND ROCKETS

Other Names Considered/Used: See below

The Story: *Love and Rockets* is the name of an underground comic.

More stuff: The previous incarnation of the band was Tones on Tail, who descended from Bauhaus.

Ed Kowalczyk of Live ➔

L7

Other Names Considered/Used: Camel Lips

The Story: "L7" is '50s sign language slang for "square." It works like this: using the thumb and forefinger of your left hand, form an "L." Then with the right, make a "7." Bring the two together and you form a square.

MADNESS

Other Names Considered/Used: The Invaders

The Story: "Madness" was the name of a song by Jamaican ska pioneer Prince Buster.

More Stuff: Frontman Suggs is really Graham MacPherson

MARILYN MANSON

Other Names Considered/Used: Marilyn Manson and the Spooky Kids

The Story: This is an amalgamation of the names of two of the most famous people in American popular culture: Marilyn Monroe and Charles Manson. The band's original name was shortened for convenience.

THE MEAT PUPPETS

Other Names Considered/Used: None

The Story: The group had a song entitled "Meat Puppets," which is what they considered themselves to be—they were made of meat and puppets of the world around them.

THE MEKONS

Other Names Considered/Used: ?

The Story: If you look back at an English comic of the '50s called "Dan Dare," you'll find that a Mekon is a really evil space alien dude.

MIDNIGHT OIL

Other Names Considered/Used: ?

The Story: It's from the phrase "burning the midnight oil."

MINISTRY

Other Names Considered/Used: Ministry of Fear, Ministry of Truth, Ministry of Canned Peaches

The Story: One night, Alain Jourgensen was transfixed by a 1944 film starring Ray Milland entitled *Ministry of Fear*. After awhile, all the variations on that title were shortened to just "Ministry."

THE MINUTEMEN
Other Names Considered/Used: ?
The Story: It's simple. They were a punk band that played songs that lasted less than a minute.

MOBY
Other Names Considered/Used: Richard Hall (his real name).
The Story: Richard is the great-great-grandnephew of Herman Melville, the author of *Moby Dick*.

THE MOCK TURTLES
Other Names Considered/Used: ?
The Story: The name is from a character in *Alice in Wonderland*.

MUDHONEY
Other Names Considered/Used: ?
The Story: This is the title of a Russ Meyer movie.

MY BLOODY VALENTINE
Other Names Considered/Used: ?
The Story: The band found inspiration in the title of the 1981 slasher flick of the same name.

NED'S ATOMIC DUSTBIN
Other Names Considered/Used: The Spy: Or Who Is the Pink Oboe
The Story: "Ned's Atomic Dustbin" was the title of an episode of the old BBC Radio series *The Goon Show* which starred Peter Sellers and Spike Milligan. "The Spy: Or Who Is the Pink Oboe" was the name of another episode. "Ned's Atomic Dustbin" was judged sillier, so it won.
More Stuff: Rat's proper name is Gareth Pring.

NEW FAST AUTOMATIC DAFFODILS ("NEW FADS")
Other Names Considered/Used: ?
The Story: "New Fast Automatic Daffodils" is the title of a poem by Adrian Henri.

NEW MODEL ARMY
Other Names Considered/Used: ?
The Story: The "New Model Army" was the name of Oliver Cromwell's forces in the English civil war.

NEW ORDER
Other Names Considered/Used: They used to be Joy Division before singer Ian Curtis died on May 9, 1980.
The Story: Manager Rob Gretton found the name in a *Manchester Guardian* article about Cambodia. Prince Sihanouk had just formed a new division of soldiers he called "the new order." Since the band was reorganizing in the wake of Curtis' death, it seemed perfect.
More Stuff: See Joy Division.

THE NEW YORK DOLLS
Other Names Considered/Used: None
The Story: There were two sources for the name. Guitarist Sylvain Sylvain was a big fan of Russ Meyer films, especially *Beyond the Valley of the Dolls*. "Dolls" also used to be slang for "pills."
More Stuff: Sylvain Sylvain's real name is Syl Mizrahi. David Johansen sometimes works under the name Buster Poindexter.

NINE INCH NAILS
Other Names Considered/Used: Over 200, allegedly.
The Story: There are three rumors and the truth. The rumors are: (1) The Statute of Liberty has nails that are nine inches long. (2) The nails used to seal coffins are nine inches long. (3) Christ was crucified with nine inch nails. Those are all great stories—but none of them are true. According to Trent, he came up with Nine Inch Nails when he was trying to come up with a name for his project. He decided to keep this one after he discovered it looked good in print, could be abbreviated—and after he realized that he wasn't sick of it after two weeks.
More Stuff: Trent's full name is Michael Trent Reznor.

NIRVANA
Other Names Considered/Used: Skid Row, Ted Ed Fred, Throat Oyster, Pen Cap Chew, Windowpane
The Story: It was Kurt's choice. He liked the dictionary definition of "nirvana" which read "the extinction of desire, passion, illusion and

244

attainment of rest, truth and unchanging things."

More stuff: Before Nirvana, Kurt was in bands with names like Fecal Matter, Brown Towel and Brown Cow. There were also at least two other bands with the name "Nirvana." One was an English band who released an album called *Rainbow Chaser* in 1968. When the Seattle Nirvana hit it big, their record company reached an out-of-court settlement over use of the name.

OASIS

Other Names Considered/Used: Rain

The Story: The banned copped "Oasis" from a chain of women's clothing stores.

OFFSPRING

Other Names Considered/Used: Manic Subsidal

The Story: There are suspicions that the band borrowed the title of a 1986 film starring Vincent Prince and Lawerence Tierney.

More Stuff: Singer Dexter Holland uses a different first name for every album. For *Ignition* in 1992, he went by "Keith." His real first name is Bryan. Bassist Greg K's proper surname is Krisesel. "Noodles" is really Kevin Wasserman.

OINGO BOINGO

Other Names Considered/Used: See below

The Story: Oingo Boingo actually began as a comedy act. The Mystical Knights of the Oingo Boingo had quite the cult following in L.A. back in the '70s. Eventually, the group turned to music and shortened its name.

ONE DOVE

Other Names Considered/Used: ?

The Story: "One Dove" was Elvis Presley's great-great-great-grandmother who was a Cherokee Indian who lived on the Mississippi Delta in the early 19th century.

1000 HOMO DJs

Other Names Considered/Used: See Ministry.

The Story: Alain Jourgensen has some songs left over from the sessions that produced Ministry's *Land of Rape and Honey* album and wanted to release them under another name. He was discussing the possibility at the offices of Wax Trax records one afternoon when someone played an unauthorized dance remix of a Revolting Cocks song entitled "We Shall Cleanse the World." Jourgensen hated it—but he was reassured by Wax Trax staff that the only people that would hear it would be "a thousand homo DJs." The name stuck and the leftover *Land of Rape and Honey* material was released under that name.

ORCHESTRAL MANOEUVERS IN THE DARK
Other Names Considered/Used: The Id, Dalek I Love You, VCL XI
The Story: They wanted something that sounded pretentious. Mission accomplished.
More Stuff: VCL XI is a transistor part.

PEARL JAM
Other Names Considered/Used: Mookie Blaylock (NBA guard who currently plays for the Atlanta Hawks, but at the time was on the New Jersey Nets.)
The Story: Unsure whether Mookie would be flattered or sue, the group opted for a name change at the last minute. They took the name from a fruit preserve that Eddie Vedder's grandmother used to make using peyote. Her name was Pearl, hence "Pearl Jam."
More Stuff: Mookie wasn't completely left out. The title of the "Ten" album comes from his uniform number. And things really get confusing when you try and pin down the name of Pearl Jam's singer. When he was born, his full name was Edward Louis Severson. When he was growing up, he used Edward Mueller, taking the last name of his stepfather. But when he was a teenager, he adopted "Vedder," which was his mother's maiden name.

PERE UBU
Other Names Considered/Used: Rockets from the Tombs
The Story: Pere Ubu was the hero of a play entitled *Ubu Roi*. It was written by the French absurdist Alfred Jarry.

PET SHOP BOYS
Other Names Considered/Used: West End
The Story: Chris Lowe had a couple of friends who owned a pet shop. They were referred to as "the pet shop boys."

THE PIXIES

Other Names Considered/Used: None

The Story: Guitarist Joey Santiago used to carry around a dictionary wherever he went. English was his second language and he was determined to learn to speak it properly. Whenever he came across a word he didn't understand, he'd look it up and memorize it. When the Pixies were coming together, the band plucked that word out of Joey's dictionary for two reasons. First, the word didn't seem relevant to the group's sound. And secondly, it was kind of funny to name a band the Pixies when you had a big guy like Black Francis out front.

More Stuff: It's Charles Michael Kittridge Thompson IV aka Black Francis aka Frank Black.

THE POGUES

Other Names Considered/Used: The Chainsaws

The Story: "Pogue ma hone" is Gaelic for "kiss my ass."

More stuff: Shane McGowan used to be in a band called "The Nipple Erectors."

THE POLICE

Other Names Considered/Used: Strontium 90

The Story: Drummer Stewart Copeland's father worked for the CIA as a spy. The name "The Police" was a cheeky shot at that.

More Stuff: Sting's real name is Gordon Sumner. The proper spelling of Andy Summers' last name is "Somers."

IGGY POP

Other Names Considered/Used: James Jewell Osterberg (his real name).

The Story: One of James' first bands was called The Iguanas. It wasn't long before people started calling him "Iggy." The "Pop" part was borrowed from Jim Popp, a local junkie.

POP WILL EAT ITSELF

Other Names Considered/Used: ?

The Story: The guys took the name from a newspaper article entitled "Will Pop Eat Itself?"

Other stuff: The subject of the article was a group called Jamie Wednesday. They eventually broke up and re-formed as Carter USM.

PORTISHEAD
Other Names Considered/Used: None
The Story: Portishead is the name of the band's hometown. It's a suburb of Bristol, England.

PREFAB SPROUT
Other Names Considered/Used: ?
The Story: Founder Paddy McAloon must have bad hearing. That line in the Nancy Sinatra song features the words *pepper sprout.*

THE PRETENDERS
Other Names Considered/Used: ?
The Story: Chrissie Hynde once knew a member of a particularly tough bike gang. But unlike some of his brothers, this guy liked music of black performers, including Sam Cooke. In fact, his favorite song of all time was "The Great Pretender." That's where Chrissie got the idea for the name for her new band.

THE PRIMITIVES
Other Names Considered/Used: None
The Story: The Primitives were one of Lou Reed's pre-Velvet Underground bands. They released a single in 1964 titled "The Ostrich."

THE PSYCHEDELIC FURS
Other Names Considered/Used: ?
The Story: All the members of the band were huge fans of the Velvet Underground. "Psychedelic Furs" was inspired by the Velvet song "Venus in Furs."

PUBLIC IMAGE, LTD.
Other Names Considered/Used: None
The Story: The name was chosen by Johnny Lydon as a sarcastic jab at those who questioned his attitude towards the music industry.

PULP
Other Names Considered/Used: Arabicus Pulp
The Story: In 1977, Jarvis Cocker was studying economics and started a band named at first after the coffee-bean commodity, but they quickly shortened the name.

RADIOHEAD

Other Names Considered/Used: On a Friday
The Story: They're named after the Talking Heads song on the *True Stories* album.

THE RAMONES

Other Names Considered/Used: At least 50, including Spice.
The Story: There were two sources for the name "Ramones." First, Paul McCartney once used the name "Paul Ramone" as a pseudonym during the days of the Silver Beatles. Secondly, all the guys were big fans of famed '60s producer Phil Ramone.
More Stuff: Why do all the members of the band have the same last name? Because in the beginning, they thought it made them sound like a bunch of outlaws. For the record, though, here are real names of all the guys that have been in the Ramones:
Joey Ramone: Jeff Hyman
Marky Ramone: Marc Bell
Johnny Ramone: John Cummings
Dee Dee Ramone: Douglas Colvin
Tommy Ramone: Tommy Erdelyi
CJ Ramone: Christopher Joseph Ward
Richie Ramone # 1 (1974): ?
Richie Ramone # 2 (1987): Richie Beau
Elvis Ramone: Clem Burke (ex-Blondie drummer)

RAPEMAN

Other Names Considered/Used: ?
The Story: Steve Albini co-opted the name of a Japanese comic book hero.

RED HOT CHILI PEPPERS

Other Names Considered/Used: Anthem
The Story: The band was looking for a name that captured the essence of their hot, spicy punk-funk.
More Stuff: Flea is known to his mother as Michael Balzary.

REDD KROSS

Other Names Considered/Used: The Tourists
The Story: The name was inspired by the masturbation scene in *The*

Exorcist.
More Stuff: Their name used to be spelled "Red Cross" until the blood bank people threatened to sue. Taking a cue from comedian Redd Foxx, they escaped the lawyers by adding a "d" and changing the "c" to a "k."

R.E.M.
Other Names Considered/Used: The Twisted Kites, Male Nurses, Slut Bank, Cans of Piss. They've also been known to perform under pseudonyms like Bingo Handjob; Hornets Attack Victor Mature; Pink Pajamas; The Neon Mud Men; It Crawled from the South; and Fat, Drunk, and Stupid.
The Story: At 3 am on April 5, 1980, with only a few hours to go before their first gig, Mike Mills says the band turned to the dictionary and went for the first name that appealed to them.
More stuff: R.E.M. does *not* stand for "rapid eye movement" in this case. The guys just liked the sound of those letters together. And it's a good thing the band had a good lawyer in those early days because when R.E.M. was formed in Athens, there were at least three other American groups using that name.

THE REPLACEMENTS
Other Names Considered/Used: The Impediments
The Story: As the Impediments, they were banned from playing at a bar. When they showed up the next day, they told the manager on duty that they were "the replacements" for the band that got thrown out the night before.

THE RESIDENTS
Other Names Considered/Used: ?
The Story: When the band moved from the bayous of Louisiana to San Francisco, they started sending anonymous demo tapes to all the major record companies. When Warner Brothers returned their tape with a rejection letter, it was address care of "the residents." The name stuck.

ROXY MUSIC
Other Names Considered/Used: Roxy
The Story: "The Roxy" was the name of a theater near Bryan Ferry's place. The group added the "music" part to avoid being confused with an American band called "Roxy."

SAINT ETIENNE
Other Names Considered/Used: ?
The Story: Saint Etienne is the name of a French soccer club.

THE SEX PISTOLS
Other Names Considered/Used: The Strand (after the Roxy Music song), The Swankers.
The Story: Malcolm McLaren originally envisioned the band as a living, breathing advertisement for his clothing shop which was called "Sex." The "Pistols" was a vague reference to one particularly graphic t-shirt for sale in the store that feature two gay cowboys.
More Stuff: Johnny Rotten's real name is John Lydon. Sid Vicious was born John Simon Ritchie.

SHELLYAN ORPHAN
Other Names Considered/Used: ?
The Story: They were inspired by "Spirit of Solitude," a poem by Percy Bysshe Shelley.

SHONEN KNIFE
Other Names Considered/Used: ?
The Story: The band is named after a brand of Japanese knife.

SIMPLE MINDS
Other Names Considered/Used: Johnny and the Self-Abusers
The Story: Jim Kerr found the name in a line of David Bowie's "The Jean Genie."

SIOUXSIE AND THE BANSHEES
Other Names Considered/Used: None.
The Story: The group was in a hurry to find a name because they were just days away from their first gig. Then they remembered the Vincent Price film they had just seen on television, *Cry of the Banshee.*
More Stuff: Siouxsie Sioux's real name is Susan Dallion. She adopted the "Siouxsie" spelling because she was "always on the Indians' side in westerns. I thought the cowboys were extremely suspicious, even without knowing the historical genocide that went on." Steve Severin once used the name Steve Havoc. His real name is Steven Bailey.

SISTERS OF MERCY
Other Names Considered/Used: The Sisterhood
The Story: There are two stories about this one. One says that Andrew Eldritch spotted the phrase in a newspaper story about a convent run by an order known as "The Sisters of Mercy." Another says he stole the phrase from a Leonard Cohen song about prostitutes.
More Stuff: Andrew Eldritch's birth certificate reads "Andrew Taylor."

SLEEPER
Other Names Considered/Used: ?
The Story: Everyone in the band is a fan of the Woody Allen movie of the same name.

SLOWDIVE
Other Names Considered/Used: None
The Story: The name comes from the title of the song by Siouxsie and the Banshees.

SMASHING PUMPKINS
Other Names Considered/Used: None
The Story: "Smashing pumpkins" was a phrase overheard by Billy Corgan one night while sitting in a friend's kitchen.
More Stuff: D'Arcy's last name is Wretzky.

THE SMITHEREENS
Other Names Considered/Used: ?
The Story: The band is a big fan of all those Bugs Bunny cartoon where Yosemite Sam threatens to blow him to "smithereens."

THE SMITHS
Other Names Considered/Used: Smithdom, Smiths' Family
The Story: There were several reasons for the choices: (1) Morrissey wanted to make a statement by choosing a name that was utterly bland, faceless, unpretentious and exquisitely English. (2) He also wanted to honor one of his idols, Patti Smith. (3) It was a tribute to fellow Mancunian Mark E. Smith of the Fall (4) There was a tie-in to David Smith, the man who exposed to the Moors Murders (5) The name was in memory of a Manchester club called "Mr. Smiths," which was hot in the '60s.
More Stuff: Morrissey's full name is Stephen Patrick Morrissey.

Johnny Marr's real last name is Maher.

SONIC YOUTH
Other Names Considered/Used: Male Bonding, Red Milk, The Arcadians, among others.
The Story: Thurston Moore came up with the name in time for a 1981 No Wave art gallery performance called the Noise Festival. He simply grafted together the names of two of his favorite groups: Sonic's Rendezvous Band (a post MC-5 band led by guitarist Fred "Sonic" Smith) and Big Youth (a late '70s reggae band.)

SOUNDGARDEN
Other Names Considered/Used: None
The Story: If you head out to 7600 Sand Point Way in Seattle, you'll find a large environmental metal sculpture entitled The Soundgarden. It gets its name from the noises it makes when the wind whistles by.

THE SOUP DRAGONS
Other Names Considered/Used: None
The Story: The group is named after characters on *The Clangers,* a kid's show on British TV.

SPANDAU BALLET
Other Names Considered/Used: The Makers
The Story: "Spandau Ballet" was a piece of graffiti written in the stall of a public washroom in Berlin. It was probably a reference to Spandau Prison.

THE SPECIALS
Other Names Considered/Used: The Automatics, The Specials aka The Automatics, The Special aka
The Story: The Automatics was the band's first choice—but they were too late. Another English band had already snagged it. That's when things got confusing. Not wanting to give up the name entirely, Jerry Dammers opted for the inconvenient The Specials aka The Automatics. When someone finally pointed out how dumb this sounded, he shortened it to simply The Specials. Later, the band retreated halfway, going under the name The Special aka. By the way, "specials" are a certain type of record made for loud Jamaican sound systems.

More Stuff: Jerry Dammers real last name is Dankey.

SQUEEZE
Other Names Considered/Used: Cum, Captain Trundlow's Sky Co. (or Skyco for short).
The Story: *Squeeze* was the title of a 1973 Velvet Underground album.

STIFF LITTLE FINGERS
Other Names Considered/Used: None
The Story: They took their name from a song they once saw the Vibrators perform.

THE STONE ROSES
Other Names Considered/Used: The Patrol, English Rose, The Angry Young Teddy Boys
The Story: The "Stone" is in tribute to the Rolling Stones. The "Rose" part comes from English Rose, a 1983 group featuring Ian Brown and John Squire. That name was derived from a Jam track on the *Setting Sons* album.
More Stuff: Mani, the bass player, is really Gary Mounfield.

STONE TEMPLE PILOTS
Other Names Considered/Used: Mighty Joe Young
The Story: The band was all set to release their debut album when they discovered that another group had laid claim to Mighty Joe Young. That meant they had to come up with something quick. Legend has it that they were inspired by an STP Oil Treatment sticker. After some discussion, they agreed that they would co-opt those initials and use them to stand for Stone Temple Pilots. (The name doesn't mean anything. The band just thought it sounded cool.)

THE STOOGES
Other Names Considered/Used: ?
The Story: Iggy Pop and the boys had just finished watching The Three Stooges on TV while on acid. Somehow, it seemed just right.
More Stuff: See also Iggy Pop.

THE STRANGLERS
Other Names Considered/Used: Johnny Sox, The Guildford

Strangers. They've also appeared under the name The Mutations and Celia and the Mutations.

The Story: They wanted something menacing. Good choice.

More Stuff: J.J. Burnel's full name is Jean Jacques Burnel. Jet Black was born Brian Duffy.

SUEDE

Other Names Considered: ?

The Story: When Justine Frischmann (now of Elastica) was a member of the band, it was she who came up with the name after she openly admired Brett Anderson's new suede jacket.

TALK TALK

Other Names Considered/Used: Reaction

The Story: No story. They just liked the sound of it.

TALKING HEADS

Other Names Considered/Used: The Artistics

The Story: A friend suggested the name after he saw the term in a *TV Guide* article on news anchors.

THE TEARDROP EXPLODES

Other Names Considered/Used: See below.

The Story: The name comes from a panel in a DC Comics book.

More Stuff: Julian Cope also appeared in bands with names like the Crucial Three, Mystery Girls and Nova Mob.

TEARS FOR FEARS

Other Names Considered/Used: Graduate (a pre-Tears for Fears ska band).

The Story: Both Roland Orzabal and Curt Smith suffered unhappy childhoods. Their salvation was found in Arthur Janov's book on "primal scream" therapy entitled *Prisoners of Pain*. "Tears for Fears" was extracted from a line in the book that reads "*Tears* as a replacement *for fears*."

TEENAGE HEAD

Other Names Considered/Used: See below

The Story: In 1971, the Flaming Groovies issued an album called

Teenage Head. A total of six copies were sold in Hamilton, Ontario—and they were all bought by guys who would end up being associated with Teenage Head.

More Stuff: When Teenage Head secured an American record deal, the label insisted that their name was sexually offensive. That forced the group to change their name to Teenage Heads for awhile.

TELEVISION

Other Names Considered/Used: The Neon Boys

The Story: It sounded good to bassist Richard Hell. It stuck.

More Stuff: Tom Verlaine's real last name is Miller. He adopted Verlaine as a tribute to his favorite French poet. Richard Hell is actually Richard Meyers.

10,000 MANIACS

Other Names Considered/Used: Still Life.

The Story: It was a mistake. The actual name of the B-movie that inspired the name was *2,000 Maniacs*.

THE THE

Other Names Considered/Used: The center of the band has always been Matt Johnson. Before settling on The The, Matt used names like Roadstar (when he was 11) and the Marble Index (when he was 16).

The Story: The name is a statement. At time when every band picked a name that started with "The" (The Cars, The Shirts, The As, etc), Matt decided to take it to the extreme and call his band The The.

THEY MIGHT BE GIANTS

Other Names Considered/Used: Dumptruck

The Story: *They Might Be Giants* was the title of an obscure George C. Scott film from 1972. There's also a passage in Don Quixote that reads "they might be giants."

THOMPSON TWINS

Other Names Considered/Used: None.

The Story: Check the names of a couple of characters in the French comic strip *Tin Tin*.

THROBBING GRISTLE
Other Names Considered/Used: ?
The Story: The guys were looking for a name that would embarrass record store clerks.

TOAD THE WET SPROCKET
Other Names Considered/Used: None
The Story: Back in 1987, the group got a job as the house band at a place in Santa Barbara, California called the Shack. Once they got the gig, they realized that they needed a name. Looking to their heroes in Monty Python for inspiration, they adopted the name of a fictitious band mentioned in a skit called "Rock Notes" that appears on the *Contractual Obligation* album. Listen for the mention right at the beginning—and beware: Eric Idle speaks very quickly.

TOM TOM CLUB
Other Names Considered/Used: None.
The Story: "The Tom Tom Club" was the name of the band's rehearsal space.

TOO MUCH JOY
Other Names Considered/Used: None
The Story: In hopes of finding a name, all three members got high on mushrooms. When they came to, the only name any of them could remember was "Too Much Joy." It won by default.

UB40
Other Names Considered/Used: None.
The Story: If you want to go on the dole in England, you have to fill out form number UB-40. Since all the members of the band were unemployed squatters, the name was a perfect fit.

ULTRAVOX
Other Names Considered/Used: Tiger Lily, The Zips, London Soundtrack and Fire of London.
The Story: They wanted something glam and futuristic.
More Stuff: John Foxx was born Dennis Leigh. Bassist Chris Cross' real name is Chris St. John. And no one names their son "Midge." Midge Ure's proper first name is James.

UTAH SAINTS

Other Names Considered/Used: None
The Story: Watch for the reference to "Utah Saints" near the very end of the Coen brothers movie *Raising Arizona*, starring Nicolas Cage and Holly Hunter.

U2

Other Names Considered/Used: The Hype, Feedback
The Story: The guys had the nerve to consult an acquaintance who worked at an advertising agency.
More Stuff: Bono's real name is Paul Hewson. The Edge was born Dave Evans.

VELVET UNDERGROUND

Other Names Considered/Used: None
The Story: *The Velvet Underground* was the title of a trashy, pseudo-scientific book on S&M and wife-swapping in suburbia by Michael Leigh.
More stuff: Lou Reed's real name is Louis "Butch" Firbank. Nico's full name was Christine Paffgen.

VERUCA SALT

Other Names Considered/Used: None
The Story: Veruca Salt was the name of the spoiled brat in the book *Charlie and the Chocolate Factory* by Roald Dahl. Veruca also appeared in the 1971 movie version, which was entitled *Willy Wonka and the Chocolate Factory*, starring Gene Wilder.
More Stuff: Nina Gordon and Jim Shapiro are actually brother and sister. "Gordon" is their mother's maiden name.

VIOLENT FEMMES

Other Names Considered/Used: Nude Family Portrait, Hitler's Missing Teste, the Romboids.
The Story: There's nothing to report. Gordon Gano says he just blurted out the name one day and it stuck.

WALL OF VOODOO

Other Names Considered/Used: Three Little Pigs, Come On Inn
The Story: "Wall of Voodoo" was actually a take-off of legendary

producer Phil Spector's famous "wall of sound."

WANG CHUNG
Other Names Considered/Used: Huang Chung
The Story: According to leader Jack Hues, "wang" is the sound of a guitar being played on the downstroke; "chung" is the sound of the upstroke.

WEEZER
Other Names Considered/Used: None
The Story: "Weezer" used to be Rivers Cuomo's nickname when he was a kid.

WHITE ZOMBIE
Other Names Considered/Used: ?
The Story: All the members of the band are big fans of Z-grade horror films. Thus it should come as no surprise that *White Zombie* was an old monster movie from 1932 starring Bela Lugosi.

XTC
Other Names Considered/Used: Stiff Beach, Star Park, Skyscraper, The Helium Kidz, Fat Fruit, The Dukes of Stratosphere.
The Story: XTC was inspired by Jimmy Durante's search for the lost chord. When he found it, he exclaimed "Dat's it! I'm in ecstasy!"
More Stuff: Andy Partridge eventually used the Dukes of Stratosphere as the name of an XTC side project.

YO LA TENGO
Other Names Considered/Used: ?
The Story: It means "I have it" in Spanish.

Plus...
A Guy Called Gerald: Gerald Simpson
Adam Ant: Stuart Goddard
The Aphex Twin: Richard James
Stiv Bators (The Dead Boys): Stivin Bators
Beck: Beck Hansen
Bjork: Bjork Gudmundsdottir

← Brian Bell of Weezer

Black: Colin Vearnocombe
Buster Bloodvessel (Bad Manners): Douglas Trendle
Cheetah Chrome (The Dead Boys): Gene Connor
Dr. Robert (Blow Monkeys): Bruce Robert Howard
Thomas Dolby: Thomas Morgan Robertson
Enya: Enya Ni Bhraonain
Exene (X): Christine Cervenka
Nick Fiend (Alien Sex Fiend): Nick Wade
G. Love: Garrett Dutton
Robert Gotobed (Wire): Mark Field
PJ Harvey: Polly Jean Harvey
Lux Interior (The Cramps): Erick Lee Purkhiser
Jona Lewie: John Lewis
Lora Logic (X-Ray Spex): Susan Whitby
M: Robin Scott
Richey Manic: Richey James
Handsome Dick Manitoba (The Dictators): Richard Blum
Elton Motello: Alan Ward
The Normal: Daniel Miller

Gary Numan: Gary Anthony James Webb
Blackie Onassis (Urge Overkill): Johnny Rowan
Genesis P Orridge (Throbbing Gristle): Neil Megson
Poison Ivy Rorschach (The Cramps): Kirsty Marlana Wallace
Sonic Boom (Spaceman 3): Pete Kember
Steve Strange (Visage): Steve Harrington
Poly Styrene (X-Ray Spex): Marion Elliot
Tad (Tad): Tad Doyle
Toyah: Toyah Ann Wilcox
Butch Vig: Brian Vig
Dean Ween (Ween): Mickey Melchiondo
Gene Ween (Ween): Aaron Freeman
Jah Wobble: John Wardle
Wreckless Eric: Eric Goulden

Section 4

A Glossary of Musical Terms

A lternative music has its own language and sometimes it can get confusing. Here is a dictionary featuring some of the more common terms.

AAA Adult Album Alternative. It's a radio format aimed at the over-30 crowd who's not quite ready for Whitney Houston and Michael Bolton. AAA stations focus on the softer sort of alternative music. (i.e. Crash Test Dummies, Sarah McLachlan, etc.)

A&R A music industry term. It stands for Artists and Repertoire. These are the people entrusted with discovering and developing new talent.

ACTRA Association of Canadian Television and Radio Artists.

Advance The money a record label fronts a band in order that they may record an album and tour to support it. The label gets their money back by deducting it from any future profits the band may see.

AFM American Federation of Musicians.

AFTRA American Federation of Television and Radio Artists.

Ambient A calming and soothing form a background instrumental music originally devised by Brian Eno in the '70s. Ambient house and ambient dub are just two sub-genres. (i.e. The Orb)

Analog The old way of doing things. Analog recordings are made by converting sound to electrical impulses and then transferring those impulses to magnetic tape that's being drawn across a recording head.

Anarcho-Punk Non-compromising punk music that has nothing to do with the system or the establishment. (i.e. Crass, Chumbawamba)

AOR A radio industry term that describes a type of music format Album Oriented Rock. In Britain, many people take this to stand for Adult Oriented Rock.

Backwards Masking The practice of burying covert messages within a song by recording it backward and dropping it in the mix. Parents and religious groups like to freak out over things like this.

Bluebeat The ancestor of ska.

BMI Broadcast Music, Inc. They administer performing rights.

Body Surf The upper layer of a mosh pit. The aim of a body surfer is to be lifted up over the heads of the people in a mosh pit and stay that way for as long as possible.

BPM Beats Per Minute.

b/w Backed with. A-sides of singles are "backed with" a b-side.

CAPAC Composers, Artists and Publishers of Canada Ltd.

CARAS Canadian Academy of Record Arts and Sciences.

CHR Contemporary Hit Radio. What we used to called Top 40.

CIRPA Canadian Independent Record Producers Association.

Cold Wave A late '70s/early '80s spin-off of techno-pop and a pre-cursor to industrial music. Cold wave bands were into stark, passionless electronic music that occasionally had sci-fi trappings. (i.e. The Normal, Gary Numan)

Compact Disc The storage medium of the moment. It's a five inch piece of pitted plastic with an aluminum coating. A laser reads the binary information stored in the pits and converts that to electrical energy—which then ends up coming out your speakers. The CD was a co-invention of Sony and Philips.

Copyright Legal protection given to authors and composers of an original work.

CRIA Canadian Recording Industry Association.

Crusty A sub-species of anarcho-punk and the indie rock scene.

Crusties tend to be very communal and nomadic, spending most of their time following the summer concert circuit their vans and caravans. They tend to be very earthy and quite left-wing in their politics. (i.e. The Levellers)

Cuddlecore A form of poppy indie rock. (i.e. Cub)

Cyberpunk A sub-genre of electronic industrial music. (i.e. Front Line Assembly)

Death Metal A very intense and very form of heavy metal headquartered in Florida. (i.e. Deicide and (to a certain extent) Marilyn Manson)

Demo The first draft of a recording.

Demo Tape A tape (usually self-financed) used by a new act to attract the attention of a record company.

Diamond Record A Canadian recording industry award that says you've sold 1 million copies of your album or single.

Digital The new way of doing things. Information is transformed into binary code which is then stored on tape or on a computer hard drive.

Dream Pop Mellow, ethereal, artsy form of alternative pop based on the traditions of the Cocteau Twins and Kate Bush. The goal is to achieve a dreamy and blissful aural effect.

Electric Body Music The style of industrial music made by a variety of European bands, especially Front 242.

Engineer The guy who actually operates and manipulates the equipment in a recording studio. He follows the producer's instructions.

EP A CD or vinyl record that features more than two songs but fewer tracks than what you'd find on a full album.

EQ Equalizer.

Faders Individual volume controls on the mixing console in a recording studio or for a PA system. These controls are used to blend instruments and recorded tracks to achieve the overall desired sound.

Fairlight A digital sampler that made New Order and the Pet Shop Boys into what they are today. A Fairlight can sample, store, manipulate and reproduce any sound you care to feed it.

Farfisa Organ A really cheesy-sounding, '60s style keyboard that turned up a lot in early Elvis Costello recordings.

Flange See "phasing."

Garage Band A term from the early '60s used to describe the rough and raw sounds of all those pre-punk bands that spend their Saturdays rehearsing in the garage and drinking beer. (i.e. The Kingsmen)

Glam Rock A type of early '70s British rock that was very theatrical and often very campy. The wilder the stage costume, the better. Some glam acts became notorious for suggesting things like androgyny, homosexuality and bisexuality. (i.e. David Bowie's "Ziggy Stardust" period, T. Rex, the Sweet)

Glitter Rock Similar to glam rock but aimed at a younger, less sophisticated audience. (i.e. Gary Glitter)

Gold Record A recording industry award which certifies sales of a significant number of records. In the US, a gold record is awarded once you've sold 500,000 copies of an album or 1 million copies of a single. In the UK, it's 100,000 copies of an album or 400,000 copies of a single. In Canada, it's 50,000 copies of either.

Goth A gloomy, introspective form of theatrical post-punk music featuring trappings of the supernatural. (i.e. Sisters of Mercy, Christian Death, Sex Gang Children, Alien Sex Fiend)

Grebo High-powered, in-your-face thrash-pop from the UK that features a lot of the same attitudes as grunge with some added exuberance. (i.e. Pop Will Eat Itself, Ned's Atomic Dustbin)

Grindcore An intense form of heavy metal related to death metal. (i.e. Morbid Angel, Carcass)

Grunge A type of loud, chunky, American guitar-based music that originated from the state of Washington that incorporated influences of the traditional metal-tinged rock bands of the '70s with hardcore punk of the '80s. It is said that Mark Arm of Mudhoney was the first to describe this music as "grunge" c. 1987.

Hardcore Whenever you call *any* band or any type of music "hardcore," you're indicating that this is serious stuff—an example of the true essence of whatever you're talking about.

Hardcore Punk Balls-to-the-wall, no compromise punk music. (i.e. Black Flag, SNFU, Circle Jerks, the Minutemen)

Home Taping The thing that the record industry says is killing them.

Homocore A mainstream media term used to label hardcore punk bands with one or more openly homosexual members and who are pro-active in homosexual rights issues. (i.e. Extra Fancy, Fifth Column, Girl Jesus)

Indie This used to be the abbreviation for "independent record label," i.e. a company that wasn't associated with a major label. Now we also use the word to describe a type of non-mainstream music that finds favor among cult followings.

Industrial Music Throbbing Gristle once defined this music as "entertainment through pain." The term was coined by San Francisco artist Monte Cazazza who once said "industrial music for industrial people." After Throbbing Gristle named their record label Industrial Records and called their first album *Second Annual Report*, the term began to be used for all bands whose music is louder and heavier than what you'd find in a steel foundry. (i.e. Ministry, Test Department, KMFDM, Nine Inch Nails)

Licensing Permission to use and market a recording for a commission.

Major Label There aren't that many of them but they (and their subsidiaries) rule the world: Warner, BMG, Polydor, MCA, Sony.

Mastering The final step in the recording process. After all the editing, overdubbing and mixing, you end up with a "master tape" which is then sent off to the pressing plant where it is transferred to compact disc or vinyl.

Mechanical Royalty Money earned from the sales of recorded music.

MIDI Musical Instrument Digital Interface. It's a computerized system that allows keyboards, samplers and drum machines to talk to each other.

Monitors Those backwards-facing speakers you see on stage. They allow the singers and musicians hear themselves.

Mosh The frantic and intense dancing that you see right down front at certain high-energy concerts. People are packed in so tight that they spend the gig banging into each other. Some people squirt up above the crowd and "body surf" until they get to the stage or everyone gets tired of holding them up—whichever comes first.

Mosh Pit That pulsating, squirming area right in front of the stage where concertgoers *really* get to know each other.

Music Publisher The company a musician entrusts to collect income generated by their songs. The publisher also protects the musician against copyright infringement.

NAIRD National Association of Independent Record Producers.

NARAS National Academy of Recording Arts and Sciences.

NARM National Association of Record Merchandisers.

NAS National Academy of Songwriters.

NMPA National Music Publishers Association.

New Romantic An early '80s new wave spin-off that featured well-dressed pop groups playing keyboard-based music. (i.e. ABC, Spandau Ballet)

New Wave A marketing term invented by some label executive while trying to find some way to sell punk to the masses. Generally, new wave acts had the same sensibilities as punks but without the rough edges, rage or violence.

New Wave of New Wave A label invented by the British music press to describe a series of mid-'90s indie bands that were obviously influenced by the original post-punk new wave groups. (i.e. Elastica, Supergrass, Shed Seven, Menswear, Oasis)

No Wave A late '70s/early '80s art-punk movement based in New York City. (i.e. early Sonic Youth, Teenage Jesus and the Jerks)

Outboard Equipment All the gear that you use to add effects to your sound either in the studio or on stage.

Overdub Extra layers of vocals or instrumentation added to a song during the recording process.

Paisley Underground A short-lived American movement in the '80s that revived some of the psychedelic pop sounds of the '60s. (i.e. Dream Syndicate)

Phasing An effect similar to flanging which is created by adding a very short delay to an instrument. The result is a "whooshing" sound that can be controlled in terms of speed and intensity.

Performing Rights Organization A company that collects income from the public performances of a musician's songs. The company then distributes this money to everyone who has a piece of the song's copyright.

Platinum Record A recording industry award which certifies sales of

a significant number of records. In the US, a platinum record is awarded once you've sold a million albums or two million singles. In the UK,
a platinum award is worth 300,000 albums or 600,000 singles. In Canada, it's 100,000 of either.

Playlist The list of songs a radio station will play.

PMRC Parents Music Resource Center. Tipper Gore's bunch and those
responsible for warning labels on music.

Pogo A type of punk dance, allegedly invented by Sid Vicious. Since
many punk gigs were held in places with low stages or no stages at all,
the only way you could catch a glimpse of what was going on was to
jump up and down. Eventually, people started doing this in time to the
music and *voilà*, a new dance.

Pre-Production All the jamming, rehearsing, writing and arranging
that goes on before you book a recording studio.

PROCAN Performing Rights Association of Canada Ltd.

Producer The guy who oversees every aspect of a recording session.
He is responsible for everything from the sound of the song, to the performance of the material, to the attitude of the musicians.

Post-Punk Everything that's happened in alternative music since
1978.

PRS Performing Rights Society of England.

Pub Rock A type of pre-punk (early '70s) music played by bands in
UK pubs. It marked a return to raw, sweaty, feel-good music. (i.e.
Brinsley Schwarz, Dr. Feelgood)

Punk Originally, this was a term used to describe the leather-clad, ne'r-
do-well, James Dean wannbe American garage bands of the '60s (Examples: The Barbarians, The Seeds, ? and the Mysterions). The term made
a comeback in the mid-'70s after the Ramones showed up in their
leather jackets. From there, "punk" was applied to everything loud and

snotty in the 1976-78 explosion of back-to-basics rock/pop music.

Reggae A form of Jamaican music with strong, syncopated rhythms. (i.e. Bob Marley, Peter Tosh, UB40)

Remastering Making another master recording, hopefully improving on things in the process. Old analog recordings are remastered before being transferred to compact disc.

Remixing Going back to the master tape with the basic tracks and putting all back together in a different form with a variety of sound enhancements.

Retro-Nuevo Recycling old ideas and giving them a slightly modern twist. (i.e. Lenny Kravitz)

RIAA Recording Industry Association of America. They're in charge of awarding gold and platinum records.

Rockabilly A sort of modern hillbilly music that was all the rage in the early '80s. (i.e. The Stray Cats, The Shakin' Pyramids)

ROIR Reach Out International Records. Independent NYC label specializing in cassette releases founded in 1980 by Neil Cooper. (i.e. Suicide, Lydia Lunch and the Fleshtones)

Royalties The money a songwriter or musician gets from record sales.

Sampling Extracting a sound or segment of music for use in your own composition.

Sequencer A machine that can be programmed to play a series of notes when you tell it to. This is especially helpful when you need a cycle of notes to be played over and over again.

Shoegazer A foggy, droning, swirling type of guitar-based alternative rock from the UK. (i.e. My Bloody Valentine, Ride, Curve)

Silver Record A Canadian record industry award for selling 25,000 copies of either a single or an album. In Britain, you get a silver award for selling 60,000 albums or 200,000 singles.

Ska Basically, ska is a type of choppy, danceable music written in 4/4 time where the beat is emphasized on the second and fourth beats of the bar. Ska began as an early form of reggae in the '50s and '60s in Jamaica before being exported to England where it enjoyed a huge resurgence centered around the 2 Tone movement in Coventry. Examples of early ska include Desmond Dekker and Prince Buster. Modern ska bands include the Specials and the English Beat.

Skatecore Punk music to ride your skateboard to. (i.e. early Suicidal Tendencies)

Speed Metal Really fast heavy metal. (i.e. Slayer)

Surfcore Similar to skatecore but at the beach. (i.e. Surf Punks)

Techno A type of high-energy electronic dance music with roots in Detroit. Originally called "brutal house." (i.e. Prodigy, the Aphex Twin)

Thrash Punk-influenced speed metal.

Part 2

LISTS & STUFF

10 Classic Alternative Albums

Every genre of music has its foundations. To help appreciate how we got to where we are today, here are the ten albums that should be included in every comprehensive alternative music collection.

1. *The Velvet Underground and Nico*— The Velvet Underground (Verve/Polygram, released March 1967)

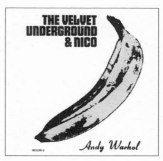

Here is a record that was very ahead of its time (including the innovative Andy Warhol "peel the banana" album cover). While most of the world was still recovering from the British Invasion, Lou Reed, John Cale, Sterling Morrison and Maureen Tucker were taking music in a totally different direction. Although most everyone dismissed the Velvets' music as too weird and a bunch of noise, they were actually laying the foundations for what would become known as alternative music. All Velvet Underground albums were commercial disasters the first time around. Now they're considered to be among the most important records ever made. Also recommended is *White Light/White Heat* from 1968.

2. *Trout Mask Replica*—Captain Beefheart and His Magic Band (Reprise, released May 1969)

If you want to clear out a room fast, put on this album. It is, admittedly, one of the most disagreeable records ever recorded and is certainly difficult to listen to. However, it has become somewhat of a cultural landmark. The abrasive nature of *Trout Mask Replica* was big with people who were into disagreeable things. In many cases, these were people who bought and played the album precisely because they knew it annoyed other people. For example, Johnny Lydon wore out several copies of the album as he was growing up. Joe Strummer was also a dedicated Beefheart fan. As a result, elements of Captain Beefheart's musical vision were instrumental in laying the foundations for the attitudes which resulted in the punk revolution of the mid-'70s.

3. *The Rise and Fall of Ziggy Stardust and the Spiders from Mars*—David Bowie (Rykodisc, released June 1972)

As of 1972, David Bowie had been making records since 1964 with only occasional commercial success. But this album turned out to be the one that established him as a worldwide superstar. Bowie introduced everyone to Ziggy Stardust, the doomed, space-aged alien rock star—part science fiction and part *A Clockwork Orange*—the first pre-packaged rock persona. According to Bowie, a portion of the character was based on the life of an obscure American singer named Vince Taylor. The "Stardust" part was inspired by another singer on Bowie's label, The Legendary Stardust Cowboy. Ziggy added a sense of theater that had never before been seen in rock music. Ziggy's fatalism and sense of style ended up having a tremendous effect on the kids that would form the foundation of the British punk movement a few years later. Since Ziggy first appeared, books and Ph.D. dissertations have been written on him and psychologists, sociologists and serious musical scholars have pronounced Ziggy to be the most profound invention in the history of rock music.

4. *The Ramones*—The Ramones (Sire, released April 1976)

Recorded between February 2 and February 17, 1976, for a total cost of $6,400, The Ramones documented most of what the band had been doing at CBGBs since they made their debut in August 1974. Using *Meet the Beatles* as a model, they did two takes of each song and at one point burned off seven in a row. The master tapes were recorded so loud that when it came to press the album, the cutter head on the machine blew apart. At first, almost every self-respecting rock fan hated the record. Here was a band that didn't believe in ballads, guitar solos, drum solos or songs much longer than two minutes—in short, the Ramones were the exact opposite to what was happening in American rock 'n' roll in the mid-'70s. The album served as a wake-up call, a demand that rock go back to its roots and start over. Those who answered the call helped The Ramones kick off the entire punk revolution. *The Ramones* was so different and so fresh that wherever the album went, new bands would pop up. The Sex Pistols copied the way the Ramones held their guitars. The early Clash used to have a jukebox filled with Ramones singles. Everyone from the Cult, Nirvana and Sonic Youth to Metallica, Guns N' Roses and Def Leppard will tell you that if it weren't for The Ramones, they wouldn't be around. To put it another way, what Johnny Appleseed was to apple trees, *The Ramones* was to alternative music.

5. *Talking Heads 77*—Talking Heads (Sire, released September 1977)

The Talking Heads were the band that inject-ed some art school sensibilities into the CBGBs scene in the mid- and late-'70s. They were different from most of the groups that played in the Bowery. First of all, the guy at the center of it all wasn't some leather-clad punk—it was a geeky, twitchy, high-strung guy named David Byrne. And while they were still into individual self-expression and all that other punk stuff, their shows came off more like presentations by conceptualist performance artists. It was this innova-tive approach to pop music (beginning with this 1977 debut album) that influenced a lot of new wave groups for years to come.

6. *Never Mind the Bollocks–Here's The Sex Pistols*—The Sex Pistols (Warner Bros., released November 1977)

The Sex Pistols only managed to release one official album—but it has gone down in his-tory as the most famous album of the origi-nal British punk era. *Never Mind the Bollocks* was perhaps the most exciting album of the '70s, and it forever changed the course of music. The Pistols went through three record companies (EMI, A&M and Virgin) and thousands of pounds in advances (more than £100,000, according to some reports) on the way to releasing the album. *Never Mind the Bollocks* documented that special freedom of spirit that had been missing from rock for so long. A lot of the credit for the album's power has to go to producer Chris Thomas who created Steve Jones'

amazing guitar sound by overdubbing the guitar lines a total of twenty-one times. It took about ten years for *Never Mind the Bollocks* to be declared a gold album in America (which means it sold about 50,000 copies a year between 1977 and 1987)—but for some reason, it sold twice as fast (100,000 copies per year) from 1987 to 1992.

7. *This Year's Model*—Elvis Costello (Columbia, released February 1978)

Declan McManus was a full-time computer operator for Elizabeth Arden cosmetics and a part-time musician. But the morning after seeing the Sex Pistols on Bill Grundy's *Today* program on December 1, 1976, he decided to get involved in the burgeoning punk rock scene. Changing his name to Elvis Costello, he released *My Aim is True* in 1977 and established himself as punk's premier singer-songwriter and Angry Young Man. *This Year's Model* was a remarkable follow-up made even more powerful by his new backing band, The Attractions. The album is tight, nasty and features two of his best singles, "Pump It Up" and "Radio Radio."

8. *Unknown Pleasures*—Joy Division (Qwest, released May 1979)

The summer of 1978 was particularly miserable in Manchester. Unemployment was high, the weather was hot and the city's ancient sewer system was crumbling so there was that constant *smell* hanging in the air. This was the backdrop for the debut of Joy Division. The members weren't particularly good musicians and the singer didn't always manage to stay in key—but their music was very different from all the punk stuff that was making the rounds. It has this unique dark quality and when the band played live, they performed mostly in shadows. They didn't look much like punks, either, preferring to appear on-stage in ordinary black, grey and dark green street clothes. Producer Martin Hannet captured this bleak, desperate mood perfectly with *Unknown Pleasures*. The bass and drums were treated as lead instruments while guitars and keyboards were used mainly as accents. The result was cold, dark, and full of genuine anguish. Meanwhile the design team at Factory Records created a package that was unlike anything ever seen before. *Unknown Pleasures* came in a black album jacket with nothing more than a drawing of a radio pulse in the front. On the back, in white letters, the band's name, the album title and the label's name. On the inside, there were hardly any liner notes and on the record itself, no track listings. *Unknown Pleasures* became the blueprint for all post-punk minor-key angst.

9. *The B-52's*—The B-52's
(Warner Bros., released July 1979)

It was fun, campy and silly but someone had to do it. The B-52's showed everyone that punk didn't have to be serious and angry all the time. The goofy nature of *The B-52's* provided a big boost to new wave just when it seemed in danger of bottoming out in 1979. The subsequent success of the album showed others from Athens, Georgia, that it was possible to make it big, which provided a lot of encouragement for another group that hung around the University of Georgia that was just starting out— R.E.M.

10. *London Calling*—The Clash
(Epic, released December 1979)

Rolling Stone magazine named this one the best album of the '80s—and with good reason. Originally released on vinyl as a double album, *London Calling* was the band's masterpiece, not only establishing them as major-league contenders commercially, but also showing the world that punk could be a driving force in mainstream music. The entire album bears the Clash's unique approach to music and never wavers from their musical manifesto. It also features the mystery track "Train in Vain," which ended up as the band's first Top 40 hit in North America.

10 More Essential Alternative Albums

1. *The Pretenders*—The Pretenders
(Sire, released January 1980)

Chrissie Hynde spent a good part of the '70s knocking around London, trying to get a music gig. After several false starts (including a job as a clerk in Malcolm McLaren's clothing store, a music critic, and answering phones at an architectural firm), she formed The Pretenders, After several terrific singles (including the Kinks' "Stop Your Sobbing"), the Pretenders lived up to their potential by releasing an album that provided a vital bridge between punk, new wave and mainstream pop. It also established Chrissie as one of post-punk's best songwriters.

2. *The Smiths*—The Smiths
(Sire, released February 1984)

In 1984, British music was awash with synthesizers and pop bands like Duran Duran. Enter the Smiths with Morrissey's poignant lyrics and Johnny Marr's tasteful guitar playing. The Smiths were so different from what everyone else was doing that it was impossible not to notice. Over the next few years, the Smiths became one of the most influential bands in the history of British music. Their effect is still evident years after they broke up.

3. *Staring at the Sea*—The Cure
(Elektra, released 1986)

This is a collection of The Cure's best-known singles from the early and mid-'80s. The CD version follows the order of the *Staring at the Sea* video collection. It is, however, worth trying to track down the cassette (known as *Standing on a Beach*) because it adds a dozen B-sides.

4. *Substance*—New Order
(Qwest, released 1987)

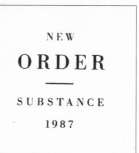

New Order's greatest contributions to alternative music often came in the form of 12" remixes. *Substance* (not to be confused with the Joy Division collection of the same name) contains full-length versions of New Order's biggest remixes up to 1987, including "Blue Monday," "Bizarre Love Triangle," and "Perfect Kiss." Take note that the version of "Temptation" is not the original remix, but it is the best-known version. This is also one of the few releases that were made available to consumers on DAT.

5. *The Stone Roses*—The Stone Roses
(Silvertone/RCA, released May 1989)

Nothing says "Manchester" like this brilliant debut album. It must have been brilliant— why else would their fans wait six years for the second one? And here's an interesting bit of trivia: While the album sold like crazy in the UK and turned the band into major stars, it barely caused a ripple in America. Best estimates say that it sold 250,000 copies.

6. *Pretty Hate Machine*—Nine Inch Nails
(TVT, released 1989)

What the Beatles and Elvis were to rock and pop, Trent Reznor was to industrial music, taking it to the masses to an extent that few people believed possible. *Pretty Hate Machine* took musical angst to a new level and immediately established Trent as not only a great lyricist and composer but as a studio whiz. At the time he recorded this album, Trent was working two jobs: as a salesperson at a Cleveland music shop called Pi Keyboards and as an engineer's assistant at a recording studio called The Right Track. After everyone went home for the day, Trent would spend most of the night experimenting with new keyboards and outboard gear in the studio. Those nights evolved into an album that was picked up by TVT Records (aka Tee-Vee Tunes, a label specializing in re-releasing old TV theme songs). Although the label hated the record and eventual forced Trent into taking legal action, it became one of the biggest-selling industrial record to date and helped set the stage for the revolution in alternative music in the '90s.

7. *Violator*—Depeche Mode
(Sire, released March 1990)

Although Depeche Mode was wildly popular in Britain and parts of Canada from the start, it took until the late-'80s for them to build up a significant fan base in America. *Violator* was their first platinum album in the US and their second gold record (the first was *Music for the Masses*). When the band showed up to do an autograph session at a record store in Los Angeles, thousands of fans were involved in a riot. The success of *Violator* was another early indication that alternative music was about to break big.

8. *Nevermind*—Nirvana
(DGC, released September 1991)

This is the album that changed everything. Recorded with producer Butch Vig for $130,000, the album has so far generated more than $50 million in gross revenues. Sales estimates vary, but it's safe to say that *Nevermind* has sold at least 8 million copies. Nirvana proved to be so successful that the music industry began to shift much of its attention from mainstream and classic rock artists to the so-called "alternative" scene.

9. *Out of Time*—R.E.M.
(Warner Bros., released September 1991)

After years of releasing quality material, *Out of Time* was the album that finally made R.E.M. a household word. Videos such as "Losing My Religion" not only became MTV staples but set new standards for the medium.

10. *Ten*—**Pearl Jam**
(Epic, released September 1991)
When *Ten* was recorded in March and April
1991, the band was known as Mookie Blaylock, their favorite NBA player (then on the
New Jersey Nets. By the way, Mookie's uniform number was 10, hence the title of the
album). "Alive" was the first single, but was
pre-released as part of a Coca-Cola music

promotion. At first, the album was lost in the swirl of Nirvana hype.
However, word of mouth on the band was so strong that sales began to
pick up quickly, especially after a long tour in early 1992 that stretched
into a stint on that summer's Lollapalooza tour. Eventually, *Ten* would
outsell *Nevermind*.

20 Mystery Tracks

Have you ever been listening to a CD only to find that there was more
to the disc than the liner notes indicated?

A compact disc can safely hold between 75 and 79 minutes worth of
music. Since most single albums aren't this long, some artists have tried
to make creative use of that extra space on the disc by adding little sur-
prises at the end.

Here are some examples of unlisted and uncredited songs that may
appear in your record collection:

1. *Another Music in a Different Kitchen*—**The Buzzcocks (1978)**
Listen for a semi-reprise of "Boredom."

2. *London Calling*—**The Clash (1979)**
When the Clash released *London Calling*, the liner notes listed 18
songs—but if you counted up all the tracks on the vinyl itself, you
found that there were actually 19. The final track was entitled "Train in
Vain" and was never listed on any version of *London Calling* because
the Clash decided to include the song at the last minute after all the artwork for the sleeve had been completed. When the album was transferred to CD, the original liner notes were kept intact and "Train in
Vain" remained unlisted.

3. *Life's Rich Pageant*—R.E.M. (1986)

R.E.M. decided to include two more songs after the artwork for the album had been completed. To make things even more confusing, the track listings on the CD don't match up with the actual running order of the songs. For example, a version of *Life's Rich Pageant* might list "Fall on Me" as track 9—but it actually comes up on track 3.

Here's what's going on. The first extra song is found on track 6. It is mostly instrumental and goes by the name "Underneath the Bunker." According to R.E.M. fans who know, it was written as a sort of a tribute to Camper Van Beethoven, a wonderfully quirky band from the San Francisco area. Track 12 is "(I Am) Superman," which was the B-side of a 1969 single by a Texas band called Clique. Peter Buck discovered the song while he was working at an Athens record store. R.E.M. started by using the song as a warm-up in rehearsals—but they liked playing it so much that they figured it should be on the album. (By the way, that sound at the beginning is a talking Godzilla doll that the band picked up during a tour of Japan.) The song marks the first time Mike Mills took a shot at lead vocals.

4. *Green*—R.E.M. (1988)

The band dropped another little surprise on this album but neglected to give it a title. Song number 11 is not listed in the liner notes—but if you look at the CD itself, you'll see that there's space for a track 11 but with no title. R.E.M. has never had a name for the song. Officially, they call it "Untitled," although when the song turned up as the B-side to the 12" of "Stand," it was listed as "The Eleventh Untitled Song."

5. *This Is The Hour...This Is The Hour...This Is This*—Pop Will Eat Itself (1989)

Track 15 is an amazing extended remix of "Wise Up! Sucker!" by Youth.

6. *Nevermind*—Nirvana (1992)

The original release of *Nevermind* featured an even dozen songs. However, subsequent editions featured a six-minute track entitled "Endless, Nameless" which roars out of the silence some 10 minutes and 3 seconds after the end of "Something in the Way." At the 19:32 mark, you can hear Cobain smashing his guitar. By the way, Weird Al Yankovic makes fun of "Endless, Nameless" on his *Off the Deep End* album. It's unlisted, naturally.

7. *Broken* EP—Nine Inch Nails (1992)

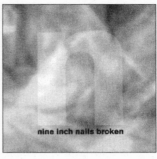

This CD came out in at least four versions. All contained the six songs listed on the cover but three of them came with two unlisted bonus tracks. The first edition featured the songs on a separate 3" CD included with the original 5". The second edition featured the bonus songs on tracks 98 and 99 while the third version of *Broken* put the two songs at tracks 6 and 7. No matter what version you have, the songs are the same: "Suck" (an old Pigface song) and "Physical" (originally done by Adam Ant).

8. *Gish*—Smashing Pumpkins (1992)

About 30 seconds after "Daydream," you'll hear a quick one minute song that doesn't seem to have a title.

9. *Dear Dear*—54-40 (1992)

Listen for the musical interlude at the end of track 11. The official title of the song is "Social Work" and was inspired by the fact that singer Neil Osborne's wife is a social worker.

10. *Kerosene Hat*—Cracker (1993)

When you put this CD in your machine, it tells you that there are 99 songs on the disc. Tracks 1-12 are obvious but then tracks 13 and 14 are blank. There's music on track 15 ("Hi-Desert Biker Meth Lab") but once it's over, the tracks keep clicking by at the rate of one every three seconds. All of them are blank until you come to track 69, which is the full eight-minute version of "Eurotrash Girl." There is also an unlisted song on track 88 that runs a little over six minutes and then there's an informal studio jam on track 99.

11. *Saturation*—Urge Overkill (1993)

Most editions of the album feature 8 minutes of messing around long after (20 minutes?) the final track fades out.

12. *No Alternative*—Various Artists (1993)

The liner notes list 18 songs, yet the track counter on the CD player says there are 19. When you skip ahead, it takes you all of three seconds to realize that the mystery song is from Nirvana. They contributed "Verse Chorus Verse" to the project on the condition that it not be listed in the liner notes because Kurt Cobain felt that the hype surrounding a new Nirvana song would almost certainly overshadow the work of the other groups on the CD.

13. *Fumbling Towards Ecstasy*—Sarah McLachlan (1993)

On most versions of the CD, there's a lovely acoustic version of "Possession" about 20 seconds after track 12 fades out.

14. *Very*—Pet Shop Boys (1993)

Look for an untitled track right after "Go West."

15. *Bang!*—World Party (1993)

A very limited number of *Bang!* CDs came with a song entitled "Kuwait City" that showed up 27 minutes after the final song faded out.

16. *Scream in Blue Live*—Midnight Oil (1993)

There's an acoustic version of a song called "Bernie" that pops up after the crowd fades out. The song originally appear on the band's 1981 album, *Places Without a Postcard*.

17. *Purple*—Stone Temple Pilots (1994)

Although the liner notes list 11 songs, there's also a picture of a cake decorated with icing that says "12 Gracious Melodies." Skip to the end of track 11 and let 33 seconds go by. That's when you'll hear "The Second Album," a song originally recorded and written by Richard Peterson. Richard is a disabled and rather eccentric street musician from Seattle whose record fell into the hands of the Pilots. They started to play the song over the PA once the lights went up at the end of their gigs—and when it came time to record their second album, it only made sense that they include Richard's song. He was paid a lump sum by the band and also gets royalties from every copy of *Purple* sold.

18. *Smash*—Offspring (1994)
The band says good-bye with a message that starts with about 7:46 remaining on the disc. That's followed by an instrumental that runs about a minute. If you let it run, you should find a mellow sitar version of "Come Out and Play" with about 1:30 left on the counter.

19. *Second Coming*—The Stone Roses (1994)
Track 90 is a song entitled "The Fox." It features the band messing around with some instruments they found in a Welsh pub.

20. *The Rembrandts LP*—The Rembrandts (1995)
Track 15 is unlisted. It's the band doing "I'll Be There For You," the theme from the NBC hit show, "Friends."

Other albums to investigate: *Experimental Jet Set, Trash and No-Star* (Sonic Youth), *Sleeping Bootie* (Bootsauce), *Aurora* (Crash Vegas), *Throwing Copper* (Live), *F-Punk* (Big Audio Dynamite).

3 Examples Of Mystery Audio
Not all buried treasure on CDs are proper songs. There are many cases where artists drop in something really strange and leave it to the listener to figure out what the hell is going on.

1. *Undertow*—Tool (1993)
"Disgustipated" is listed as track 10—but it actually comes up on track 69. The composition runs almost 16 minutes, including some 6 minutes of night-time sounds. With 1:52 left, a narrator comes on. The effect is chilling.

2. *Come On, Feel the Lemonheads*—Lemonheads (1993)
Scan through the last part of the disc and you'll uncover all sorts of weird studio noise.

3. *Beer Can and More* EP—Beck (1994)
About 23 seconds after "Spanking Room" (track 5), you hear a very rough, very experimental jam. Is this an early demo of "Loser"?

Several CDs That Contain More Than Just Music

In the era of the multimedia CD-ROM, it's not unusual for to find a disc that contains everything from audio and full-motion video to still pictures and interactive interfaces. However, some artists were incorporating non-audio information on their CDs long before the CD-ROM became chic. Here are several examples.

1. *Naked*—Talking Heads (1988)
When David Byrne was with the Talking Heads, he was determined that the band always be ahead of their time. But there was one occasion where the band was too far ahead. When *Naked* was released in 1988, it was encoded with a "graphics-ready" interface. This meant that if you were to buy a CD player with a special decoder, you could watch the lyrics pass by in real time on your television. You could also watch of a list of which instruments were playing and went. Unfortunately, these CDs players were not available in 1988 and few people make use of this feature. And since technological standards have changed so much over the years, today there might not be a piece of consumer electronics that can properly decode this part of the Talking Heads disc.

2. *The Breathtaking Blue*—Alphaville (1989)
The German band included a selection of clip art on a track of the CD.

3. *Sound + Vision*—David Bowie (1989)
There's some CD video available on one of the discs that came with the original release of this collection. A CD-ROM track has since replaced it.

4. *Dollars and Sex*—The Escape Club (1991)
The band encoded a fax transmission on the final track of this album. If you managed to decode it, you'll get a printed story about a roadtrip through Brazil.

8 Bands Who Recorded Cheap

1. *The Ramones*—The Ramones (1976)
The Ramones are one of the stingiest bands in the world when it comes to spending money on recording sessions. Their first album was recorded in 17 days and cost $6,400. That included $125 for the artwork.

2. *Spiral Scratch*—The Buzzcocks (1977)

Knowing that most major record companies weren't going to touch their stuff, the Buzzcocks became one of the first punk bands to form their own label. *Spiral Scratch* appeared on their New Hormones label in January 1977. Total cost for the recording, manufacturing and formation of the label: $1,000.

3. "Money"—The Flying Lizards (1978)
David Cunningham loved novelty songs. In 1978, he and Deborah Evans recorded a cover of "Money" using an upright piano filled with rubber toys, sheet music, cassettes and a telephone directories which gave it a peculiar muted sound. A few pots and pans served as percussion instruments. The whole thing was committed to tape on David's porta-studio. The result was a worldwide smash single. Total cost: $14.

4. "Rock Lobster"—The B-52's (1979)
The original version of "Rock Lobster" (the one that help land them a major record deal) was funded by a fan who had a big crush on Kate Pierson. Danny Beard ran a used record shop in Athens, Georgia, called Wax 'n' Facts and was one of the band's first big fans. After one particularly good show, Danny offered to cover the costs of recording a single. The cost to record and release 2,000 copies of that first version of "Rock Lobster" was $1,500. The re-recording that appeared on the band's major label debut helped the album go platinum.

5. *Garlands*—The Cocteau Twins (1982)
4AD was a struggling indie label and couldn't afford to advance their acts a lot of money to make records. No problem. The Cocteaus burned through *Garlands* in nine days and spent about $2,000.

6. "Upside Down"—The Jesus and Mary Chain (1984)

The Chain's first single not only launched their career but helped establish Creation Records as one of the coolest indie labels in Britain. Some of the costs were covered by Creation boss, Alan McGee. The rest of the money came from William Reid (courtesy his job at the cheese-packing plant) and Jim Reid (thanks to his job with Rolls-Royce). "Upside Down" eventually sold 35,000 copies and both the band and the label were on their way. Total cost: $350.

7. *The Trinity Session*—Cowboy Junkies (1988)

On November 27, 1987, the Cowboy Junkies held a one day recording session at the Church of the Holy Trinity in downtown Toronto, a place they chose on the basis of its interesting acoustics. To keep things as simple as possible, everything was recorded using one digital tape deck and one overhead microphone. The group ran through a bunch of songs over about nine hours and then called it a day.

When the resulting album came out, its popularity built slowly. Eventually, *The Trinity Session* climbed onto the album charts and stayed their for 29 weeks. "Sweet Jane" (the single) landed the Cowboy Junkies on MTV and "Saturday Night Live"—plus it took them on an 18-month world tour. By the end of 1989, the album had sold well over a million copies. Not bad for a record that cost a grand total of $162 to make.

8. *Bleach*—Nirvana (1989)

Bleach took three sessions and 30 hours beginning on Christmas Eve, 1988. When the bill came in, none of the members had any money to pay it. That's when their friend Jason Overman fronted them the cash. He had spent a lot of time up in Alaska as a commercial fisherman and had a little extra in the bank. As a result, Jason is credited with playing guitar on the album. In fact, he didn't play a note—but he did pay for the record.

For the longest time, it seemed like a bad investment. But when *Nevermind* broke big, *Bleach* also took off, eventually selling more than a million copies and bringing in millions of dollars in revenue for Sub Pop. Total cost to record: $606.17. (By way of comparison, *Nevermind* cost $130,000—but it's generated more than $50 million in revenue!)

11 Cases of Censorship

1. Boys Shouldn't Wear Dresses (1971)

The sight of David Bowie wearing a long, flowing blue dress on the cover of *The Man Who Sold the World* was just too much for most record stores. They refused to stock the album until the cover was changed.

2. The Sex Pistols Offend Monarchists (1977)

Because it came out during the Queen's Silver Jubilee, the BBC refused to play "God Save the Queen" and most British record stores refused to stock it. Still, the song sold well enough to make it into the Top 20 on the singles charts—except that even the charts wouldn't list the song. A blank space appeared at the position where the song was.

3. The Sex Pistols Break an Ancient Law (1977)

A policewoman took offense the word "bollocks" when she saw a window display for the album *Never Mind the Bollocks*. Invoking the Indecent Advertisements Act from 1889, the store owner was arrested and charged. The whole thing was later thrown out of court.

4. The Smiths and the Moors Murders (1984)

"Suffer Little Children" (the B-side of "Heaven Knows I'm Miserable Now") is based on the infamous Moors Murders in Manchester back in the mid-'60s. Morrissey was fascinated by the case and wrote the song to mourn the victims. But one evening, a relative of one of the murdered children heard the song on the jukebox at a local pub. Outraged by what he felt was insensitive exploitation, he went to the local newspaper which ran the story on the front page.

Large chain stores began banning the single and The Smiths' debut album. Parents of the murdered children accused The Smiths of sensationalism and opening old wounds. Morrissey took all these accusations quite seriously and spent a considerable amount of time writing and talking to the parents, assuring them that his intentions were honorable and that the song was intended as a memorial to the children. Eventually, the controversy died down—especially after The Smiths agreed to donate some of the royalties from the song to charity.

5. How a Ban on "Relax" Made Frankie Rich (1984)

According to Holly Johnson, it all began when the producer of a BBC radio program came home to find his children watching the "Relax" video over and over. Outraged by the song's homo-erotic overtones, he took his complaint to Mike Reed, a BBC Radio 1 DJ. Mike agreed that the song was offensive and he began a one-man campaign to get the song banned. His efforts were successful—but the single still sold 2 million copies in five weeks and Frankie Goes to Hollywood went on to become one of the biggest groups of the year.

6. The *Frankenchrist* Trial (1986-87)

In April 1986, Jello Biafra, along with other members of the Dead Kennedys, their record label, and their associates were charged with "trafficking in harmful" matter. The charges related to a poster titled "Landscape No. XX" by H.R. Giger that was included with the DK's *Frankenchrist* album. (H.R. Giger is a Swiss surrealist artist who, among other things, designed the monster for the movie *Alien*). Determined the fight the charges, the band took the SFPD to court and after months of testimony and thousands of dollars, the jury was deadlocked at 7-5 in favor of acquittal. The judge dismissed a motion for a retrial and the case was dropped.

7. The "Dear God" Threats (1987)

Many people considered "Dear God" by XTC to be blasphemous and complained to radio stations whenever they heard it. One Florida radio station received a series of bomb threats and in Binghampton, New York, a high school student took a secretary hostage in the principal's office and demanded that "Dear God" be played over the school's PA system. Heat like this caused many radio stations to drop the song from their playlists.

8. The Replacements Get the Boot (1987)

MTV refused to air the video for "The Ledge" saying that it will encourage kids to commit suicide.

9. Morrissey Speaks to the Dead (1989)

Morrissey's "Ouija Board, Ouija Board" single was banned by the BBC because it allegedly promoted the occult.

10. Jane's Addiction Recalls the First Amendment (1990)

The original cover of *Ritual de lo Habitual* album featured a stylistic painting of three nude people: one man and two women. But because there was a hint of genitalia, many of the big record stores refused to carry the record. The outcry was so strong that the album was recalled and reissued with a plain white cover. The only thing it featured was the band's name, the title of the album and, in very small type at the bottom, the text of the First Amendment of the US Constitution—the one dealing with free speech.

12. Adam's Naughty Bits (1992)

The montage of pictures that made up the cover of U2's *Achtung Baby* had to be modified when it was discovered that one pictured featured a full frontal nude shot of bassist Adam Clayton.

11. Kurt Cobain's Sense of Art Questioned (1993)

The fetus-and-mother themes of the artwork of *In Utero* got Kurt Cobain into a lot of trouble. Many stores (including the giant Wal-Mart chain and K-mart) refused to stock it. They also weren't crazy about the song "Rape Me."

10 Places to Visit on Your Vacation

1. CBGBs, 315 Bowery, New York, NY

The place where many people say punk was born still exists, although for such a famous site, it sure is scuzzy. It's a long, narrow room with a tiny stage and some horrendous bathrooms. The walls seem held together by a quarter century of posters for long-forgotten gigs and the floor probably hasn't had a good scrub in decades. But still, it's a mecca for alternative music fans and a bit of living history.

2. The Chelsea Hotel, 222 West 23rd Street, New York, NY

The Chelsea has always been a hangout for strange and wonderful people. Bob Dylan lived here for a while and so did Joni Mitchell (who was inspired to write the song "Chelsea Morning"). Janis Joplin had a quickie affair with Leonard Cohen at the Chelsea, which inspired

Leonard to write "Chelsea Hotel." Members of the Velvet Underground used to visit poet Delmore Schwartz, who was a long-time resident. If you choose to stay at the hotel, see if you can book Room 101; that's where Sid Vicious allegedly murdered his girlfriend Nancy Spungen on October 13, 1979.

3. R.E.M. World Headquarters, 250-252 West Clayton, Athens, GA
This is a great old house, built sometime around 1890. This is where you'll find R.E.M.'s management offices, their official fanclub, a rehearsal space and a recording studio. Next door at 256 Clayton is the 40 Watt Club, which is a good place to spot members of the band. Wuxtry Records (where Peter Buck met Michael Stipe) is down the street on the corner of College. If you get hungry, there's always Guaranteed, the vegetarian owned eatery (and occasionally patronized by Michael Stipe) located at 167 East Broad St. A little further down, at 1016 East Broad St., is Weever D's, the restaurant whose motto is "Automatic for the People," which was used as the title for the band's 1992 album. Finally, the old church where R.E.M. played their first gig in April 1980 used to be at 394 Oconee Street.

4. The Soundgarden, 7600 Sand Point Way, Seattle, WA
This is where you'll find a giant environmental metal sculpture that makes a sound when the wind whistles by—and yes, this is where the group got their name.

5. The Cobains, 171 Lake Washington Boulevard East, Seattle, WA
The latest address of Courtney Love and the last of Kurt Cobain. If you look carefully through the trees, you can see the apartment above the garage.

6. The Gilman Street Theatre, 924 Gilman Street, San Francisco, CA
Behind the wicker shop is the punk club that gave birth to Green Day, Rancid, and many other punk bands.

7. Pig West Studios, 10050 Cielo Drive, Beverly Hills, CA
Sharon Tate and her guests were murdered here by the Manson Family. In 1993, the house was rented out to Trent Reznor who recorded most of *The Downward Spiral* here, which he dubbed Pig West Studios. The house was destroyed in an earthquake in January 1994.

8. Sex, 430 The King's Road, London, England
This was the site of Malcolm McLaren's shop. Johnny Lydon auditioned for the Sex Pistols in the front room by singing along to Alice Cooper's "I'm Eighteen," which was playing on the jukebox.

9. The Hacienda, Manchester, England
This is the club co-owned by the members of New Order.

10. Morrissey's Boyhood Homes, 384 King's Road, Stretford, Manchester, England
Morrissey lived at 17 Harper Street until he was five. That's when the family moved to this address.

15 Crimes and Misdemeanors

1. The Clash with the Law
The Clash were forever getting into trouble with the authorities. The first real incident happened on June 10, 1977, when Joe Strummer and Topper Headon appeared in court on charges of spraying "Clash" graffiti on a wall somewhere in London. They were fined £5. The very next night, they were thrown in jail in Newcastle on robbery charges, accused of stealing a pillowcase from a Holiday Inn. And that's not all. In March 1978, Topper and bassist Paul Simonon were arrested in London on charges of criminal damage. They had been hunting racing pigeons with air rifles. The fine this time was £800. In July, Joe and Paul were taken into custody for being drunk and disorderly following a show in Glasgow. And then on July 21, Joe nailed a fan with his guitar during a particularly violent show in Hamburg, Germany. He was arrested for assault and then released once it was proven that he acted in self-defense.

2. Johnny Meets Some Monarchists
On June 18, 1977, Johnny Lydon, producer Chris Thomas, and engineer Bill Price stopped by a local pub in North London for a few pints. When they left, they were jumped by a dozen thugs armed with razors and knives. Johnny, Chris and Bill managed to escape by locking themselves in a car but not before Johnny took a stiletto through his left hand. He would have been wounded even more had his thick leather pants not stopped another knife slash. The next night, drummer Paul

Cook was attacked by five guys with knives and an iron bar. He got banged up pretty good, but fortunately, none of his injuries were life-threatening. Why were the Sex Pistols being hunted? Not everyone was pleased with the sentiments of the new Pistols single which was released during the Queen's Silver Jubilee, "God Save the Queen."

3. UB40

In the beginning, all the guys in the band were dirt poor. They grew up in Balsall Heath, a particularly nasty section of Birmingham, England, full of drug dealers and hookers. The members of the band were basically homeless. They'd squat in abandoned buildings powered by stolen electricity from a jury-rigged meter. Food was stolen and occasionally, they'd resort to the odd break-and-enter and stick-up. The only legitimate money they had was what they received in unemployment benefits: about £8 a week. So where did they get the money for instruments? Only people who had the nerve to *steal* their gear was allowed in. And one other thing: in July 1988, bassist Earl Falconer was jailed for six months for his role in a car accident that killed his brother.

4. Don't Mess With Chrissie

In May 1980, Chrissie Hynde of The Pretenders got into a fight with a bouncer at a club in Memphis. When the cops came to take her away, she kicked the window out of the cruiser. That cost her a night in jail. Then there was the famous McDonald's event in 1989. On June 8, Chrissie spoke at a Greenpeace press conference in London and she mentioned that, as a committed vegetarian and animal rights activist, she once participated in the fire-bombing of a McDonald's restaurant. The very next day, a McDonald's was fire-bombed in Milton Keynes. Chrissie was questioned by police and then sued by McDonald's. The suit was later dropped when Chrissie agreed to sign a statement that said she would never repeat what she said about McDonald's ever again.

5. Kate Pierson vs. *Vogue.*

Kate Pierson of the B-52's was arrested on Sept. 30, 1993, when a large group of anti-fur protesters invaded and occupied the offices of *Vogue* in New York.

6. U2 and the Law

During a surprise show in San Francisco in November 1987, Bono felt the urge to spray some graffiti on a public fountain at Justin Herman Plaza. The message read "Stop the Traffic, Rock and Roll." The mayor was outraged, especially since the city had been waging war against graffiti artists at the time. U2 later issued a press release that read "Ooops! U2 would like to apologize for any upset they caused. We got carried away by what was a great day and a great gig." Bono explained his actions by saying that he was suffering from "tour madness."

7. Martin Gore Should Have Turned Down His Stereo
During a stop in Denver on the 1993 *Songs of Faith and Devotion* tour, guests at Depeche Mode's hotel complained about loud music coming from one of the rooms. Even though it was four in the morning, Martin refused the front desk's request that he turn down the stereo. The cops were called, Martin was arrested and thrown in the overnight lockup at Denver City Jail. He was released in the morning after being fined $50 for disturbing the peace.

8. The Chain Do Time
The Jesus and Mary Chain are easily one of the "most-arrested" bands in the history of alternative music. In fact, they incited a riot at their very first gig. They were unhappy with the quality of the PA system with which they had been supplied, so at the end of their set, they trashed it. In March 1985, a London show was cut short when the venue was badly oversold. The crowd caused more than £8,000 in damage and four people were sent to the hospital. The most infamous incident in North America occurred in Toronto at a club called RPM in November 1987. The band was out promoting their *Darklands* album and things weren't going well. The whole show consisted of Jim and William Reid playing along to a rhythm track from a cassette that was played through the PA. The crowd wasn't into it and people often shouted out that the band was boring. After a while, Jim snapped and brained a member of the audience with his mike stand. Running off stage, the band tried to make break for it in their tour bus, but a member of the club's security staff blocked their escape route with his car. Jim Reid was arrested and charged with assault and ordered to appear in court the following February. He was eventually given a full discharge after he agreed to donate $1,000 to the Salvation Army.

9. The Cult's PNE Riot

On August 29, 1987, Ian Astbury invited members of the audience up on the stage for the final encore of a show at the PNE in Vancouver. More than a hundred people took him up on it and things very quickly got out of hand. Security people started tossing people left and right and at one point, Ian decided to come to the aid of one fan that was taking a particularly bad beating. Once he made it to the dressing room, Ian was confronted by five cops who arrested him for assault. He spent the night in jail.

10. Henry Rollins' Terrible Ordeal

On December 19, 1991, Henry Rollins and his friend Joe Cole were on their way back to their house after shopping for groceries at a local store in Venice, California when they were ambushed by a gang. They were taken back to the house and forced to lie on the floor while the place was ransacked. Then something went very wrong—Joe tried to fight back and was shot to death.

11. Eddie and Black Jack

On November 18, 1993, Eddie Vedder of Pearl Jam was out with his new buddy, Jack McDowell, (at the time pitching for the Chicago White Sox). They went to a restaurant in New Orleans for a few drinks, but very soon, things were completely out of hand. Their waiter was James Gorman, and he said that a fight broke out after Eddie spit in his face. Eddie was arrested on charges of battery but the case was thrown out before he had a chance to appear in court.

12. Revenge of The Stone Roses

In 1987, the Stone Roses had a deal with a label called FM Revolver to release just the 12" single entitled "Sally Cinnamon." Once the record was out, the Roses moved on to their ill-fated deal with Silvertone. Three years later, at the height of the Stone Roses popularity, FM Revolver decided to capitalize on the situation by re-releasing "Sally Cinnamon" along with a video. However, they did this without the band's permission and the Roses went ballistic. To exact a little revenge, the group visited the FM Revolver offices with the purpose of doing a little remodeling. By the time they were done, they had caused £23,000 in damage. They were later fined £3,000 each and spared a jail term because the judge was afraid it might just add to the group's notoriety.

13. Rob Collins Gives a Friend a Lift
It was December 3, 1992. The Charlatans UK had just returned from a successful tour of Japan, and keyboardist Rob Collins was spending a few days catching up with old friends. Rob drove over to see Michael Whitehouse, an old school friend, and the two of them went out for drinks. At about 9:15 that night, Michael asked Rob to pull up in front of a liquor store. Michael went inside and after a few minutes there was a bang. Suddenly, Michael ran out of the store shouting for Rob to start the car. Rob, not really believing what was happening, did as he was told. However, someone had noted his license plate and just after midnight, Rob was arrested and taken into custody. He was kept at the station for five days while the police waited for Michael to talk. When he confessed, he told the cops that he had robbed the liquor store in order to impress his friend the pop star. The original charges against Rob were reduced from armed robbery and possession of a firearm to assisting an offender after a crime. When the trial finished up on September 21, 1993, Michael was sentenced to four years in prison while Rob was given eight months. He spent his time at Redditch Open Prison and was known as Prisoner RD 1533.

14. Hugh's Bad Business Deal
When the Housemartins broke up, most of the band went on to form the Beautiful South. However, drummer Hugh Whittaker was one of the people who got left behind. Determined to start a new career, he invested his life savings in a car dealership. Unfortunately, his partner turned out to be a bad money manager and the whole venture went bust. That's when Hugh began seeking revenge. First, he poured gasoline into his ex-partner's mailbox at least twice. When that failed to do any damage, he fire-bombed his house. And when that didn't have the desired effect, Hugh attacked his partner with an axe. Hugh was sentenced to six years for assault.

15. Problems with The Farm
This band has had their problems. In 1986, original drummer Andy McVann was killed in a police chase. He had been driving a stolen car. And in 1989, keyboard player Ray Toohey was charged with safe-cracking.

303

15 Delightful Oddities

1. The Trent Reznor Snuff Film

Around the time *Pretty Hate Machine* was released, the FBI got a tip that Trent Reznor had been murdered. An undercover agent stumbled across raw footage from the "Down In It" video—but he didn't know it was a video. After viewing the shot of Trent being thrown off a building and the shot of his bloody corpse on the sidewalk, the agent thought he had a genuine snuff film. He was sure that the guy in the film had actually been killed in front of the camera. The FBI investigated the case for six months, examining the film one frame at a time. Finally, someone clued into the fact that they were studying a music video. The whole time, Trent was alive and well and living in Cleveland.

2. The Clash vs. Flushco

In 1992, Flushco (the makers of a toilet bowl cleaner) sued The Clash for plagiarism. They alleged that the Clash song "Inoculated City" (from 1982's *Combat Rock*) ripped off the music from one of Flushco's advertising jingles.

3. Keep Your Mouth Closed, Joe

Joe Strummer of The Clash accidentally swallowed a gob of spit hurled at the stage by a member of the audience. He contracted hepatitis.

4. The Power of Ska

In August 1992, people in an apartment building in central London thought they were feeling an earthquake. The building shook, the windows rattled and the floor rumbled. Central London doesn't see a lot of earthquakes, so scientists were very interested in checking things out. After careful investigation, they discovered that the cause of the quake was an outdoor show by Madness down the street. So many people were dancing during "One Step Beyond" that they created vibrations that simulated an earthquake for blocks.

5. Karen Carpenter Sinks the Sex Pistols

On March 9, 1977, The Sex Pistols signed a contract with A&M Records. However, other artists on the label were less than pleased. They were concerned that the Pistols were bad news and demanded they be dropped. Supertramp complained. Peter Frampton made a phone call. Rick Wakeman wrote a letter. But the final straw came when

Karen Carpenter informed label bosses that she did not want those British thugs on the roster. Six days after they were signed, the Pistols were dropped—but they were paid £75,000 to go away.

6. Nice Record. Who's in the Band?
When Elvis Costello recorded his first album in 1977, he didn't have a permanent back-up band. Instead, he hired an American band called Clover to help out with the sessions. Clover was living in London at the time and was happy to have the gig. The only guy that wasn't so pleased was the singer, mainly because with Elvis doing all the singing, there wasn't anything for him to do. When *My Aim Is True* was completed, Elvis dismissed Clover and went about auditioning people for what would eventually become The Attractions, his permanent back-up band. Clover guitarist John McFee went on to join The Doobie Brothers, while members Huey Lewis and Sean Hopper returned to the US and managed to turn things around by forming a new band, Huey Lewis and the News.

7. Another Strange Lawsuit
New Order was once sued for plagiarism by John Denver. He claimed that the song "Run" sounded suspiciously like his 1969 hit, "Leaving on Jet Plane." Believe it or not, New Order decided not to challenge the claim and settled out of court.

8. Roger's Forgotten Gig
Part of Malcolm McLaren's plan for the Sex Pistols was to have them star in a movie. He hired soft-core porn king Russ Meyer to direct and an unknown American screenwriter (whose only previous credit was Meyer's cult classic *Beyond The Valley Of The Dolls*) to come up with the script. The result was *Who Killed Bambi?* which had the Sex Pistols taking over the world and assassinating a major rock star named M.J. (Mick Jagger?). However, the whole project fell apart and the movie was never made. But don't feel bad for the writer—he still had his full-time job as a film critic to fall back on. The critic: Roger Ebert.

9. What If Kurt Had Used Right Guard?
After a night of drinking with Kathleen Hanna of Bikini Kill, she and Kurt went back to his apartment where she started spray-painting graffiti all over the walls. One of the things Kathleen had noticed that night

was that Kurt smelled like a particular brand of deodorant used by high school students called Teen Spirit. That why she wrote "Kurt Smells Like Teen Spirit" on the wall. But Kurt (who never wore deodorant) didn't get the joke and thought that she was paying him a compliment about his spirit and energy. He went on write a song based on that piece of graffiti—and the rest is history.

10. Flea and Big Bird?
The Red Hot Chili Peppers were once booked to perform as guest artists on "Sesame Street." However, the producers at the Children's Television Workshop had a change of heart, saying that the Chili Peppers would not be appropriate for the show. Oh well—at least they got to be on "The Simpsons."

11. Confusion at the Factory
In early 1987, grandparents everywhere were pleased when the Lawrence Welk Orchestra released a collection of golden greats on compact disc. All those wonderful songs performed by his big band and sung by those nice young people with the sensible haircuts were finally going to be preserved digitally for all time. However, something went wrong at the CD factory in Japan. Thousands of mislabeled albums were sent out and instead of getting Lawrence Welk's *Polka Party*, many senior citizens actually received the *Sid and Nancy* soundtrack.

12. The International League for the Preservation of Animal Filament
In 1964, David Bowie had very long hair, which was quite unfashionable for men at the time. To fight society's scorn towards men with long hair, he established this association. "The League is really for the protection of pop musicians, and those who wear their hair long," he told the paper. "Anyone who has the courage to wear hair down to his shoulders has to go through hell. It's time we united and fought for our curls."

13. Kurt Cobain's First Guitar
When he was young, Kurt's mother and stepfather got into a terrible fight which ended up with his mom throwing all her husband's guns into a river. Kurt fished them out and sold them to raise money to buy his first guitar.

14. Green Day's Deep, Dark Secret
One of Green Day's managers used to sing with the '50s revival group, Sha Na Na.

15. A Potentially Interesting Situation
When "The Barbara Mandrell Show" was looking to book a gospel group, they somehow came within a whisker of booking the Jesus and Mary Chain.

Various Superlatives

1. The Longest Album Title in Alternative Music History
In 1990, British band called Snuff released an album titled: *Snuffsaid-butgorblimeyguvstonemeifhedidntthrowawobbler-chachachachachachachachachachachachayouregoinghomeinacosmicambience.* (116 letters)

2. The Longest Band Name in Alternative Music History
These guys named released a self-titled debut album in 1982. They were called One Hundred and Fifty Murderous Passions, Or Those Belonging to the Fourth Class, Composing the Twenty-Eight Days of February Spent In Hearing the Narrations of Madame Desgranges Interspersed Among Which Are the Scandalous Doings At the Chateau That Month. (219 letters). Second places goes to Who Is That Girl in the Red Dress and Why Does She Keep Calling Me Andrew? (58 letters).

3. The First Punk Single
"New Rose" was issued by The Damned on Stiff Records on October 22, 1976.

4. The First Alternative Band to Play Carnegie Hall
The Violent Femmes played there on March 7, 1986.

5. The First British Techno-Pop Band to Have a #1 Single in North America
The Human League hit #1 in the summer of 1982 with "Don't You Want Me," opening the door for the British new wave invasion.

6. The First CD-ROM Disc to Make the Billboard Top 200 Album Chart

Sarah McLachlan's *Freedom Sessions* features live versions of songs from her *Fumbling Towards Ecstasy* album as well as CD-ROM video material.

7. The First Live Internet Concert

In the fall of 1993, a group of scientists and engineers from Apple and Xerox went on-line with a band they called Severe Tire Damage. The second Internet show has been credited to Deth Specula. Seattle's Sky Cries Mary was third with a show on November 11, 1994.

8. The World's Biggest-Selling Indie Band

By "indie band," we mean a group who, although they may have their albums distributed by a major, they still officially record for an independent label. Using this definition, the answer is the Offspring. They're still the property of Epitaph Records, the indie punk label based out of Hollywood and founded by the members of Bad Religion. Offspring have sold more than 7 million copies of *Smash*. At one point, they were selling 60,000 copies *a week*. No other indie band even comes close.

9. The World's Biggest Illegal Rave

Few records are kept of this sort of thing, but the honor seems to go to a May 1992 rave in Castlemorton in the UK. This one party featured a dozen separate sound systems which entertained 30,000 people for over eight straight days.

Trivial Trivia

1. Who's That Boy?

The boy on the cover of U2's *Boy* album is Peter Rosen. He's the brother of one of the members of Dublin's Virgin Prunes. He can also be seen in the video for "Two Hearts Beat As One," and if you ever see the movie *The Commitments,* looks for the kid on the skateboard. That's Peter.

2. Strange Gig

When Francis Ford Coppola was shooting his version of *Bram Stoker's*

Dracula, he realized that his star, Gary Oldman, couldn't scream like a vampire. Coppola's daughter suggested that he contact Lux Interior of The Cramps to do the screaming. Lux auditioned and got the part.

3. But What Kind of Glass Do You Use?
Both The Cure and New Order say that they've invented their own cocktails. Robert Smith has makes something out of rum, calvados, orange juice, lemon juice and apple slices. He calls it an "Oracle." New Order's official tour cocktail is made from white wine and Pernod. They call it a "Headache."

4. Forgotten Inspiration
The Ramones based "Blitzkrieg Bop" on the chant in the Bay City Rollers song "Saturday Night."

5. CBGB OMFUG
The full name of the club is Country Blue Grass and Blues and Other Music For Urban Gourmands.

6. Who Negotiated This Deal?
According to legend, The Pogues signed with Stiff Records after the label agreed to throw in a half a case of beer as a bonus.

7. Yeah, But What About the Rest of the Time?
There were 66 months between the first two Stone Roses albums. According to the band itself, they spent 3,470 hours in the studio recording *Second Coming*, an album that runs about 75 minutes.

8. Getting Ahead of Schedule
"Smells Like Teen Spirit" wasn't supposed to be a big hit. Nirvana's record company released the song to prepare the public for what was going to be the "real" single, "Come As You Are." No one—not even the band—felt that the song had any major potential. "Smells Like Teen Spirit" was released on September 10, 1991, and by Christmas, the song was helping *Nevermind* sell 300,000 copies *a week*.

17 Alternative Artists That Have Appeared in Movies

1. Henry Rollins
The former Black Flag singer has recently appeared in the films *The Chase* and *Johnny Mnemonic*. Oliver Stone has also said that if he had met Henry earlier, he would have cast Rollins as Mickey in *Natural Born Killers*.

2. Debbie Harry
Since Blondie disbanded, Debbie has appeared in a wide variety of films including *Roadie* (1980), *Videodrome* (1983) and *Tales from the Dark Side* (1989). She's been involved in at least 26 movies and has had screen roles in at least nine.

3. Roland Gift
The singer for the Fine Young Cannibals is actually a very talented actor. His best known role was as Bridget Fonda's boyfriend in *Scandal* (1989). The entire band also appeared in a cameo role in *Tin Men* (1987) singing "Good Thing."

4. Michael Hutchence
Michael starred as the singer of a fictitious band called The Ears in an awful 1986 movie called *Dogs in Space*.

5. L7
They appear as a band called Camel Lips in John Waters' *Serial Mom*, which starred Kathleen Turner and Ricki Lake.

6. Adam Ant
Adam Ant has had roles in an at least eight films, including *Slamdance* with Tom Hulce.

7. Flea
Flea is an excellent dramatic actor. You can see him in *My Own Private Idaho* and *Back to the Future III*.

8. Trent Reznor
Trent Reznor in a Michael J. Fox film? You bet. In 1987, he had a role in *Light of Day*. Trent was part of a band in the film called The Prob-

lems. If you ever rent the video, watch for their rendition of an old Buddy Holly song.

9. Ween
Dean and Gene had a small part in *It's Pat!* Unfortunately, the movie was such a bomb that no one saw them.

10. Blue Rodeo
Blue Rodeo appears as Meryl Streep's back-up band in the final scene of *Postcards from the Edge.*

11. The Kemp Brothers
The brothers from Spandau Ballet, Gary and Martin Kemp, turn in convincing performances as the evil twins in *The Krays*, the bio-pic based on the life of the legendary London gangsters of the '50s and '60s.

12. David Johansen
The ex-New York Dolls frontman has appeared in a number of big-budget films such as *Scrooged* (he was Bill Murray's ghostly cab driver), *Freejack* and *Car 54, Where Are You?*

13. Adam Horovitz
Ad Rock of the Beastie Boys can be seen in dramatic roles in *Lost Angels* (1989) and *Roadside Prophets* (with Nick Cave in 1992).

14. Courtney Love
Before forming Hole, Love was a bit-part actress and occasional stripper. She ended up in a couple of punk roles, most notably in two Alex Cox films, *Straight to Hell* (with Joe Strummer, The Pogues and others) and *Sid and Nancy.* She also helped compile the soundtrack for *Tank Girl* and appears in *Feeling Minnesota.*

15. Sting
Movies are a healthy second career for Sting. His first role was as the Mod bellboy in Quadrophenia (1979). That was followed by appearances in *Dune, The Bride, Plenty, The Adventures of Baron Munchausen* and *Resident Alien.*

16. David Bowie

No one in alternative music has appeared in as many movies as David Bowie. His first gig was in an obscure 1969 movie entitled *The Virgin Soldiers*. Since then, he's played everything from Thomas Newton, the friendly alien in *The Man Who Fell to Earth* (1976) to John Blaylock, the 150 year-old vampire in *The Hunger* (1983). He also played Pontius Pilate in Martin Scorsese's *The Last Temptation of Christ* (1988). Not counting his concert films or the soundtracks he has helped write, Bowie has been in at least fourteen different movies.

17. J Mascis

The leader of Dinosaur Jr. scored *Gas Food Lodging* in 1992. He also had a small part in the film.

4 Things To Do With Movies

1. *Rock 'n' Roll High School* (1979)

This is the Ramones' show. Watch for their entrance in a Cadillac convertible with leopard skin seats and a license plate that reads "NY GABBA GABBA HEY."

2. *The Last Emperor* (1987)

David Byrne shared an Academy Award for Best Original Score with Ryuichi Sakamoto and Cong Su for their score for this 1987 Bernardo Bertolucci film.

3. *Singles* (1992)

This is a great film for spotting famous Seattle people. (1) Alice in Chains performs in a bar scene. (2) Eddie Vedder, Stone Gossard and Jeff Ament of Pearl Jam are Matt Dillon's band mates in Citizen Dick. (3) Mark Arm of Mudhoney is seen hauling around some furniture. (4) Chris Cornell of Soundgarden is the guy who watches Matt destroy Bridget Fonda's car with a stereo. (5) Tad Doyle gets a wrong number from Bridget. (6) Bruce Pavitt (one of the founders of Sub Pop) is in a scene featuring a dating service.

4. *The Basketball Diaries* (1995)

This film starring Leonardo DiCaprio is based on the autobiographical writings of poet and musician Jim Carroll. Jim eventually turned to music and followed the example of his idol Patti Smith by moving to New York. His most successful project was a 1980 album titled *Catholic Boy*, which features his biggest song, "People Who Died." Jim has a cameo appearance in the film as a drug dealer.

2 Performers Who Tried Big-Time Politics

1. Jello Biafra

In 1979, the Dead Kennedys leader ran for mayor San Francisco on an anti-censorship platform. In a field of ten, he finished fourth.

2. Peter Garrett

Over the years, Peter has been very involved in a variety of political causes. Because of his uncompromising beliefs (and because he has a law degree), the singer for Midnight Oil was asked to run for a six-year term in the Australian Senate as a member of the Nuclear Disarmament Party. He didn't make it but he did receive a very respectable 200,000 votes.

Stories Behind 12 Songs

1. "She's Lost Control"—Joy Division

Ian Curtis wrote the song about epilepsy.

2. "Biko"—Peter Gabriel

Stephen Bantu Biko was a black South African committed to ending apartheid. He was the ideological leader of Black Consciousness, a political and social movement dedicated to change in South Africa. Biko's message and popularity with blacks made authorities very nervous and he was officially banned by the government. On August 18, 1977, Biko was arrested at a roadblock that had been set up especially for him. He wasn't formally charged with any crime but was held under the "Terrorism Act," which allowed for the indefinite detention of any person who was suspected of being connected with terrorism. On August 19, he was transferred to Port Elizabeth where he was left naked in his cell. On September 6, still naked, he was shackled and moved to another detention center where a five man interrogation team was waiting. By 7:00 the next morning, he was dead.

The Justice Ministry insisted that Biko's death was the result of a two-day hunger strike. The police in the interrogation room said that Stephen had "bumped his head" by accident. They also said that a doctor was called in when Stephen "appeared unwell"—but they suspected that he was almost certainly faking illness. When it became clear that he was in danger, they loaded him—still naked and still in chains—into the back of a truck and hauled him to the nearest available prison hospital, which was about 1,100 km away. That's where he died, on a mat on a stone floor.

According to the autopsy, Stephen died as the result of massive blows to the head. When the case went to court, this was the official verdict: "Death was probably caused by head injuries sustained during a scuffle with security police. The available evidence does not prove that death was brought about any act of omission involving or accounting to an offense on the part of any person." The world knew otherwise.

3. "Me and a Gun"—Tori Amos
This song is a emotional account of the time Tori was sexually assaulted.

4. "Polly"—Nirvana
In June 1987, a 14 year-old girl was kidnapped on her way home from a punk show at the Community World Theatre in Tacoma, Washington. The kidnapper was a real piece of work named Gerald Friend. He took the girl back to his mobile home where he hung her upside down from a pulley attached to the ceiling. For the next several days, he raped and tortured her using hot wax, a whip, a razor and even a blowtorch. Fortunately, the girl managed to escape one day when she was out with Gerald and he stopped for gas.

The story received a lot of attention in the Pacific Northwest. When Kurt Cobain heard what happened, he wrote "Polly," in which he takes the perspective of the sicko rapist.

5. "Suffer Little Children"—The Smiths
In October 1965, Ian Brady was working at a chemical plant in an area of Manchester known as Moss Side. All his co-workers thought that he was a little weird because Ian had a very bad temper and spent a lot of money on books about the Nazis and the Marquis de Sade. The only person who seemed to like him was Myra Hindley, who also worked at the plant.

What no one knew was that Ian and Myra were kidnapping and torturing children, Once they were dead, Ian would bury the bodies out on a bleak spot known as the Saddleworth Moors. On at least one occasion, they tape-recorded the torture session.

When Ian tried to include Myra's brother-in-law in what they were doing, he went to police. Both Ian and Myra were arrested and ordered to stand trial in the spring of 1966. The Moors Murders case was one of the most sensational in the history of Manchester and the whole city awaited the outcome. Ian and Myra were found guilty and sentenced to life in prison. When Myra found herself in Holloway (a very bleak Victorian prison for women), the other inmates would whisper one particular Bible verse to her over and over: "Suffer little children to come unto me."

Morrissey was about seven during the trial but he never forgot the horrors of the Moors Murders and in 1983, he wrote the song "Suffer Little Children" as a tribute to Leslie Ann Downey, the last of the children murdered by Ian and Myra.

6. "The Last of the Famous International Playboys"—Morrissey
The song is dedicated to the Krays, the legendary brothers who ran the crime scene in London in the '50s and '60s.

7. "Jeremy"—Pearl Jam
Jeremy Delle lived in Richardson, Texas. He was not a happy kid, mainly because things were very difficult at home. On January 8, 1991, something snapped. After his English teacher ripped into him for missing so many classes, Jeremy whipped out a loaded .357 magnum and shot himself in the head, right in front of the whole class. The story received international attention and one person who took notice was Eddie Vedder of Pearl Jam, who insisted that the song he wrote based on Jeremy Delle be included on Pearl Jam's debut album.

8. "Love Removal Machine"—The Cult
The song was inspired by the night Ian Astbury witnessed the work of a 60 year-old stripper/prostitute at a military social club.

9. "Spoonman"—Soundgarden
The Spoonman is Artis, a big, bald guy who began busking with his spoons in Seattle in 1974. For years, this was his only source of income

and he eventually became somewhat of a local legend. The guys from Soundgarden were especially impressed. Not only did they write a song about Artis, but they also got him to star in the video.

10. "And She Was"—Talking Heads
David Byrne wrote the song about a hippy girl from Baltimore. Her favorite thing was to drop acid and lie in a field all day.

11. "Valerie Loves Me"—Material Issue
When Jim Ellison was growing up, a girl named Valerie lived in the apartment above him. Everything he says in the song about her is absolutely true.

12. "Under the Bridge"—Red Hot Chili Peppers
The song describes a bridge in downtown L.A. where Hillel Slovak and Anthony Kiedis used to go to buy their drugs. Slovak died of a heroin overdose in June 1988.

7 Heroin Deaths

1. Billy Murcia and Johnny Thunders—The New York Dolls
The New York Dolls were freaks and proud of it. They started playing around New York City on Christmas Day 1971 and did whatever they could to shock an audience. Their act was totally different from everything else that was out there and quickly attracted a following of people who liked things different and strange. For awhile, it looked as if the Dolls were going to make it—but the beginning of the end came on November 6, 1972, when drummer Billy Murcia died in London. He had gone to a party where was given a drug mixture that contained heroin and washed it all down with champagne. When he passed out, someone put him in a bathtub so he could sleep it off. However, his girlfriend panicked and tried to revive him by pouring hot coffee down his throat. He died by choking on his own vomit.

After the Dolls broke up, lead guitarist and singer Johnny Thunders decided to form another band, the Heartbreakers. They released a bunch of records between 1977 and 1984, plus there were almost a dozen Thunders solo albums. However, Johnny was a habitual user and on April 23, 1991, he died of a heroin overdose in a New Orleans hotel room.

2. Sid Vicious

Few people were more interested in drugs than Sid. His downfall began when he met Nancy Spungen, an ex-hooker and full time junkie from Philadelphia. By most accounts, it was Nancy who introduced Sid to hardcore heroin use, and once they became a steady couple, their intake escalated. They were constantly being busted, hospitalized, and detoxed. In the end, they were killed by two separate fixes.

The first came in the early morning hours of October 13, 1978 in room 100 of the Chelsea Hotel in New York City. After a long, restless night of scoring drugs from visiting dealers and shooting up, Sid awoke to find Nancy dead in the bathroom. Someone had stabbed her in the stomach—and Sid couldn't remember a thing. He didn't know if he had done it or if it had been one of the dealers or if Nancy had done it herself. Sid was charged with her murder and held in detox before being discharged into his mother's custody.

Sid was never tried for Nancy's murder because on the evening of February 1, 1979, Sid's mother threw a party at the apartment of his new girlfriend. Along with a fine spaghetti dinner, Ma Vicious had thoughtfully brought along a dose of heroin her son as sort of an after dinner treat. After everyone went to bed, Sid got up and took the rest of the junk from his mother's purse and injected it. Because Sid had been detoxed, his body wasn't prepared for the fix. He died of an overdose during the early morning hours of February 2.

3. James Honeyman-Scott and Pete Farndon

In 1978, James Honeyman-Scott helped Chrissie Hynde for the Pretenders. He was a great guitar player who could also play keyboards. While Chrissie became the focal point of the band, James was a big part of the overall Pretenders sound. Unfortunately, he had a taste for heroin and cocaine which required weeks in detox programs.

Another important part of the band was bassist Pete Farndon. Pete was a complicated guy. At one point, he was romantically involved with Chrissie—but when the relationship fell apart and Chrissie began seeing Ray Davies of the Kinks, Pete began to get more and more into drugs.

Disaster struck in June 1982, beginning on the 14th. Saying that his drug use had gone too far, Pete was fired from the band. Two days later, James Honeyman-Scott died. James' body had been so weakened by a recent detox program that he couldn't handle the speedball he snorted at a party in London on the 16th.

And that's not all. After months of almost continuous substance abuse, Pete Farndon died of an overdose, ten months to the day after being fired. On April 14, 1983, Pete was having a bath after a shot of heroin. The post-mortem revealed that the drug had made him so sleepy that he slipped below the surface of the water and drowned.

4. Hillel Slovak

Hillel Slovak, Anthony Kiedis and Flea were all founding members of the Red Hot Chili Peppers. Unfortunately, they all dabbled in drugs. Hillel died of what was called an accidental heroin overdose on June 27, 1988.

5. Andrew Wood

Andrew was a big part of the proto-grunge scene in Seattle. He had always wanted to be a rock star, complete with all the trappings. By the time he was 18, Andrew had followed his brothers into heroin addiction. He was so into heroin that even a case of hepatitis in 1986 (from a dirty needle) didn't diminish his appetite for drugs.

By 1988, Andrew was part of a band called Mother Love Bone. They were quite good and by November, they had a major record deal and began work on their first full album. But on Friday, March 16, 1990— just weeks before the Mother Love Bone album was to be released— Andrew failed to show up for a band meeting. At 10:30 that night, he was discovered on the bed at his girlfriend's apartment with the needle still stuck in his arm. He had injected his first dose of heroin in more than 100 days and had overdosed.

An ambulance was called and he was immediately admitted to a hospital. By Monday, he was declared clinically dead and the life-support machines were shut off.

6. Kurt Cobain

Heroin has always been a big part of the Seattle music scene. Kurt Cobain first tried heroin soon after he started out with a dealer named Grunt in the summer of 1985. After that, he shot up whenever he could, otherwise sticking to opiate-derived drugs like Percodan.

By November 1991, he had met Courtney Love and the two of them were injecting each other and over the next year, and scoring drugs from a dealer became as routine as going out for a loaf of bread.

Kurt's problems started to become public in January 1992, just as *Nevermind* was starting to peak. He made several attempts to quit, but his habit was too strong. Even when he was in the delivery room with Courtney for the birth of their daughter, he was hooked up to a morphine drip to ease his withdrawal symptoms. And when he shot himself in April 1994, the King County coroner reported that there had been a substantial amount of heroin in his bloodstream.

7. Kristen Pfaff

The bassist for Hole was another person who fell victim to the heroin trade in Seattle. She tried several rehab programs but when they didn't work, she decided to move back home to Minneapolis to escape. The night before she was supposed to leave (June 15, 1994), she died of an overdose in her bathtub.

11 Loving Music Couples

1. Damon Albarn (Blur) and Justine Frischmann (Elastica)
2. Kim Gordon and Thurston Moore (Sonic Youth)
3. Liz Fraser and Robin Guthrie (Cocteau Twins)
4. Lux Interior and Ivy Rorschach (The Cramps)
5. Debbie Harry and Chris Stein (Blondie)
6. Siouxsie Sioux and Budgie (Siouxsie and the Banshees)
7. Elvis Costello and Kate O'Riordan (ex-Pogues)
8. Gillian Gilbert and Stephen Morris (New Order, The Other Two)
9. Allanah Currie and Tom Bailey (Thompson Twins, Babble)
10. Einar and Bragi (Sugarcubes—the first publicized gay marriage in pop music).
11. Tina Weymouth and Chris Frantz (Talking Heads, Tom Tom Club)

16 Ex-Couples

1. Mark E. Smith and Brix Smith (The Fall)
2. Annie Lennox and Dave Stewart (Eurythmics)
3. Donna Matthews and Justin Welch (Elastica)
4. Paul Weller and DC Lee (The Style Council)
5. Hope Sandoval and Dave Roback (Mazzy Star)
6. James Iha and D'Arcy Wretzky (Smashing Pumpkins)
7. Kate Bush and Del Palmer

8. Chrissie Hynde and James Honeyman-Scott (The Pretenders)
9. Chrissie Hynde and Pete Farndon (The Pretenders)
10. Chrissie Hynde (The Pretenders) and Ray Davies (Kinks)
11. Chrissie Hynde (The Pretenders) and Jim Kerr (Simple Minds)
12. Courtney Love (Hole) and Kurt Cobain (Nirvana)
13. Evan Dando (Lemonheads) and Juliana Hatfield
14. Toni Halliday and Dean Garcia (Curve)
15. Genesis P Orridge (Throbbing Gristle) and Paula (Psychic TV)
16. PJ Harvey and Mike Delanian (Gallon Drunk)

14 Miscellaneous Relationships

1. Noel and Liam Gallagher (Oasis)—brothers
2. Jim and William Reid (Jesus and Mary Chain)—brothers
3. Kristen Hersch (Throwing Muses) and Tanya Donnelly (Belly)—stepsisters
4. Rob Dickinson (Catherine Wheel) and Bruce Dickinson (Iron Maiden)—cousins
5. Nina Gordon and Jim Shapiro (Veruca Salt)—brother and sister
6. David Sylvian and Steve Jansen (Japan)—brothers
7. Paul Weller and his manager, John Weller—father and son
8. Jay and Michael Aston (Gene Loves Jezebel)—brothers
9. Margo and Michael Timmins (Cowboy Junkies)—brother and sister
10. Kelly and Kim Deal (Breeders)—sisters
11. Cindy and Ricky Wilson (B-52's)—brother and sister
12. Mike and Alastair Score (A Flock of Seagulls)—brothers
13. Sean and Paul Ryder (Happy Mondays)—brothers
14. Martin and Gary Kemp (Spandau Ballet)—brothers

4 Bad Career Moves

1. The Happy Mondays

Just as the band was about to sign a lucrative long-term record deal, Sean Ryder asked to be excused from a meeting with label executives. Everyone waited and waited for him to return, but they eventually got tired and went home. As a result, no record deal was signed.

2. Walt Must Be Spinning in His Cyrogenic Chamber

None of the three dozen artists signed to Disney's Hollywood Records have ever had a major hit. What's worse is that the company turned down opportunities to sign Nirvana and the Smashing Pumpkins.

3. Simon Wolstencraft
Simon started out in 1981 by playing drums for The Patrol and English Rose. However, he wasn't happy, so he quit to join another group. Bad move. English Rose eventually evolved into The Stone Roses. Simon's second group was called Freaky Party, but before things really got going, Simon quit. Freaky Party featured Johnny Marr and Andy Rourke—and it wasn't long before they were renamed The Smiths. In the space of two years, Simon bailed out of what would become two of the biggest groups in the history of Manchester. Fortunately, though, Simon found steady work with The Fall.

4. A Whopper of a Mistake
Aaron Bruckhard worked at the Burger King in Aberdeen, Washington. He was also the drummer for an early version of Nirvana. Although he had a reputation as someone who got into trouble (he once drove a car through the front of a convenience store and was also involved in a car accident where the driver was killed), he was the only drummer Kurt Cobain and Krist Novoselic could find.

Aaron played a series of gigs with Nirvana in 1987. He was a good enough drummer—but he hated to rehearse, something that really irked Kurt, who was totally committed to making the band work. Aaron also wasn't in a hurry to upgrade his ramshackle drum kit, part of which was purchased from Sears. For awhile, an old music stand held up his cymbal.

The final straw came when Aaron borrowed Kurt's car to go buy some beer. Instead of bringing it right back, he went for a tour of the local taverns and on the way home was pulled over by the police. After mouthing off to the cop, Aaron was arrested and charged with DUI. Kurt's car was impounded. He didn't find out about what happened until Krist phoned him, saying that Aaron was asking for bail money. The next day, Kurt called a band rehearsal and Aaron didn't show. He said he was too hungover to make it. That did it. Aaron was out for good.

Who knows? Had Aaron brought Kurt's car right back inside of hitting the bars, he might be a millionaire now. Instead, he's gone down in history as the Pete Best of Nirvana.

11 Great Indie Labels

1. Sub Pop

Sub Pop was formed in 1986 in the warehouse of Muzak Corporation in Seattle. The founders were Bruce Pavitt and Jonathan Poneman, who scraped together $20,000 to start things up. Although the label was on the brink of financial ruin for years, Pavitt and Poneman managed to establish the company as one that cared about documenting the emerging grunge scene in the Pacific Northwest. One of the label's great innovations was the Sub Pop singles club where subscribers were regularly sent cool 7" singles.

Sub Pop was also the label that took a chance on Nirvana. Once *Nevermind* hit it big, the company's financial problems were over for good. Pavitt and Poneman eventually sold a majority stake in the company to Warner Bros. for $20 million.

2. Factory Records

Factory was the idea of Tony Wilson, a TV reporter based out of Manchester. He had a couple of part-time jobs, including hosting a couple of TV shows that spent a lot of time showcasing punk and new wave bands. He also ran a place called The Russell Club. It was through his TV work and his club that he met up with Alan Erasmus, the manager for the Duritti Column. They struck up a partnership whereby Tony would act as promoter for the club while Alan would run the place. Everything was subsidized by Tony's day jobs with the TV station.

The first thing they did was rename The Russell Club. It became The Factory. Second, Tony decided that since all the major labels were snapping up the new wave bands, he needed to get a piece of the action by forming his own label. He started by signing some of the groups that appeared at his club.

From that moment on, everything Factory did was assigned a catalogue number that began with FAC. FAC 1 was the poster that announced the opening of the club. FAC 2 was the label's first release. One of the acts that appeared on that compilation was Joy Division.

Joy Division established Factory as a player in the world of indie labels. Other bands quickly joined the fold, including OMD, A Certain Ratio and Cabaret Voltaire. And when Joy Division evolved into New Order, the money really started to flow in. The Happy Mondays provided the label with some serious success in the late '80s. Unfortunately, mismanagement led to cashflow problems in 1991 and by November

1992, things were desperate. Factory was forced to close down. However, the label has since been resurrected under the name Factory Too.

3. 4AD

There are few indie labels that have as much to brag about as 4AD. The label's roster reads like a "who's who" of alternative music: The Pixies, Bauhaus, Modern English, The Cocteau Twins, Lush, The Wolfgang Press, The Breeders, Xymox, Red House Painters, The Birthday Party, Pale Saints, Ultravivid Scene, and Dead Can Dance. The label really has released some wonderful music over the years.

4AD started in early 1980 by Peter Kent and Ivo Watts-Russell, two guys who worked for Beggar's Banquet. They had heard a demo tape by Modern English and were so impressed by what they heard, they convinced their bosses to let them set up a new label called Axis. Unfortunately, Axis ran into problems with their name. People get getting them confused with someone else. That's when they came up with "4AD." Beggar's Banquet gave then £2,000 to get started.

From then on, 4AD became known as the label that signed groups who refused to compromise when it came to their music. So far, that philosophy has served everyone very well.

4. Stiff

In 1977, the British music scene was pretty stale. The only real action was happening down in the streets, and that action could be roughly divided into two parts. On one side, you had the Ziggy Stardust wannabes; on the other, rough and raw groups that played American style R&B in the pubs. The most famous of the pub rockers was Dr. Feelgood. His manager was very upset that none of the major labels were paying attention to his star. Jake Riviera got together with Dave Robinson, the manager of Brinsley Schwartz, and worked out a scheme whereby they could set up headquarters at the Hope and Anchor. They formed a label so that they could sign bands as they pleased.

Borrowing £400 from the singer of Dr. Feelgood, they began to recruit talent for the label. The only guy they could find was the bass player of Brinsley Schwartz, a talented songwriter named Nick Lowe. On August 16, 1976, Stiff Records released their first single, Nick Lowe's "So It Goes." It just cost £45 to release that record, but that took up 11% of the companies assets.

"So It Goes" established Stiff as a label that was a little wonky—

which was perfect because punk was starting to break. Stiff soon became known as one of the few labels that would support punk acts. In fact, the Damned issued "New Rose," the first official punk single on Stiff Records. After The Damned came Elvis Costello, Ian Dury and the Blockheads, Lene Lovich and Madness.

Unfortunately, Stiff started to stagnate after a 1983 merger between Stiff and Island Records didn't work out. The partnership was dissolved and Stiff was left to struggle on their own.

5. Mute

Daniel Miller has been in charge of Mute from the beginning. He started the label with the proceeds from "Warm Leatherette," the single he released as The Normal. However, Daniel soon realized his limitations as a musician and decided to stick with managing his label. He stuck with the emerging synthesizer trend, signing bands like Fad Gadget, DAF and most importantly, Depeche Mode.

Depeche Mode's relationship with Mute is nothing short of remarkable. They trusted Daniel so much that they didn't even sign a formal contract with him until 1986, despite the fact that every major label in the world was chasing after them. All profits generated for the label by the sales of Depeche Mode records were plowed back into the company in order to develop new synthesizer-based bands. Beneficiaries of that policy have included Yazoo, Erasure, Nitzer Ebb, Renegade Soundwave and even the Inspiral Carpets.

These days, Mute has an extremely eclectic roster of artists, ranging from techno groups to experimental types like Diamanda Galas. The company also owns the back catalogue of some of the most influential experimental electronic groups of the past, including Throbbing Gristle, Cabaret Voltaire, and Can.

6. Beggar's Banquet

Beggar's Banquet has been around since late 1977 and actually began as a side project of a record shop. Martin Mills owned a bunch of record stores and was continually pestered by customers who wanted to buy some of this new punk rock music that everyone was talking about. The problem was that there was very little of this product available. The major labels considered punk to be nothing more than a passing fad and the young indie labels (Stiff, Factory and Rough Trade) weren't sufficiently established to be able to distribute their product efficiently.

Martin saw this as a big hole in the market—and since he already owned a chain of record stores, he had a makeshift distribution system already in place. The clincher came when he was approached by Pete Stride, who played in the Lurkers. He convinced Martin to invest a few hundred pounds into the production of the Lurkers' first single, which in turn would be sold in Martin's shop on a label created by Martin.

Once word got out, dozens of punk and new wave bands started looking to Martin for help. The most successful of the bunch was Gary Numan and the Tubeway Army, who had a huge hit with "Are Friends Electric?" Less than eighteen months after it was established on the front counter of a record store, Beggar's Banquet was on its way.

Most of the profits were reinvested right back into the label. The Icicle Works, Bauhaus, Tones on Tail and the Cult eventually followed. In the late '80s, the label was responsible for signing the Charlatans UK, one of the best bands to emerge from the so-called Manchester scene. The company remains alive and well today.

7. Wax Trax

Wax Trax began as a record store on Lincoln Avenue in Chicago. Jim Nash and Danny Fletcher ran the place and they were constantly besieged with requests for records by some of the more active local bands. Unfortunately, none of these groups had any product available. So, in 1980, Jim and Danny decided to do what Martin Mills had done at his Beggar's Banquet store in England. They formed a label that would specialize in releasing of the music their clientele kept asking for. Wax Trax played a very big part in the evolution of industrial music— although that's not how things started out. It's true that one of their first projects was Ministry, but back in the early '80s, Ministry was indistinguishable in sound from Depeche Mode, OMD and a hundred other polite techno-pop bands. That all began to change when Ministry and Wax Trax started to get into more aggressive dance floor sounds with songs like "All Day" and "Every Day is Like Halloween."

When those releases proved to be popular, Wax Trax began issuing records by American and European acts who liked their beats computerized and heavy. Agreements were reached with Front 242, KMFDM, My Life With the Thrill Kill Kult, The Revolting Cocks, Lead Into Gold and many others. The goofiest Wax Trax signing was Divine, the 400 pound transvestite.

8. SST

SST was one of the most influential of all the American post-punk records labels, What began as an act of defiance, ended up playing an integral role in the development of grunge and the generation of post-Nirvana bands in general.

Los Angeles was the home to dozens of punk bands in the late '70s, and they had a reputation of doing things on their own terms. The best of the bunch was Black Flag. In 1977, Bomp Records was all set to release the group's debut single—but then someone told the label that punk was dead and that it wasn't worth getting involved. That's when the master tapes were returned to the band.

Needless to say, Black Flag was pretty freaked out at this turn of events, and it got even worse when they couldn't interest another label in their material. So, faced with no other option, Black Flag decided to form its own label. They called it SST after an old electronics company called "Solid State Tuners." Everything was handled by guitarist Greg Ginn, bassist Chuck Dukowski, the band's soundman and one of the group's roadies. SST 1 was a collection of four songs on a 7" in 1978.

Things got pretty scary for a while. There was a two-year gap between SST 1 and SST 2 along with an ugly legal battle with MCA Records, which almost killed both the label and Black Flag. Eventually, though, things worked out, and by the mid-'80s, the SST catalogue featured releases by such legendary American punk bands as Bad Brains, Sonic Youth, the Meat Puppets and Hüsker Dü. Soundgarden and Dinosaur Jr. have also had material out on SST. The company is still going strong and is based out of Lawndale, California.

9. Rough Trade

Geoff Travis was on his way to becoming a teacher at a girls' school, but he wasn't too keen on the deal. One morning, while waiting for the bus, he decided that if the bus didn't show up in the next five minutes, he was going to give up teaching. The bus didn't come and Geoff ran off to America.

During his trip, he bought an awful lot of records. But when he got back to England, he realized that he didn't have room for them all. Since they only cost twenty-five cents apiece, he decided to sell them at a slight profit. Very soon, Geoff was running a record shop in Kensington Park Road that he called Rough Trade (the name game from a slang term used by gay prostitutes to describes clients who would beat them up). The shop was up and running by mid-1976, just in time for the punk explosion. Soon, Geoff was dealing in the latest UK releases and all sorts of imports. This led to the establishment of an independent distribution network called "The Cartel." The next logical step was to form a label.

The first group to release a single on Rough Trade was a French band called Metal Urbain. The first group to release an album was Stiff Little Fingers. Other early Rough Trade signings included Pere Ubu, The Fall and The Slits. However, it took 91 single releases before anything from Rough Trade made the charts. Scritti Politti managed to make it all the way to number 64 in 1981 with a song called "The Sweetest Girl."

The big break came along in 1983 when a guitarist from Manchester cornered Geoff in his kitchen and demanded that he listen to a tape of his new group. The band was The Smiths. At first, Rough Trade and The Smiths got along fairly well but the relationship soon turned stormy. By 1987, The Smiths were gone and the label was reeling from the loss of his bread and butter. For awhile, it looked as if The Sundays may be the answer to Rough Trade's problems, but the money problems were too severe. The label never recovered and the distribution network collapsed.

10. Creation Records
Creation was the product of Alan McGee, a Scottish musician and club owner. He had always wanted to be a concert promoter. Once he started with that, he decided that it was time that he open his own nightclub. It was a tiny back room place in central London called The Living Room. The club was so popular that it was turning a profit in less than six months. That's when he decided to start a label that would showcase the bands that he liked.

The first release on Creation Records was "73 in 83" by The Legend. A thousand copies were pressed up, but they didn't sell. Alan ended up storing most of the inventory under his bed and when he and The Legend had a big fight, Alan had the remaining records melted down.

His first long-term project was The Jasmine Minks. They were followed by The Pastels, a pop group from Scotland. Eleven singles went by without much happening for Creation. But things took off with release number twelve. The name of the band was Jesus and Mary Chain and their first single, "Upside Down." It sold 50,000 copies and established Creation in the record shops.

Since then, the labels has had its ups and downs. There were big successes like the House of Love and Primal Scream and then miserable failures like Baby Amphetamine and Momus. Then there was the ill-advised deal with Elevation Records, followed by the bank-breaking recording bills for My Bloody Valentine's *Loveless* album. But Alan McGee had learned from the experience of Rough Trade and Factory. Rather than see his label go down, he accepted an offer from Sony and sold 49% of Creation for £3.5 million. Since then, things have been much better and Creation has been free to sign new and exciting bands like Oasis. Other major Creation acts have included Ride, Adorable and the Boo Radleys.

11. Epitaph Records

In 1981, Bad Religion found itself in the same position as Black Flag— they had a lot of great music but they couldn't find a label that was interested. So, with typical "do it yourself" spirit, Bad Religion also formed their own indie label. They scraped together enough money to put out a single and an album, and Epitaph was on its way.

Guitarist Brett Gurewitz was the man in charge of the label, but it wasn't until he overcame his long-term drug addiction in 1988 that he was able to devote all his energies to the company. Epitaph began releasing all sorts of punk albums by bands like L7 and NOFX and although radio and MTV almost totally ignored Epitaph acts, the word of mouth on the label within the punk community was excellent. By 1993, Epitaph was shipping about a million punk records a year.

Things really shifted into high gear when Epitaph spent $5,000 to make a video for Offspring's "Come Out and Play." MTV picked it up and suddenly, punk was hotter than ever and Epitaph could barely keep up with demand. Offspring's *Smash* album sold more than seven million copies, turning Epitaph into one of the most successful indie operations ever.

Still, Epitaph (and most of the label's roster) remains true to its punk roots and while other American indie labels are looking to make deals with a major, Epitaph remains fiercely independent. Gurewitz once rejected a $50 million buy-out offer from Maverick Records, a label controlled by Madonna.

Lollapalooza

1. Origins

Most people don't realize that the whole Lollapalooza thing might not have happened if Perry Farrell had not come down with a case of laryngitis. Jane's Addiction was in England for the 1990 Reading Festival. The night before their appearance, they played a club show in a very hot, very sweaty room. This didn't help Perry who had a cold. By the following morning, laryngitis had set in and Jane's Addiction had to cancel their Reading appearance. While Perry was recovering, the rest of the band and their management decided to cruise through the festival. They were so impressed by what they saw and by the general vibe of the event that they decided to try and organize a traveling version of Reading for North America.

It was Perry who came up with the name. During the planning stages of the first Lollapalooza, he had stayed up all night watching a "Three Stooges" marathon on TV. The Stooges often used "lollapalooza" to describe something huge and unbelievable. Perry thought that the term was perfect. The first show was held at Compton Terrace outside of Phoenix on July 18, 1991.

2. Main Stage Line-Ups

1991: Rollins Band, Butthole Surfers, Nine Inch Nails, Ice-T and Bodycount, Living Color, Siouxsie and the Banshees, Jane's Addiction.

1992: Lush, Jesus and Mary Chain, Pearl Jam, Soundgarden, Ice Cube, Ministry, Red Hot Chili Peppers.

1993: Rage Against the Machine, Front 242, Alice in Chains, Arrested Development, Dinosaur Jr., Fishbone, Primus. (Tool also made some main stage appearances).

1994: The Boredoms (first half), Green Day (second half), L7, Nick Cave and the Bad Seeds, A Tribe Called Quest, Breeders, George Clinton and the P-Funk All Stars, Beastie Boys, Smashing Pumpkins.

1995: Mighty Mighty Bosstones, Jesus Lizard, Beck, Sinead O'Connor, Pavement, Cypress Hill, Hole, Sonic Youth.

3. Acts Who Have Performed on the Second Stage

1992: The Jim Rose Circus Sideshow, Archie Bell's Future Kulture (a dance/performance art group), various local acts.

1993: Tool, Mercury Rev, Mutubaruka (first segment), Unrest, A Lighter Shade of Brown (second segment), Cell, Royal Trux, Mosquito (third segment), Sebadoh, Tsunami, Free Kitten (fourth segment).

1994: The following joined the tour for various periods of time: The Flaming Lips, The Verve, The Souls of Mischief, Rollerskate Skinny, The Frogs, Lucious Jackson, Palace Songs, Guided By Voices, Girls Against Boys, Stereolab, Blast Off Country Style, Charlie Hunter Trio, Fu-Schnickens, Lambchop, Shudder to Think, The Boo Radleys, King Kong, The Pharcyde, Shonen Knife.

1995: The following bands joined the tour for short stints on the tour: Blonde Redhead, Brainiac, Built to Spill, Coolio, Dirty Three, Doo Rag, Helium, Laika, Mike Watt, Possum Dixon, Poster Children, Redman, St. Johnny, Superchunk, The Coctails, The Dambuilders, The Geraldine Fibbers, The Pharcyde, The Roots, Versus, Yo La Tengo.

4. Ten Statistics About the 1994 Lollapalooza Tour

Once the 1994 edition of the tour wrapped up, the organizers issued a press release detailing some interesting numbers:

Total number of miles traveled: 15,175

Total number of people traveling with the tour: 375 on 26 trucks and 22 buses

Total number of people who successfully body-surfed to the front of the stage: 6,553

Number of people who signed up for the video dating service: 2,583

Number of couples brought together: 129

Number of cases of beer consumed by festival talent: 1,548 (37,152 bottles/cans)

Number of bottles of Evian used backstage: 25,800

Number of pounds of carrots consumed by the talent: 2,365

Number times festival tents were erected and torn down: 4,128

Total amount donated to charity: $856,437.16

Lollapalooza '95

Woodstock '94

Backstage passes

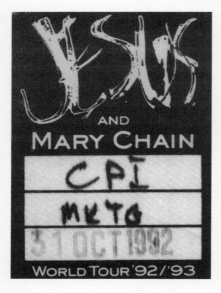

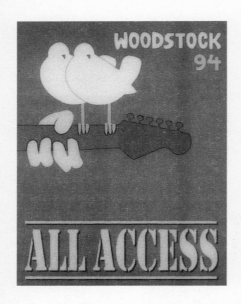

Part 3

GETTING MORE INFO

Section 1
Fanclubs

ADORABLE
Adorable
Box 2817
London N1 71X
England

A-HOUSE
A-House
Box 2795
Dublin 12
Ireland

TORI AMOS
Tori Amos Fanclub (North
America)
Box 8456
Clearwater FL 34618

BARENAKED LADIES
Page Publications
800 Steeles Ave West
Suite B10-138
Thornhill ON L4J 7L2
Canada
Notes: Write to this address for
The Barenaked Bulletin as well as
for merchandise info.

BEASTIE BOYS
Beastie Boys
c/o Grand Royal
PO Box 26689
Los Angeles CA 90026
Notes: Use a large SASE.

BEAUTIFUL SOUTH
Pumpkin Seeds
Box 19348
San Diego CA 92159

BELLY
Belly c/o Gary Smith
Fort Apache
1 Camp Street, Suite 2
Cambridge MA 02140

BETTIE SERVEERT
Under the Surface
Box 1092
BB Enschede, The Netherlands

B-52'S
B-52's Official Inter-Dimentional
Fan Club
c/o Sue-52
Box 60468
Mt. Read Station
Rochester NY 14606
Note: You must send a SASE!

JELLO BIAFRA
Alternative Tentacles Operation
Desert Scam
PO Box 11458
San Francisco, CA 94101
Notes: For Alternative Tentacles
catalogue, include 50 cents (US)

BIG AUDIO DYNAMITE
B.A.D
Box 2972
London W16 1GP
England

BLUR
Blur Information Service
Box 21
London SW11 4LZ
England

BOO RADLEYS
Club Boo!
Box 1880
London N16 0DZ
England
Notes: Send an SASE or IRC.

BUFFALO TOM
Buffalo Tom
Box 88
Backbay Annex
Boston MA 02117

BUTTHOLE SURFERS
Butthole Surfers
5913 Washington Ave
Houston, TX 77007

CARTER USM
Club Carter
PO Box 709
London SE19 1JY
England

CATHERINE WHEEL
Catherine Wheel
Box 9
Lowestoft, Suffolk NR32 3Q3
England

CHAPTERHOUSE
Chapterhouse
Box 2406
London NW10 5NE
England

CHARLATANS UK
Charlatans UK
109 PO Box 94

Northwich CW9 5TS
England
Note: SASE required.

CONCRETE BLONDE
Concrete Blonde
c/o Happy Hermit Co.
1608 North Cahuenga
Box 567
Hollywood CA 90028

CONSOLIDATED
Consolidated
PO Box 170057
San Francisco CA 94117
Notes: Send SASE

JULIAN COPE
Julian Cope
c/o Outlaw
145 Oxford Street
London W1
England

CORKY AND THE JUICE PIGS
Corky and the Juice Pigs
Legion of Gravel
PO Box 680
Station C
Toronto ON M6J 3S1
Canada

CRACKER
Cracker
c/o Home Office Management
Jackson Haring
2200 Adeline Street
Suite 330F
Oakland CA 94607-2332

CRANES
Cranes Contact
PO Box 144
Southsea Hants PO5 2PY
England

CROWDED HOUSE
Crowded House
Box 333
Prahran Vic 3181
Australia
Note: Send both an SASE and an
international reply coupon.

CYPRESS HILL
Cypress Hill
c/o Buzztone Entertainment
646 North Robertson
Los Angeles CA 90069
Notes: Merchandise hotline:
(800) 219-HILL

DEPECHE MODE
Depeche Mode Fan Club
Box 1281
London 11 9UX
England

DINK
Dink
c/o Fuck You I'm Not Sorry
Entertainment Conglomeration
Box 3341
Kent OH 44240

DISPOSABLE HEROES OF HIPHOPRISY
Hiphoprisy
PO Box 410502

San Francisco CA 94141

EINSTURZENDE NEUBAUTEN
Einsturzende Neubauten
c/o Kathleen Nizzari
PO Box 20207
London Terrace Station
New York NY 10011

ELEVENTH DREAM DAY
Friends of EDD
Box 261
Prudential Station
Boston MA 02199

ERASURE
Erasure Information Service
Box 399
London NW3 1TB
England

EURYTHMICS
Eurythmics
Box 245
London N8 9QU
England

5440
5440
c/o #707
810 West Broadway
Vancouver BC V5Z 1J8
Canada

FRENTE
Frente
PO Box 1720
Collingwood, Victoria 3066
Australia

FUGAZI
Fugazi
3819 Beecher Street
NW Washington DC 20001

PETER GABRIEL
Peter Gabriel
c/o Real World [Dept. PG]
Box 35
Bath, Avon
England

GENE
Gene
Box 4079
London SW9 0XR
England

GREEN DAY
Green Day
5337 College Ave
Suite 555
Oakland CA 94618

GUIDED BY VOICES
Guided By Voices
2109 Titus Ave.
Dayton OH 45414

THE REVERAND HORTON HEAT
The Reverand Horton Heat
Box 59031
Dallas TX 75359
Note: Send SASE

HUM
Hum
Box 666
Urbana IL 61801

HUNTERS AND COLLECTORS
Ghost Nation
Box 276
Albert Park, Victoria 3206
Australia

ICE-T/BODY COUNT
Syndicate Fan Club
1283 South LaBrea
PO Box 211
Los Angeles CA 90019

INXS
INXS
MMA Management
Box 55
Spit Junction 2008
Australia

JALE
Jale
PO Box 1601
Halifax NS B3J 2Y3
Canada

JAMES
James
Box 182
Manchester M60 4DL1
England

JESUS JONES
Jesus Jones Information Service
Box 1475
London SW3 2NP
England

KILLING JOKE
Killing Joke-Trinity Street

47 Bedord Street
Leamington Spa CV32 5D4
England
Notes: International reply
coupon required.

KINGMAKER
Kingmaker Info
Box 31
Ely, Cambs 3B6 2UW
England

KMFDM
KMFDM Enterprises
2524 North Lincoln Ave.
#44
Chicago IL 69614-2389

LENNY KRAVITZ
Lenny Kravitz Fan Club
14755 Ventura
I-710
Sherman Oaks CA 91403

DANIEL LANOIS
Daniel Lanois
Opal Information
Box 141 Leigh-on-Sea, Essex
England

LEMONHEADS
Lemonheads Box 366
Kenmore Station
Boston MA 02215
  or
Lemonheads
Box 109150
7985 Santa Monica Blvd.
West Hollywood CA 90046

LEVELLERS
Levellers
On the Fiddle
Box 266
Alliston MA 02135
Levellers Hotline:
(617) SUB-VERT

LIVE
Friends of Live
c/o Media 5 Entertainment
400 Northampton Street
Easton, PA 18042
Notes: Send a large envelope.

LOVE BATTERY
P.O Box 64737-506
Los Angeles CA 90064

L7
L7
PO Box 3928
Hollywood CA 90078

LUSH
Lush Information Service
Box 2406
London NW10 5NE
England

MANIC STREET PREACHERS
Manic Street Preachers
Box 306
London SW9 4QN
England
Notes: Send 50p and SASE

MARILYN MANSON
Marilyn Manson Fan Club

2901 Clint Moore Road
Suite 404
Boca Raton FL 33496
Notes: Marilyn Manson Family
Intervention Hotline:
(407) 997-9437

JOHNNY MARR
Johnny Marr
c/o Ignition
Box 4RU
London W1A 4RU
England

MC 900 FT JESUS
MC 900 Ft Jesus
c/o Gonga
PO Box 64716
Dallas TX 750206-0716

MEAT PUPPETS
Meat Puppets
PO Box 119
Tempe AZ 85281

THE MISSION
Mission World Information
Box HP 21
Leeds LS7 1SQ
West Yorks, England
   or
Neverland Recordings
c/o Equator Records
333 Latimer Road
London W10 6RA
Mission Hotline (Britain only):
0891 600 069

MOIST

Moist
Box 355
1195 Davie Street
Vancouver BC V6G 1N2
Canada

MORPHEINE
Morpheine
c/o P.O Box 382085
Cambridge MA 02138-2085

MORRISSEY
For North America:
Morrissey
c/o Nancy Poetner
505 South Beverly Drive
#1194
Beverly Hills CA 90212

For the UK:
Morrissey
c/o Gail Colson
81-83 Walton
London SW3 2HP

MOXY FRUVOUS
Moxy Fruvous
1436 Queen Street West
Box 90005
Toronto ON Canada M6K 1M2

MY LIFE WITH THE THRILL KILL KULT
Thrill Kill Kult
c/o Eric Kroll
464 Grand Central Station
New York NY 10016
Notes: Signed photos available.

NED'S ATOMIC DUSTBIN
Ned's Atomic Dustbin
Box 2169
Stourbridge, West Midlands DY8
1YU
England

NINE INCH NAILS
Nine Inch Nails
Box 16681
Cleveland OH 44116

NIRVANA
Nirvana
4739 University Way NE
Suite 1606
Seattle WA 98105

NITZER EBB
Nitzer Ebb Produkt
Box 867
Chelmsford, Essex, CM1 5RQ
England

NOFX
NOFX
c/o Epitaph Records
6201 Sunset Blvd
Suite 111
Hollywood CA 90028

THE OCEAN BLUE
The Ocean Blue
Box 565
Hershey PA 17055

THE ODDS
The Odds
Box 1761

Santa Monica, CA 90406-1761

OFFSPRING
c/o Epitaph Records
6021 Sunset Blvd
Hollywood CA 90028

THE ORB
The Orb Info Network
Suite 310
163 Third Ave.
New York NY 10003

OUR LADY PEACE
Our Lady Peace
Box 1263
Station B
Weston, Ontario, Canada M9L
2R9
Note: SASE required.

PAVEMENT
Pavement
9361 Cove Drive
Stockton CA 95212

PEARL JAM
Pearl Ten Fan Club
Box 4570
Seattle WA 98104

PET SHOP BOYS
Pet Shop Boys
Box 102
Stanmore, Middlesex HA7 2PY
England

THE POGUES

The Pogues Fan Club
Postfach 110705
4410 Warendorf
Germany

POP WILL EAT ITSELF
PWEI
c/o Paul Boswell
The Agency
370 City Road
London EC1
England

THE POSIES
The Posies
Box 45656
Seattle WA 98145-0656

PRIMUS
Primus Fan Club and Mail Order
Prawnsong/Club Bastardo
3470 19th Street
San Francisco CA 94110
Notes: SASE required.

THE PROCLAIMERS
The Proclaimers
Box 309
Edinburgh EH9 1JE
Scotland

PUBLIC IMAGE LTD.
PiL
132 A Bristol Road
London E78 8 QF
England

PULP
Pulp

PO Box 87
Sheffield S6 2Y2
England
  or
Pulp People
Box 84
Sheffield S10 1YQ
England

RADIOHEAD
Radiohead Information (UK)
PO Box 322
Oxford OX4 1EL
England
Answerphone: 0235 848261
  or
Radiohead (USA)
Box 3268
Hollywood CA 90078

RAGE AGAINST THE MACHINE
Rage Against the Machine
Box 2052
Los Angeles CA 90069

THE RAMONES
The Ramones
c/o Overland Productions
1775 Broadway
7th Floor
New York NY 10019

RANCID
Rancid
PO Box 4596
Berkeley CA 94704

REDD KROSS
Redd Kross

Box 803
North Hollywood CA 91603

RED HOT CHILI PEPPERS
Rockinfreakapotamus
11012 Ventura Blvd
Box 368
Studio City CA 91604

R.E.M.
R.E.M.
Box 8032
Athens GA 30603

RIDE
Ride
c/o Lesley Braden
POB 7183
Rockford IL 61126

HENRY ROLLINS/ROLLINS BAND
Henry Rollins
2.13.61
Box 1910
Los Angeles CA 90078
Hotline: (213) 462-8962

RYMES WITH ORANGE
RWO Fanclub
Citrus Soul Productions Ltd.
Box 11515
Suite 888-650 West Georgia
Street
Vancouver BC V6B 4N7

SHADOWY MEN ON A SHADOWY PLANET
Shadowy Men on a Shadowy
Planet

c/o Ted Bogues
Station C
1117 Queen Street West
Toronto ON M6J 3R9
Canada
Notes: Send SASE. Allow *4-60*
weeks for delivery.

SHED SEVEN
Shed Seven c/ Cut Throat Management
Box 777
Coventry CV7 9YZ
England

SIOUXSIE AND THE BANSHEES
Siouxsie and the Banshees File
Box 1984
London W11
England

SISTERS OF MERCY
Sisters Information Service
Box HP 29
Leeds 6 West Yorkshire
England

SLEEPER
Sleeper
Box 3305
London SW9 8BG
England

SLOAN
Sloan
c/o Brooks Diamond Productions
Suite 507
1800 Argyle Street

Halifax NS B3J 3N8

SLOWDIVE
Slowdive
Box 1880
London N16 OD2
England

SMASHING PUMPKINS
Smashing Pumpkins Fanclub
Information
Box 578010
Chicago IL 60657

SOCIAL DISTORTION
Social Distortion
c/o Rebel Waltz Management
11684 Ventura Blvd
Suite 772
Studio City CA 91604
Notes: Send $1 U.S.

SONIC YOUTH
Sonic Death
Box 6179
Hoboken NJ 07030
   or
Sonic Death
PO Box 1588
Bloomfield NJ 07003

SOUL COUGHING
Soul Coughing
Box 477
New York NY 10108
Notes: Please include prose frag-
ments, bizarre factoids, xerox
collages and snapshots.

SOUNDGARDEN
Knights of the Sound Table
Box 61275
Seattle WA 98121

SQUEEZE
Squeeze Club
Bugle House
21A Noel Street
London W1V 3PD
England

STEREO MCs
Stereo MCs
c/o Gee Street Management
Suite 151 Zecjendorf Towers
111 East 14th Street
New York NY 10003

STONE TEMPLE PILOTS
Stone Temple Pilots Info and
Stuff
PO Box 227
1118 West Magnolia Blvd
Burbank CA 41506

SUEDE
Suede Fanclub
PO Box 2384
London E2 9BE
England
   or
Suede Info Service
Box 3431
London N1 7LW
England

SUICIDAL TENDENCIES
Suicidal Tendencies

Box 5131
Playa del Ray CA 90296

SUGAR
Sugar
c/o Granary Music
PO Box 4947
Austin, TX 78765-4947
E-mail: sugarnet@aol.com

MATTHEW SWEET
Matthew Sweet
c/o Russel Carter Artist Management Ltd.
315 West Ponce de Leon Ave
Suite 755
Decatur GA 30030

SWERVEDRIVER
Swervedriver Info Service
8 Station Parade
Barking, Essex IG11 8DN
England

TEA PARTY
Tea Party
1971 Spruce Hill Road
Pickering ON L1V 1S6
Canada

10,000 MANIACS
Friends of 10,000 Maniacs
34 Canterberry Street
New Bedford MA 02746

THE THE
The The
Box 6010-901
Sherman Oaks CA 91413

THESE ANIMAL MEN
These Animal Men
Globeshine Ltd.
8 Wendell Road
London W12 9RT
England

THEY MIGHT BE GIANTS
They Might Be Giants Info Club
Box 110535 H
Williamsburgh Station
Brooklyn NY 11211-0003
Notes: Send $2 (US)—Includes newsletter, tour dates and mail order catalogue. TMBG Information Club Hotline:
(914) 359-0867
TMBG Dial-a-song service:
(718) 387-6962

TOO MUCH JOY
Too Much Joy
1780 Broadway
Suite 1201
New York NY 10019

TOOL
Tool
8391 Beverly Blvd
#298
Los Angeles CA 90048

TRAGICALLY HIP
Tragically Hip
c/o Lori Dennis
405 Wellington Street
Unit 29
St. Thomas ON N5R 5T7
Canada

or
Tragically Hipp
Box 37
Station C
Toronto ON M6J 3M7
Canada

TRASH CAN SINATRAS

Trash Can Sinatras
c/o I Hate Music
No. 1 Glencairn Square
Kilmarnock K1A 2QX
Scotland

URGE OVERKILL

Urge Overkill Fan Club
PO Box 25619
Chicago IL 60625

›U2

In North America:
U2 World Service
119 Rockland Center
Nauet NY 10954
*In the UK and the rest of the
world*:
U2 World Service
Box 18
Wellingborough NN8 3VY
England

VERUCA SALT

Veruca Salt
c/o Minty Fresh
PO Box 577400
Chicago IL 60657

VIOLENT FEMMES

14755 Ventura Blvd

I-710
Sherman Oaks CA 91403

THE WALTONS

The Waltons
Box 215
Postal Station G
Toronto ON Canada M4M 3G7

THE WATCHMEN

The Watchmen
745-740 Corydon Ave.
Winnipeg MB R3M 0Y1
Canada

THE WATERBOYS

Waterboys Information Society
Box 45
Belfast BT126 BQ
Northern Ireland

WEDDING PRESENT

Wedding Present Info and Mer-
chandise
PO Box HP 25
Leeds LS6 1RU
England

WEEN

Ween
Box 39
Trenton NJ 08601
Notes: For lyrics, send $1 U.S.

WEEZER

Weezer
6312 Hollywood Blvd
Suite 110
Los Angeles CA 90028

PAUL WELLER
Paul Weller
c/o Modern Works
nomi Studios
45153 Sinclair Road
London W14 0NS
England
Notes: Send a SASE envelope and
an internation reply coupon.

WORLD PARTY
World Party Mail
Box 18
Earls Court Road
London W8 6ED
England

XTC
The Little Express
Box 1072
Barrie ON Canada L4M 5E1
Notes: Newsletter is available.

YOUNG GODS
Young Gods
c/o Patrick Jammes
283 Faubourg St-Antoine
Paris 75011
France

Section 2

Alternative Music and the Internet

A s more people come online, the amount of information and discusson on the Internet is growing exponentially every day. As of May 1, 1995, there were at least 27,000 web sites on the Net with the number doubling roughly every fifty-three days. There is obviously much more out there than what is listed here but these addresses should get you started. Every effort has been made to make sure all the addresses are current and will be there for you in the future. (That's why I've stayed away from a lot of fan-generated web sites. How long will they last?)

Remember: Each site will link you to others. And keep in mind that if you find that a site has been moved—or if you discover something cool and you think it should appear in the next edition of this book— e-mail it to: alanc@passport.ca.

A. Artists
A-HOUSE
World Wide Web: http://radioactive.net
E-mail: radioactive@radioactive net

AMERICAN MUSIC CLUB
World Wide Web:
http://www.iuma.com/Warner/html/american_music_club.html

TORI AMOS
List address: really-deep-thoughts@gradient.cis.upenn.edu
World Wide Web:
http://www.mit.edu:8001/people/nocturne/tori.html

ADAM ANT
World Wide Web: http://caprec.com/Ant/

ART OF NOISE
List address: aon@calpoly.edu
FTP (path): ftp.uwp.edu. (/pub/music/lists/aon/*)

BAD RELIGION
E-mail: (band member's first name)@badreligion.com
FTP: badreligion.com

World Wide Web: http://nebuleuse.enst-bretagne.fr/lepoulti/bad.religion

BAUHAUS
World Wide Web: http://www.mordor.com/bauhaus

BEASTIE BOYS
Newsgroup: alt.music.beastie-boys
World Wide Web: http://www.nando.net/music/gm/BeastieBoys/

BELLY
E-mail: bellymail@aol.com

JELLO BIAFRA
Newsgroup: alt.fan.jello-biafra

BJORK
World Wide Web: http://www.centrum.is/bjork/

BLUR
World Wide Web: http://lispstat.alcd.soton.ac.uk/~prbt/blur.hmtl

DAVID BOWIE
Newsgroup: alt.fan.david-bowie

KATE BUSH
List address: love-hounds@eddie.mit.edu

CHEMLAB
E-mail: chemlin@cyberden.com

CHRISTIAN DEATH
World Wide Web: http://christian-death.acc.brad.ac.uk/

COCTEAU TWINS
World Wide Web: http://garnet.berkley.edu:8080/cocteau.html

COIL
E-mail: john@loci.demon.co.uk

CONCRETE BLONDE
List address: concrete-blonde@piggy.ucsb.edu

ELVIS COSTELLO
List address: costello@gnu.ai.mit.edu
World Wide Web:
http://www.mit.edu:8001/people/nocturne/tori.html

CRANES
E-mail: Cranes95@aol.com

DEAD CAN DANCE
World Wide Web: http://www.nets.com/dcd

DEPECHE MODE
List address: http://www.cis.ufl.edu/~sag/dm/

DEVO
Newsgroup: alt.fan.devo

DURAN DURAN
World Wide Web: http://caprec.com/Duran/

BRIAN ENO
List address: eno-l@/udlapvms.pue.udlap.mx
Newsgroup: alt.music.brian-eno

ENYA
List address: enya@cs.colorado.edu

FRONT 242
World Wide Web: http://www.ifi.uio.no/~terjesa/front242/main.html

PETER GABRIEL
Newsgroup: alt.music.peter-grabriel
World Wide Web:
http://www.cosy.sbg.ac.at/`bjelli/Gabriel/Text/pg.faq

GREG GINN (SST RECORDS, BLACK FLAG)
E-mail: bmc@cyberden.com

GOO GOO DOLLS
E-mail: googoodoll@aol.com

JULIANA HATFIELD/BLAKE BABIES
List address: listproc@mcfeeley.ccutexas.edu (Type in "subscribe juliana" and then your e-mail address)

HOLE
World Wide Web: http://geffen.com/hole.html

KMFDM
E-mail: kmfdm@sonicnet.com

LEMONHEADS
E-mail: hyf-request@kazak.nmsu.edu

ANNIE LENNOX
World Wide Web:
http://sashimi.wwa.com/hammers/pictures/annie.html

LIVE
World Wide Web: http://www.cerf.net/live.html

L7
E-mail: L7@aol.com

LETTERS TO CLEO
E-mail: cleo@world.std.com

LOTION
E-mail: lotion@sonic.net

LOW POP SUICIDE
World Wide Web:
http://underground.net:80/worlddom/lowpopsuicide

MACHINES OF LOVING GRACE
E-mail: mlginfo@emerald.net

MANIC STREET PREACHERS
World Wide Web: http://www.cs.nott.ac/~jwl/manics/
http://boris.qub.ac.uk/tony/manics

SARAH MCLACHLAN
World Wide Web: http://wimsey.com/nettwerk.com/sarpg.html
http://www.css.itd.umich.edu//~hubt/sarah/

MOBY
E-mail: tlims@phantom.com

MORPHINE
E-mail: lickme4@aol.com
Also try: morphine@sonicnet.com

NEGATIVLAND
World Wide Web: http://sunsite.unc.edu:80/id/negativland

NINE INCH NAILS
IRC: #nin
Newsgroup: alt.music.nin
World Wide Web: http://www.scri.fsu.edu/~patters/nin.html
http://www.csh.rit.edu/~jerry/NIN_RI/welcome.hmtl
http://www.fsl.orst.edu/novell/tsuga.share/rogues/rosero/nin/nin-list.html

NIRVANA
Newsgroup: alt.music.nirvana
World Wide Web:
http://www2.ecst.csuchico.edu//~jedi/nirvana.html
http://www/ludd.luth.se/misc/nirvana/
http://american.recordings.com/wwwofmusic/ubl.html

OASIS
World Wide Web: http://www.cts.com/browse/ginger

SINEAD O'CONNOR
List address: jump-in-the-river@presto.ig.com

THE ORB
World Wide Web: http://www.hyperlink.com/orb/

PEARL JAM
Newsgroup: alt.music.pearl-jam
World Wide Web: http://tiac.net/biz/applwood/vitalogy.html

PERE UBU
E-mail: pereubu@projex.demon.co.uk

LIZ PHAIR
E-mail: guyville@aol.com
World Wide Web: There are Web pages in the U.S., France, Africa and Australia (which seems to be the best one).
Try the following:
http://magna.com.au/woodwire/index.html

THE POGUES
World Wide Web: http://daneel.acns.nwu:8082/kultur/pogues/pogue-root.html

THE POLICE
List address: police@cindy.ecst.csuchico.edu
Newsgroup: alt.music.the.police
alt.fan.sting

POP WILL EAT ITSELF
World Wide Web: http://elmail.co.uk/music/pwei

QUICKSAND
E-mail: quicksand@sonicnet.com

RADIOHEAD
Newsgroup: alt.music.radiohead
World Wide Web: http://musicbase.co.uk/music/radiohead/

R.E.M.
Newsgroup: rec.music.rem
World Wide Web: http://www.halcyon.com/rem/index.html
Song lyrics available at:
http://www.sys.uea.ac.uk//~u9333975/rem_lyrics.html

THE REMBRANDTS
E-mail: globecool@aol.com

THE RESIDENTS
E-mail: crypticcor@aol.com

SENSER
E-mail: senser@underground.net

SEVERED HEADS
List address: adolph-a-carrot@andrew.cmu.edu

THE SHAMEN
World Wide Web:
http://www.demon.co.uk/drci/shamen/nemeton.html

SINGLE GUN THEORY
E-mail: pete.rivett-carnac@f406.n712.z3.fidonet.org

SISTERS OF MERCY
World Wide Web: http://www.cm.cf.ac.uk./Sisters.of.Mercy/

SKINNY PUPPY
E-mail: puppy@netcom.con

SKY CRIES MARY
E-mail: toddr@halcyon.com

SMASHING PUMPKINS
Newsgroup: alt.music.smashing.pumpkins

SONIC YOUTH
Newsgroup: alt.music.sonic-youth

SPIRITUALIZED ELECTRIC MAINLINE
E-mail: purephase@aol.com

SUGAR
E-mail: sugarnet@aol.com

10,000 MANIACS
World Wide Web:
http://www.nd.edu/StudentLinks/mecheves/misc.10000.html

THEY MIGHT BE GIANTS
Newsgroup: alt.music.tmbg

TRAGICALLY HIP
E-mail: thehip@hookup.net
World Wide Web: http://cimtegration.com/ent/music/hip/hip.html

U2
Newsgroup: alt.fan.u2
alt.music.u2

VERUCA SALT
World Wide Web: http://www.gordian.com/users/daniel/veruca

THE VERVE
World Wide Web: http://vmg.co.uk/

SID VICIOUS
World Wide Web:
http://alfred1.u.washington.edu:8080/~jlks/pike/svicio.html

VIOLENT FEMMES
World Wide Web: http://www.gl.umbc.edu/~mmerry2/femmes/html

WEEN
Newsgroup: alt.music.ween

B. Record Companies:

AJAX RECORDS
E-mail: ajax@ripco.com

AMERICAN RECORDINGS
World Wide Web: http://american.recordings.com
E-mail: american@american.recordings.com

ATLANTIC
E-mail: atlgrp@aol.com

BOMP
E-mail: orbit23@aol.com

CAROLINE
E-mail: caroline@sonicnet.com

CLEOPATRA
E-mail: cleopatra@cyberdeen.com

CREATION
World Wide Web: http://www.musicbase.co.uk/music/creation/
To subscribe: cremktg@cityscape.co.uk

DISCHORD
E-mail: dischordr@aol.com

EARACHE
E-mail: earacher@aol.com

EAST/WEST
World Wide Web: http://www.music.net

ELEKTRA
World Wide Web: http://elektra.com

ffrr
E-mail: ffrr@aol.com

FIFTH COLUMN
E-mail: fifthcolvmn@cyberden.com

4AD
World Wide Web: http://www.evo.org:80html/eyesore.html

GEFFEN/DGC
World Wide Web: http://geffen.com/

GO! DISCS/LONDON RECORDS
E-mail: ffrr1@aol.com
World Wide Web: http://www.godiscs.co.uk/godiscs/index.html

INTERSCOPE
E-mail: jenboddy@aol.com

KILL ROCK STARS
E-mail: kllrck-strs@aol.com

KNITTING FACTORY
E-mail: knitting@knittingfactory.com

MAMMOTH
World Wide Web: http://www.nando.net/mammoth/mammoth.html
E-mail: info@mammoth.com
Also try: ftp.nando.net

MATADOR
E-mail: matadorrec@aol.com

MCA
World Wide Web: http://musicbase.co.uk/music/mca

MUTE
E-mail: mute@mute.com
mutenews@mute.com
Also try: ftp.mutelibtech.com

NETTWERK
BBS: (604) 731-7007
E-mail: nettwerk@mindlink.bc.ca
World Wide Web: http://www.wimsey.com/nettwerk

RADIOACTIVE
World Wide Web: http://radioactive.net
E-mail: radioactive@radioactive.net

RESTLESS
E-mail: restrecord@aol.com

ROADRUNNER
E-mail: roadrun@ix.netcom.com

SIDE EFFECTS AMERICA
E-mail: soleilmoon@aol.com

SILENT
World Wide Web: http://www.iuma.com/Silent/

SIRE
World Wide Web: http://www.iuma.com/Warner/

SONY
World Wide Web: http://www.sony.com

SUB POP
E-mail: info@subpop.com
loser@subpop.com
FTP: ftp.subpop.com
World Wide Web: http://www.subpop.com

TAANG!
E-mail: taang2@aol.com

VIRGIN/HUT
World Wide Web: http://vmg.co.uk/

C. Other Interesting Sites

102.1 THE EDGE

The official web page of CFNY-FM in Toronto offers dozens of links to individual bands. Start browsing with the home page and move out from there.

World Wide Web: http://passport.ca:80/edge

ADDICTED TO NOISE

A digital magazine put together by a contributing editor to *Rolling Stone*. The music news is very up-to-date.

World Wide Web: http://www.addict.com/ATN/

AMERICAN RECORDINGS' "WORLD OF MUSIC"

Rick Rubin's company has put together a nice resource archive that has links to many other sites. It's worth browsing.

World Wide Web:
http://american.recordings.com/wwwofmusic/ubl.html

CENSORED MUSIC PAGE

Stuff that they don't want you to hear (or even know about).

World Wide Web: http://fileroom.aaup.uic.edu/FileRoom/documents/Mmusic.html

C.G. PUBLISHING

An excellent publishing house when it comes to books on music. (Okay, so I'm biased because they had the good taste to publish this book). Lots of links to interesting sites.

World Wide Web: http://www.icom.ca/cgpinc

COMPACT DISCS

A general discussion of CDs including what's available and what's new out there.

Newsgroup: rec.music.cd

CONCERT INFORMATION

Get access to tour itineraries for hundreds of bands.

World Wide Web: http://akebono.stanford.edu/yahoo/Entertainment/Music/Concert_Information

DISCOGRAPHIES
Looking for a list of all the records put out by your favorite band? Try the net.
FTP (path): ftp.spie.com (/library/music/label/*)

GOTH MUSIC
Information and discussion of Alien Sex Fiend, Sisters of Mercy, Christian Death and more.
IRC: #gothic
World Wide Web: http://akebono.stanford.edu/yahoo/Entertainment/Music/Gothic
World Wide Web: http://www.acs.csu;b.edu/~vamp/Gothic/

GRUNGE
Just because you like flannel shirts doesn't mean you don't know how to use a computer!
List address: grunge-l@ubvm.cc.buffalo.edu

INTERNET UNDERGROUND MUSIC ARCHIVE
This is a music resource based in Santa Cruz, California that's home to hundreds of digitized songs from hundreds of unsigned bands. The sound is CD-quality and there are loads of graphics.
World Wide Web: http://www.iuma.com/IUMA/index_graphic.html

THE LIST OF MUSIC MAILING LISTS
This is great. This site regularly compiles the details of dozens of lists that cover everything from various musical styles to specfic artists.
World Wide Web: http://server.berkeley.edu/~ayukawa/lommi

LOLLAPALOOZA
This is the official web site of the annual Lollapalooza tour. It features graphics, rumors, official press releases and more.
World Wide Web: http://www.lollapalooza.com

LYRICS
If you've been looking for the words, they could be here.
FTP (path): ftp.uwp.edu (/pub/music/lyrics/*)
FTP (path): ocf.berkeley.edu (/pub/Library/Lyrics)

Gopher—University of Wisconsin Parkside: gopher.uwp.edu (select "music archives")
World Wide Web: http:/anxiety-closet,mit.edu:8001/activities/russian-club/catalog.html
http://www.mcc.ac.uk./Lyrics

MUSIC ARCHIVES

This is huge. You might not know what you're looking for until you start browsing. Only 50 users can be on line at a time, so be prepared to wait.
FTP (path): ftp.uwp.edu (/pub/music/*)

MUSICBASE

A great UK web site. This is the offical home page to a number of bands (The Stone Roses, Human League and *lots* more) and record companies (Creation, Motown). If you like British music, then this page is for you.
World Wide Web: http://www.musicbase.co.uk/music/

MUSIC CHATS

Meet like-minded people and talk about music.
IRCs: #altmusic
#music
#punk
#realpunk
#trax
Newsgroups: alt.music.alternative

MUSIC DATABASE

Search material by artist, title, track, language, style or whatever. Information uploads are welcome.
World Wide Web:
http://www.cecer.army.mil/~burnett/MDB/musicResources.html

MUSIC FACTS

Surf this one and get lost in lists.
FTP (path): quartz.rutgers.edu (/pub/music/*)

MUSIC FAQS

Got a question? The answer might be here. Topics include industrial, goth, ska grunge and more.
World Wide Web: http://www.cis.ohio-state.edu/hypertext/faq/usenet/music/top.hmtl

MUSIC HARMONY LIST

A great compilation detailing what's out there. There are files on labels, local scenes and radio stations. The second web page is a collection of artists and web sites with everything sorted alphabetically.
World Wide Web: http://orpheus.ucsd.edu/mbreen/music_links.html
World Wide Web: http://orpheus.ucsd.edu/webmaster/artists.html

MUSIC INDEX

Another giant megalist of stuff. Browse away.
World Wide Web: http://www.cc.columbia.edu/-hauben/music-index.html

MUSIC KITCHEN

Everything from discographies, audio files and pictures to press releases and movies. The Beastie Boys hang out here, too.
World Wide Web: http://www.nando.net/music/gm/

MUSIC LIBRARY ASSOCIATION

Like looking through other people's stuff? You should enjoy this tour through music libraries around the world.
Newsgroup: bit.listserv.mal-l

MUSIC LISTS

There are enough subjects here to keep you surfing for hours.
List address: mlol@wariat.org

MUSIC NEWS

Why wait for the papers and magazine? Get the news *now*.
Newsgroup: rec.music.info

MUSIC REVIEWS

Find out what others think of the latest releases. All genres covered.
World Wide Web: http://www.dcs.ed.ac.uk/students/pg/awrc/review/

MUSIC VIDEOS

This is where people go to discuss videos and how to make them.
Newsgroup: rec.music.videos

POLLSTAR

Pollstar is a trade magazine that specializes in the concert industry. This site will give you free access to the latest concert tour information. The information is always kept current because music industry professionals rely on it.
World Wide Web: http://www.pollstar.com

PUNK

Punk is *not* dead—it's on the net!
Newsgroup: alt.punk

STROBE

A bi-monthy cyber fanzine on alternative music. There are lots of soundbites for downloading.
World Wide Web: http://www.iuma.com/strobe/

TICKETMASTER

The world's biggest ticket seller offers listings of concerts and sporting events along wtih descriptions of more than 400 venues. Keep in mind that you still have to order tickets over the phone with a credit card.
World Wide Web: http://www.ticketmaster.com

TOP 100 LISTS

Some people are addicted to ranking things. If you're into this kind of list-making, check out this site.
FTP (path): ftp.spies.com (/Library/Music/Lists/*)

THE WEB WIDE WORLD OF MUSIC

Lists and links and trivia and discussions and more.
World Wide Web:
http://www.galcit.caltech.edu/~ta/music/index.html

Find Any More Interesting Sites? List Them Here

Section 3

Record Label Guide

Contary to what you might think, record companies love getting mail. Sometimes, they'll even write back—especially if you ask for a catalogue or to be included on their mailing list. Another thing to remember: If you're trying to reach a specific band but you don't have the address of their fanclub or official information service, write their label. If they care anything about their artists, they'll see to it that all letters are forwarded.

A&M
1416 North LaBrea Ave.
Hollywood CA 90028

ACE
46-50 Steele Road
London NW10 7AS
England

AJAX
Box 805293
Chicago IL 60680-4114
Catalogue: Free

ALTERNATIVE TENTACLES
Box 424756
San Francisco CA 94142
Catalogue: 50 cents (US)

AMERICAN RECORDINGS
3500 West Olive Avenue
#1550
Burbank CA 91505

AMPHETIMINE REPTILE
2645 First Avenue South
Minneapolis MN 55408

ARISTA
6 West 57th Street
New York NY 10019

ASPHODEL
Box 51
Old Chelsea Station
New York NY 10113-0051

ATLANTIC
75 Rockefeller Plaza
New York NY 10014

AVANT
c/o Sphere
Cargo Building 80
Room 2A
JFK Airport
Jamaica NY 11430

BAR NONE
Box 1704
Hoboken NJ 07030

BEAR FAMILY
Eduard Grunow Strasse 12
2800 Bremen 1
West Germany

BEAR RECORDS
511 Sixth Avenue
Suite 321
New York NY 10011
Catalogue: Free

BEGGAR'S BANQUET
274 Madison Avenue
Suite 804
New York NY 10016

BIZARRE/PLANET
740 North LaBrea
Los Angeles CA 90038-3339

BLAST FIRST
262 Mott Street
#324
New York NY 10012
Catalogue: Free

BOMP
PO Box 7112
Burbank CA 91510
Catalogue: Sends SASE or two
International Reply Coupons.

CANDY-ASS
Box 42382
Portland OR 97242

CAPITOL RECORDS
1750 North Vine Street
Hollywood CA 90028

CARGO
4901-906 Morena Blvd
San Diego CA 92117-3432

CAROLINE
114 West 26th Street
11th Floor
New York NY 10001
Catalogue: Free

CD PRESENTS
1317 Grant Ave.
Suite 531
San Francisco CA 94133
Catalogue: Free

CHAINSAW
Box 42600
Portland OR 97242

CLEOPATRA
8726 South Sepulveda
Suite D-82
Los Angeles CA 90045
Catalogue: Free

COLUMBIA
550 Madison Avenue
New York NY 10022

CREATION
83 Clerkenwell Road
London EC1
England

CRUZ RECORDS
Box 7756
Long Beach CA 90807
Catalogue: Free

CRYPT
c/o Matador
676 Broadway
4th Floor
New York NY 10012

DB RECS
432 Moreland Ave. NE
Atlanta GA 30307

Catalogue: Free

DECEPTIVE
The Sunday School
Rotary Street
London SE1 6LG
UK

DEJADISC
537 Lindsey Street
San Marco TX 78666

DGC
9130 Sunset Blvd.
Los Angeles CA 90069

DISCHORD
3819 Beecher Street NW
Washington DC 20007
Catalogue: Free

DOCTOR DREAM
841 West Collins
Orange CA 92667
Note: Write for a product list or call (800) 45 DREAM.

DRAG CITY
Box 476867
Chicago IL 60647

DRUNKEN FISH
8600 West Olympic Bvld.
Los Angeles CA 90035

DUTCH EAST INDIA TRADING
Box 800
Rockville Center NY 11571-0800

DYNAMICA
c/o CBM Inc.
8721 Sunset Blvd
Suite 7
West Hollywood CA 90069

EARACHE
295 Lafayette Street
Suite 915
New York NY 10012

ELEKTRA
75 Rockefeller Plaza
New York NY 10019

EMI
1290 Avenue of the Americas
42nd Floor
New York NY 10012

EPIC
550 Madison Avenue
New York NY 10012

EPITAPH
6201 Sunset Blvd.
Suite 111
Hollywood CA 90028

FAX USA
c/o Instinct
26 West 17th Street
Suite 502
New York NY 10011

FFRR
825 8th Avenue
New York NY 10019

FIFTH COLUMN RECORDS
Box 787
Washington DC 20044
Catalogue: Free

FLYDADDY
Box 43542
Philadelphia PA 10106

FLYING NUN
Box 677
Auckland, New Zealand

4AD
Box 3813
London SW18 1XE
England
Catalogue: £2.00

FUTURIST
6 Green Street
2nd Floor
New York NY 10013

GEFFEN
9130 Sunset Blvd
Los Angeles CA 90069

GIANT
8900 Wilshire Blvd
Suite 200
Beverly Hills CA 90211

GRAND ROYAL
Box 26689
Los Angeles CA 90026

GRASS
81 North Forest Avenue

Rockville Center NY 11570

GREEN LINNET
43 Beaver Brook Road
Danbury CT 06810

HOMESTEAD RECORDS
Box 800
Rockville Center NY 11571
Catalogue: Free

INTERSCOPE/NOTHING
10900 Wilshire Blvd.
Suite 1230
Los Angeles CA 90024

INVISIBLE
Box 16008
Chicago IL 60616

IRS
Catalogue: Call (800) 336-2IRS

ISLAND
400 Lafayette Street
5th Floor
New York NY 10003

K
Box 7154
Olympia WA 98507

KILL ROCK STARS
120 NE State Avenue
Suite 418
Olympia WA 98501
Catalogue: Send $1 (US)

KNITTING FACTORY RECORDS
47 East Houston Street
New York NY 10012
Catalogue: Free

LOOKOUT!
Box 11374
Berkeley CA 94712

LOTUS RECORDS
Box 669
Ansonia Station
New York NY 10023

MAG WHEEL
Box 15
Boston MA 02133

MAMMOTH
Carr Mill
2nd Floor
Carrboro NC 27510
Catalogue: Free

MATADOR
676 Broadway
4th Floor
New York NY 10012
Catalogue: Free

MCA
70 Universal City Plaza
Universal City CA 91608

MERCURY
825 Eighth Avenue
New York NY 10019

MERGE
Box 1235
Chapel Hill NC 27514

MINT
699-810 West Broadway
Vancouver BC V5Z 4C9
Canada

MOONSHINE
8391 Beverly Blvd
Suite 195
Los Angeles CA 90028

MOTOWN
6255 Sunset Blvd
Hollywood CA 90028

NORTON
Box 646
Cooper Station
New York NY 10003

PEARLS FROM THE PAST
Box 54133 LWPO
1562 Lonsdale Avenue
North Vancouver BC V7M 3L5
Canada

PIAO!
BM Nancee
London WC1N 3XX
England

POWER MUSIC
648 Broadway
Suite 600
New York NY 10012

PRIORITY
6430 Sunset Blvd
Suite 900
Hollywood CA 90028

PROJECKT
Box 1591
Garden Grove CA
92642-1591
Catalogue: Free

QBADISC
Box 1256
Old Chelsea Station
New York NY 10011

QWEST
3800 Barham Blvd
Suite 503
Los Angeles CA 90068

REGURGITATED SEMEN
07819 Mittelpollnitz
Str. d. Friedens 45
Germany

RELATIVITY/EARACHE
187-07 Henderson Avenue
Hollis NY 11423
Catalogue: Free

REPRISE
3300 Warner Blvd
Burbank CA 91505

RESTLESS
1616 Vista Del Mar
Hollywood CA 90028

REVELATION RECORDS
Box 5232
Huntington Beach CA 92615-5232
Catalogue: Send $1 (US)

RHINO
2225 Colorado Avenue
Santa Monica CA 90404

RIGHT STUFF
1750 North Vine Street
Hollywood CA 90028

RIOR (REACH OUT INTERNATIONAL RECORDS)
611 Broadway
Suite 411
New York NY 10012
Catalogue: Free

ROAD CONE
Box 8732
Portland OR 97297

ROCKVILLE RECORDS
PO Box 800
Rockville Center NY 11571-0800
Catalogue: Free

ROOF BOLT
Box 3565
Oak Park IL 60303

ROUNDER RECORDS
1 Camp Street
Cambridge MA 02140

RYKODISC
Pickering Wharf
Building C
Salem MA 01970
Catalogue: Free

SCAT
5466 Broadway
#220
Cleveland OH 44127

SHANACHIE
27 East Clinton Street
Newton NJ 07860

SHIMMY DISC
JAF
Box 1187
New York NY 10116
Catalogue: SASE requried.

SIDE EFFECTS AMERICA
Box 83296
Portland OR 97283

SIDE EFFECTS EUROPE
Kettelerstrasse 4
D-95952
Germany

SILENT
101 Townsend Street
Suite 206
San Francisco CA 94107
Catalogue: Free

SIRE
75 Rockefeller Plaza
21st Floor

New York NY 10019

SONY
550 Madison Avenue
New York NY 10022

SPINART
Box 1798
New York NY 10156

SST
Box 1
Lawndale CA 90802
Catalogue: Free

STRANGE FRUIT RECORDS
PO Box 800
Rockville Center NY 11571-0800

SUB POP
1932 First Avenue
Suite 1103
Seattle WA 98101
Catalogue: Send $1 (US) or three
IRCs for catalogue and discount
coupon.

SUGAR HILL
Box 55300
Durham NC 27717

SUNDAZED
Box 85
Coxsackie NY 12051

SUPERLUX
Box 291
North Chester NY 10573

SYMPATHY FOR THE RECORD INDUSTRY
4901 Virginia Avenue
Long Beach CA 90805

TEC TONES/RALPH RECORDS
109 Minna
#391
San Francisco CA 94105
Catalogue: Free

TEENBEAT
Box 3265
Arlington VA 22203

TOUCH AND GO
Box 25520
Chicago IL 60625

TRANCE SYNDICATE
Box 49771
Austin TX 78789

TRIPLE X RECORDS
Box 862529
Los Angeles CA 90086-2529
Catalogue: free

TUMBLE GEAR
138 Duane Street
New York NY 10013

TVT
23 East 4th Street
New York NY 10003

TWIN/TONE
2217 Nicollet Ave. South
Minneapolis MN 55404

ULTRASOUND
215 10th Avenue #7
Olympia WA 98501

UMBRELLA
Box 41269
Providence RI 02940-1269

VARESE SARABANDE
11746 Ventura Blvd
Suite 130
Studio City CA 91604

VERVE
825 Eighth Avenue
26th Floor
New York NY 10019

VHF
Box 7365
Fairfax VA 22039

VIRGIN
338 North Foothill Road
Beverly Hills CA 90210

VINYL JAPAN
281 Camden High Street
Camden Town
London NW1 7BX

WARNER BROTHERS
3300 Warner Blvd
Burbank CA 91505

WAX TRAX!
1659 North Damen Avenue
Chicago IL 60647
Catalogue: Free

Section 4

Recommended Reading

A. General Topics

ANTI-ROCK: THE OPPOSITION TO ROCK 'N' ROLL
Linda Mawrtin and Kerry Segrave
Da Capo Press (1993)
Synopsis: A history of objections to rock through its many phases.

ART INTO POP
Simon Frith and Howard Horne
Methuen Press (1987)
Synopsis: The art school influence on British pop music.

BAT CHAIN PULLER: ROCK AND ROLL IN THE AGE OF CELEBRITY
Kurt Loder
St. Martin's Press (1990)
Synopsis: A collection of essays and interviews featuring David Bowie, the Pretenders, Iggy Pop, Blondie, the Ramones and others.

BITCH BITCH BITCH
Mike Wrenn
Omnibus Press (1988)
Synopsis: A collection of insulting and vindictive remarks about and from those in the music business.

THE COMPLETE ROCK FAMILY TREES
Peter Frame
Omnibus Press (1993)
Synopsis: A well-presented series of genealogy charts involving well-known artists and groups. The carefully-drawn charts and family trees make this book worth the price.

DANCING IN THE DISTRACTION FACTORY: MUSIC TELEVISION AND POP CULTURE
Andrew Goodwin
University of Minnesota Press (1992)
Synopsis: Analysis and study of MTV along with the impact of music videos.

THE DARK STUFF: SELECTED WRITINGS ON ROCK MUSIC 1972-1993
Nick Kent
Penguin Books (1994)
Synopsis: A compilation of his writing from years with *NME* among other places.

THE DEATH OF ROCK 'N' ROLL
Jeff Pike
Faber and Faber (1992)
Synopsis: A look at how, why and when rock stars died and whether its an occupational hazard.

DISPATCHES FORM THE FRONT LINE OF POPULAR CULTURE
Tony Parsons
Virgin Books (1994)
Synopsis: A collection of essays by freelance writer Tony Parsons. His subjects range from Kurt Cobain to *A Clockwork Orange*.

ENCYCLOPEDIA OF CANADIAN ROCK, POP & FOLK MUSIC
Rick Jackson
Quarry Press (1994)
Synopsis: An overview of everyone from Barenaked Ladies to Neil Young. A good music resource for fans of Canadian music.

EXPENSIVE HABITS
Simon Garfield
Faber and Faber (1986)
Synopsis: The dark side of the music business.

FROM VELVETS TO THE VOIDOIDS
Clinton Heylin
Penguin (1993)
Synopsis: Pre-punk history for a post punk world. Covers the CBGBs era very well.

GETTING IT ON...THE CLOTHING OF ROCK AND ROCK
Mablen Jones
Abbeville Press (1987)

Synopsis: A look at the how the look changed with the music. The book covers everything from rock and pop to punk and new wave.

GOTHIC ROCK
Mick Mercer
Cleopatra Press (1993)
Synopsis: A dictionary of music, magazines and a discography. The writing style is a little cheeky, but there is definitely some good information here. Available mainly through mail order.

GREAT RECORD LABELS
Al Cimino
Chartwell Books (1992)
Synopsis: A history of all the big labels and some of the small cooler ones (4AD, SST, etc.)

THE GUINNESS WHO'S WHO OF INDIE AND NEW WAVE MUSIC
Colin Larkin
Guinness (1992)
Synopsis: A excellent guide to indie and new wave music featuring tons of band biographies. Definitely recommended.

THE HISTORY OF SCOTTISH ROCK AND POP: ALL THAT EVER MATTERED
Brian Hogg
Guinness Publishing (1993)
Synopsis: This starts in the '50s, but moves quickly to talk about new music artists like Simple Minds, Teenage Fan Club and the Jesus and Mary Chain. It includes some photos and album reviews.

HIT MEN
Fredric Dannen
Random House (1990)
Synopsis: More on the seamy side of the music business.

HOLLYWOOD ROCK: A GUIDE TO ROCK 'N' ROLL IN THE MOVIES
Marshall Crenshaw
Harper Collins (1994)
Synopsis: Starting in the '50s, this is a movie-by-movie listing of when

and where rock songs show up, as well as which musicians appeared in what movies, including cameos.

INDUSTRIAL REVOLUTION
Dave Thompson
Cleopatra Press (1993)
Synopsis: A history of the industrial movement, complete with the bands and discography. Industrial fans should own a copy. Available mainly through mail order.

INSIDE POP MUSIC
Compiled by Johnny Black and International Association of Fan Clubs
CHW Roles & Associates Ltd. (1984)
Synopsis: A basic rundown of how the industry works.

INTERNATIONAL DISCOGRAPHY OF THE NEW WAVE: VOLUME 2
B. George and Martha Defoe
Omnibus Press (1982)
Synopsis: Look back at the compilations of punk, new wave, futurist and hard core.

IRISH ROCK
Tony Clayton-Lea and Richie Taylor
Sidgwick and Jackson (1992)
Synopsis: The history of Irish rock with a focus on the usual suspects like U2 and Sinead.

THE ISLE OF NOISES: ROCK 'N' ROLL'S ROOTS IN IRELAND
Mark J. Prendergast
St. Martin's Press (1990)
Synopsis: A look at the music of Ireland, starting in the '50s, but with heavy focus on modern stars like Sinead O'Connor, the Boomtown Rats, the Pogues and U2. Also included a list of Irish music charts and of Irish artists who crossed over onto British charts.

LIPSTICK TRACES-A SECRET HISTORY OF THE 20TH CENTURY
Griel Marcus
Harvard University Press (1989)

Synopsis: A scholarly look at societal development in the 20th century.

MANIC POP THRILL
Rachel Felder
Ecco Press (1993)
Synopsis: Analysis of various genres of alternative music. Includes a brief discography.

THE MUSIC ADDRESS BOOK
Michael Levine
Harper and Row (1989)
Synopsis: A directory on how to reach all kinds of people in the industry. Try to get the latest edition.

THE NEW BOOK OF ROCK LISTS
Dave Marsh and James Bernard
Fireside Books (1994)
Synopsis: A great book to pick up when you have a few minutes and want to know the 10 worst things about MTV or the 10 most innovative record companies.

THE NEW ROCK AND ROLL: THE A-Z OF ROCK IN THE '80S
Stuart Coupe and Glenn A. Baker
Sound and Vision Press (1983)
Synopsis: A dictionary of rock and roll in the 1980s

1988: THE NEW WAVE PUNK ROCK
Caroline Coon
Omnibus Press (1982)
Synopsis: A look at punk and new wave from the inside.

ON RECORD
Simon Frith and Andrew Goodwin
Pantheon Books (1990)
Synopsis: A survey of critical approaches to pop music.

PARTY OUT OF BOUNDS
Roger Lyle Brown
Plume (1991)

Synopsis: A history of the scene in Athens, Georgia, home of the B-52's and R.E.M.

PRESENT TENSE: ROCK & ROLL AND CULTURE
Anthony De Curtis
Duke University Press (1992)
Synopsis: Various essays on rock and roll

PUNK DIARY: 1970-1979
George Gimarc
St. Martin's Press (1994)
Synopsis: A daily listing of what happened in punk in the '70s; includes a CD. Old time punk fans *will love it.*

RANTERS AND CROWD PLEASERS: PUNK IN POP MUSIC 1977-1992
Griel Marcus
Doubleday (1993)
Synopsis: A collection of Marcus' essays on music.

ROCK AND ROLL: THE 100 BEST SINGLES
Paul Williams
Carroll & Graf Publishers (1993)
Synopsis: An arbitrary selection, ranging from "Peggy Sue" to "Smells Like Teen Spirit." It includes the stories behind the songs.

ROCK BOTTOM
Muck Ranker
Proteus Books (1981)
Synopsis: Obscene and boorish moments of rock 'n' roll history.

ROCK MOVERS AND SHAKERS
Dafydd Rees and Luke Crampton
Billboard Books (1991)
Synopsis: An A-Z of the people who make the music. Great reference work. Highly recommended.

ROCK MUSIC: CULTURE, AESTHETICS AND SOCIOLOGY
Peter Wicke

Cambridge University Press (1991)
Synopsis: A study of the public's fascination with rock.

ROCK 'N' ROLL ROAD TRIP
A.M. Nolan
Pharos Books (1992)
Synopsis: An excellent guide to just about all the addresses you will ever want to visit from Seattle to Athens, Georgia; from CBGB's to its west coast equivalent Club 88, complete with photos and the significance of the venues.

ROCK NAMES
Adam Dolgins
Citadel Press (1993)
Synopsis: A guide to where bands got their names.

ROCKONOMICS: THE MONEY BEHIND THE MUSIC
Marc Eliot
Franklin Watts (1989)
Synopsis: A must read for anyone who thinks "it's about the music, man."

ROUTE 666: ON THE ROAD TO NIRVANA
Gina Arnold
St. Martin's Press (1993)
Synopsis: A look at new music from punk to present, from Sex Pistols to Nirvana with a focus on how this affected a disaffected generation.

SHE'S A REBEL: THE HISTORY OF WOMEN IN ROCK 'N' ROLL
Gillian G. Gaar
Seal Press (1992)
Synopsis: From Chantels to Sinead, this overview is divided by era not genre.

SHOTS FROM THE HIP
Charles Shaar Murray
Penguin (1991)
Synopsis: The history of pop music and its evolution over the last two decades.

SMASH THE STATE
Frank Manley
No Exit (1993)
Synopsis: A discography of Canadian punk 1977-92.

TROUSER PRESS RECORD GUIDE 4TH EDITION
Ira A. Robbins
Collier MacMillan (1991)
Synopsis: A guide and review of alternative music. Make sure you buy the latest edition available. The best record guide out there.

THE ULTIMATE GUIDE TO INDIE RECORDS LABEL AND ARTISTS
Norman Schreiber
Pharos Books (1992)
Synopsis: A guide to indie record labels and their artist rosters.

WILL POP EAT ITSELF?
Jeremy J. Beadle
Faber and Faber (1993)
Synopsis: The history of pop music with particular attention paid to sampling.

WOMEN, SEX AND ROCK 'N' ROLL: IN THEIR OWN WORDS
Liz Evans
Pandora (1994)
Synopsis: Everybody from Bjork to Dolores O'Riordan has something to say about the role women have played in music and their fight to break out of certain stereotypes. Recommended.

B. Biographies

—BAUHAUS
BAUHAUS
Bruna Zarini
Watermelon-Milano (1989)
Synopsis: A history and discography of the band. Translated into English from Italian. Includes a special 3" CD.

—BOWIE, DAVID
BACKSTAGE PASSES
Angela Bowie and Patrick Carr
G.P. Putnam and Sons (1993)
Synopsis: Dave's first wife talks about their life together. Lots of gossip along with a little insight.

THE BOWIE COMPANION
Edited by Elizabeth Thomson and David Gutman
MacMillan (1993)
Synopsis: A collection of essays and articles that form an overview of Bowie's career.

—BUSH, KATE
KATE BUSH: A VISUAL DOCUMENTARY
Kevin Cann & Sean Mayes
Omnibus Press (1988)
Synopsis: Lots of glossy photos and a look at Kate's life and career, with a discography, videos and contacts for fanzines and her fan club.

THE ILLUSTRATED COLLECTOR'S GUIDE TO KATE BUSH
Robert Godwin
Collector's Guide Publishing
Synopsis: A comprehensive discography, along with lists of videos, lasterdiscs, interview discs, bootlegs, books, fanzines and even her television appearances. A must-have for Kate Bush fans.

—BYRNE, DAVID
DAVID BYRNE
John Howell
Thunders Mouth Press (1992)
Synopsis: The life of David Byrne, complete with photos, an interview and entries from his personal diary written during the *Rei Momo* tour.

—THE CLASH
THE CLASH: THE NEW VISUAL DOCUMENTARY

John Tobler and Mal Peachy
Omnibus Press (1983)
Synopsis: A bio of the band with lots of pictures and a discography.

–THE CURE

THE CURE: A VISUAL DOCUMENTARY
Dave Thompson & Jo-Ann Greene
Omnibus Press (1988)
Synopsis: A biography of the band, with quotes, interviews, album and concert reviews, a discography and full listing of almost every show they did in the '80s.

THE CURE: FAITH
Dave Bowler and Bryan Dray
Sidjwick and Jackson (1995)
Synopsis: A basic biography of The Cure with a helpful index and list of magazine articles.

–DEPECHE MODE

DEPECHE MODE: SOME GREAT REWARD
Dave Thompson
St. Martin's Press (1994)
Synopsis: A reasonably comprehensive biography pieced together from various magazine interviews and record company bios. Contains some interesting stories about Mute Records. Depeche Mode fans should own a copy.

–FRANKIE GOES TO HOLLYWOOD

A BONE IN MY FLUTE
Holly Johnson
Random House (1994)
Synopsis: Johnson tells his story from growing up in Liverpool in the '60s to his musical success, and his positive HIV test. Lots of pictures and a discography.

—THE JAM
THE JAM: OUR STORY
Bruce Foxton & Rick Buckler
Castle Communications (1993)
Synopsis: The guys talk about how the band got started and what happened along the way.

—JOY DIVISION
JOY DIVISION
Alfredo Suantoni
Black Ink Studios (1987)
Synopsis: A history and discography of the band. Translated into English from Italian. Comes with a 3" CD featuring the original Warsaw demos.

TOUCHING FROM A DISTANCE
Deborah Curtis
Faber and Faber (1995)
Synopsis: Biography of Ian Curtis of Joy Division, written by his widow. Lots of detail about the Ian, Joy Division, New Order and Factory Records. Recommended.

—MARLEY, BOB
CATCH A FIRE: THE LIFE OF BOB MARLEY
Timothy White
Henry Holt and Company (1993)
Synopsis: A basic biography of the singer.

—NEW ORDER
NEW ORDER AND JOY DIVISION
Brian Edge
Omnibus Press
Synopsis: The history of both bands with a discography. One of the best books out there on the subject.

—NIRVANA

COME AS YOU ARE: THE STORY OF NIRVANA
Michael Azerrad
Doubleday (1993)

Synopsis: The story of the band complete with photos and a discography and original lyric sheets. All band biographies should be this honest and comprehensive. You'll love the book even if you aren't a fan of Nirvana. Make sure you buy the edition with the extra chapter that was added after Cobain's suicide.

NIRVANA AND THE SOUND OF SEATTLE
Brad Morrell
Omnibus Press (1993)

Synopsis: A look at how and why the band changed new music and their Seattle-based descendants, along with a discography, photos and a guide to essential grunge albums.

NIRVANA TRIBUTE: THE LIFE AND DEATH OF KURT COBAIN
Suzi Black
Omnibus Press (1994)

Synopsis: Lots of color photos and a run-down of the events leading up to Kurt's suicide, as well as the aftermath of the tragedy on new music and those who knew him.

—PEARL JAM

PEARL JAM
Nick Wall
Sidgewick & Jackson Ltd. (1994)

Synopsis: The story of the band including photos, a discography and a geneological chart of the Seattle music scene.

—RAMONES

RAMONES: AN AMERICAN BAND
Jim Bessman
St. Martin's Press (1993)

Synopsis: A history of the band, compiled with their help, and complete with photos, a tour schedule and a discography. Essential reading for the Ramones fan.

–R.E.M.

R.E.M. – BEHIND THE MASK
Jim Greer
Little, Brown and Co. (1992)
Synopsis: A bio of the band.

AN R.E.M. COMPANION – IT CRAWLED FROM THE SOUTH
Marcus Gray
Da Capo Press (1992)
Synopsis: A collection of articles and essays on a variety of R.E.M. topics. Tons of trivia. Recommended.

THE STORY OF R.E.M.
Tony Fletcher
Omnibus Press (1993)
Synopsis: A bio, discography, a list of videos and more.

TALK ABOUT THE PASSION – R.E.M.: AN ORAL HISTORY
Denise Sullivan
Underwood-Miller (1994)
Synopsis: The band's story as told by friends and associates featuring direct quotes.

–SEX PISTOLS

ENGLAND'S DREAMING: SEX PISTOLS AND PUNK ROCK
Jon Savage
Faber and Faber (1991)
Synopsis: A colorful history of a colorful band. Contains a tremendous amount of information on the original punk movement. Highly recommended.

ROTTEN: NO IRISH – NO BLACKS – NO DOGS
John Lydon
St. Martin's Press (1994)
Synopsis: Johnny's life story in his own words. He tends to ramble—

THE ALTERNATIVE MUSIC ALMANAC

but it's still entertaining.

12 DAYS ON THE ROAD: THE SEX PISTOLS AND AMERICA
Noele Monk and Jimmy Guterman
Quill (1990)
Synopsis: A diary of the band's ill-fated tour with some great stories.

—SISTERS OF MERCY
THE SISTERS OF MERCY: LIFE
Alberto Lutriani and Nino LaLoggia
Watermelon-Milano (1988)
Synopsis: A history and discography of the band. Translated from Italian. Comes with a 3" CD.

—SMASHING PUMPKINS
SMASHING PUMPKINS
Chris Charlesworth, ed.
Omnibus Press, 1994.
Synopsis: A glossy soft cover filled with pictures and stories about the band and a discography.

—THE SMITHS/MORRISSEY
MORRISSEY: IN HIS OWN WORDS
Morrissey
Omnibus Press (1988)
Synopsis: Quotes and various words of wisdom from the Mozzer.

MORRISSEY AND MARR: THE SEVERED ALLIANCE
Johnny Rogan
Omnibus Press (1992)
Synopsis: An incredibly detailed account of the rise and fall of one of Britain's most influential bands. Rogan is so candid that Morrissey still hasn't forgiven him. Recommended reading for Smiths fans.

THE SMITHS 1982-87
Bruna Zarini
Watermelon-Milano (1987)

Synopsis: A history and discography of the band. Translated from Italian.

THE SMITHS: THE VISUAL DOCUMENTARY
Johnny Rogan
Omnibus Press (1994)
Synopsis: The history of the band, complete with unpublished interviews, a list of the Smiths' performances, a discography, and lots of new photos. Contains much of the information in *Morrissey and Marr: The Severed Alliance* but in and easy to read day-by-day chronological order.

–SONIC YOUTH
CONFUSION IS NEXT: THE SONIC YOUTH STORY
Alec Foege
St. Martin's Press (1994)
Synopsis: A bio of the band with some snaps, a discography, and a foreword by Thurston Moore.

–U2
U2 LIVE: A CONCERT DOCUMENTARY
Pimm Jal del la Parra
Omnibus Press (1994)
Synopsis: The focus is on U2's live shows, complete with anecdotes, stories, attendance, opening acts, sets and lots of photos. Mind-boggling detail.

OUTSIDE IS AMERICA (U2 IN THE US)
Carter Alan
Faber and Faber (1993)
Synopsis: A look at how the band conquered the New World.

THE UNFORGETTABLE FIRE: THE DEFINITIVE BIOGRAPHY OF U2
Eamon Dunphy
Warner Books (1987)
Synopsis: A well-written and fairly comprehensive biography of U2.

U2 AT THE END OF THE WORLD
Bill Flanagan
Delacore Press (1995)
Synopsis: Flanagan was allowed to follow the band around the world for two years on the *Zoo-TV* tour. The result is more than 500 pages of stories and observations.

–VELVET UNDERGROUND
VELVET UNDERGROUND HANDBOOK
M.C. Kostek
Black Spring Press (1992)
Synopsis: A run down of the band's history in all media, including films and Lou Reed's poetry, as well as some rare photographs, and a discography. See also *From the Velvets to the Voidoids*.

–XTC
XTC CHALKHILLS AND CHILDREN: THE DEFINITIVE BIOGRAPHY
Chris Twomey
Omnibus Press (1992)
Synopsis: A complete biography of the band, with pictures and discography.

ABOUT THE AUTHOR

Alan Cross is from an incredibly normal small town on the Canadian Prairies called Stonewall, Manitoba. When he's not out walking the dog, he can be heard every weekday afternoons on 102.1 The Edge (CFNY-FM)/Toronto, one of North America's oldest commercial radio stations devoted to alternative music. Once a week, he's the host, producer and writer of *The Ongoing History of New Music,* a one hour documentary on alternative music.

Alan Cross (left) with the Police's Stuart Copeland

Alan Cross with Ministry's Alain Jourgensen (middle)

UPCOMING RELEASES FROM COLLECTOR'S GUIDE PUBLISHING

The Illustrated Book Of Nazareth
By Michael D. Melton

A comprehensive guide to, and in appreciation of Nazareth, the band and their music. Every Nazareth album, from their 1971 self-titled debut to the recent release of Move Me, is included in this 172 page guide; numerous rarities, singles, solo material, special releases, and more are also included, documented in over 100 photos.

The Illustrated Collector's Guide To Wishbone Ash (w/ CD)
By Andy Powell

Written by Ash guitarist Andy Powell, this extensive book features over 100 photos, with a comprehensive discography of the group, along with complete listings of band line-ups, tours and concert dates, set lists, tour programs and posters, catalogue numbers, videos, songbooks, fanzines, memorabilia, and much more. Also included in the box set is the CD BBC Radio 1 Live In Concert, which was originally recorded at the Paris Theatre in 1972.

The Progressive Rock Book, Vol. 1 – North & South American Editon
By Ron Johnston

This incredibly exhaustive book contains complete single and album listings for hundreds of progressive rock bands hailing from North and South America. The listings include LPs, cassettes, CDs, EPs, 45s, bootlegs, imports, and so on, and extend to such diverse musical styles as jazz, new age, blues-rock, electronic, cosmic and space music, acid and psychedelic, and folk..

The Illustrated Collector's Guide To Ian Gillan (w/ CD)
By Mary Gear

Legendary Deep Purple frontman Ian Gillan is the subject of this extensive book about the man and his music. This guide features a full Gillan discography spanning his entire career, including his stints in Episode Six, Black Sabbath, along with his solo works. The book also has listings of rare imports, videos, tour dates and posters, postcards, magazines, and so on. Comes packaged in a box set with the CD Trouble: The Best of Ian Gillan.

Books For The Music Collector

COLLECTOR'S GUIDE PUBLISHING
ORDER FORM

TITLE		PRICE (U.S.)	QTY.
Black Market Beatles	paperbk.	$14.95	_____
By Jim Berkenstadt & Belmo	hardcvr.	$19.95	_____
The Collector's Guide To Progressive Rock, Vol. 1			
By Ron Johnston		$14.95	_____
The Hitchhiker's Guide To Elvis			
By Mick Farren		$12.95	_____
Hot Wacks Books:			
Hot Wacks XV – The Last Wacks		$22.95	_____
Supplement 1		$12.95	_____
Supplement 2		$14.95	_____
Supplement 3		$15.95	_____
The Illustrated Collector's Guide To Kate Bush			
By Robert Godwin		$10.95	_____
The Illustrated Collector's Guide To Hawkwind			
By Robert Godwin		$12.95	_____
(box set—w/ *Warriors On The Edge Of Time* CD)		$28.98	_____
The Illustrated Collector's Guide To Led Zeppelin	paperbk.	$17.95	_____
By Robert Godwin	hardcvr.	$21.95	_____
The Illustrated Collector's Guide To Motorhead			
By Alan Burridge & Mick Stevenson		$12.95	_____
(box set—w/ *The Best Of Motorhead* CD)		$28.98	_____
The Illustrated Collector's Guide To Nazareth			
By Michael D. Melton		$14.95	_____

The Illustrated Collector's Guide To Punk, Vol. 1
By Dave Thompson $14.95 _____
(w/ *The Very Best Of UK Punk* CD) $28.98 _____

The Illustrated Collector's Guide To Wishbone Ash
By Andy Powell $14.95 _____
(w/ *Live In Chicago* CD) $28.98 _____

Led Zeppelin Live
By Luis Rey $17.95 _____

Michael Moorcock box set
(incl. *New World's Fair* CD and *Death Is No Obstacle* book) $28.98 _____
Death Is No Obstacle (interview with Michael Moorcock) $16.95 _____

Olivia: More Than Physical – A Collector's Guide
By Gregory Branson-Trent $12.95 _____
(box set—w/ *Have You Never Been Mellow* CD) $28.98 _____

Phillip Lynott – The Rocker
By Mark Putterford $12.95 _____

Queens of Deliria
By Michael Butterworth $12.95 _____
(box set—w/ *Quark, Strangeness & Charm* CD) $28.98 _____

The Time of the Hawklords
By Michael Butterworth $12.95 _____
(box set—w/ *Astounding Sounds, Amazing Music* CD) $28.95 _____

Shipping & handling   + _$5.00_, $3
                                                              each
                                                              add.
                                                              book
Total   _____